AI and Society

Navigating Ethics, Governance and Trust

Otega Wisdom Efe

DEDICATION

To God Almighty,
the source of wisdom, understanding, and purpose.
For His divine guidance, endless grace, and boundless love,
which have illuminated this journey and made all things possible.
May this work be a reflection of the gifts He has bestowed,
and may it serve to enlighten minds and inspire hearts.
With deepest gratitude and reverence.
— Otega

Preface

In the ever-evolving landscape of technology, few advancements have had as profound an impact on our lives as Artificial Intelligence (AI). From its theoretical origins to its practical applications in everyday life, AI has emerged as a pivotal force, driving innovation and challenging our fundamental understanding of the world. This book, AI and Society: Navigating Ethics, Governance, and Trust, is my attempt to delve into the multifaceted dimensions of AI and its implications for our society.

My journey into the world of AI began with a deep curiosity about how machines could emulate human intelligence. This curiosity led me to pursue an MBA in Artificial Intelligence at Nexford University, where I immersed myself in data science, robotics, and the ethical considerations of AI technology. Through this academic and professional journey, I have witnessed firsthand the transformative potential of AI, as well as the ethical dilemmas and challenges it presents.

This book is structured to take you through a comprehensive exploration of AI, starting with its historical genesis, and its applications across industries and moving through the critical issues of misinformation, ethical concerns, trust, economic impact, human rights, environmental sustainability, and the essential need for effective regulation and governance. Each chapter is designed to provide a balanced perspective, offering both the promise and the perils of AI technology.

I have endeavored to make this book accessible to a broad audience, from AI enthusiasts and policymakers to anyone interested in the future of technology and its societal impact. I aim to demystify AI, presenting complex concepts in a manner that is both engaging and informative.

As we stand at the frontier of human progress, AI beckons us to navigate its complexities with care and foresight. It is my hope that this book will serve as a guide, inspiring thoughtful consideration and informed dialogue about the role of AI in our society. Together, let us explore the ethical pathways and governance frameworks that will shape a future where AI contributes to a safer, more equitable, and connected world.

Thank you for joining me on this journey.

Sincerely,

Otega Wisdom Efe

Table of Contents

ACKNOWLEDGMENTS

I extend my heartfelt gratitude to Fadl Al Tarzi, CEO of Nexford University, for his unwavering support throughout the writing of this book. His encouragement, insights, and belief in the pursuit of knowledge have been instrumental in shaping this work. To my beloved family, who have stood by me through the years, offering their endless love, patience, and understanding—this journey would not have been possible without you. Your strength and support have been my greatest foundation.
With deep appreciation,
— Otega

Chapters Introduction

In the annals of human history, few innovations have sparked as much intrigue, debate, and transformation as Artificial Intelligence (AI). From its humble beginnings in academic circles to its pervasive presence in our daily lives, AI has evolved into a force that shapes industries, influences societal norms, and challenges our understanding of what it means to be human.

Chapter One: The Genesis of Artificial Intelligence

Imagine a world where machines can think, learn, and adapt. This is not the realm of science fiction but the reality of AI. In this chapter, we delve into the scholarly definitions and scope of AI, tracing its origins from early theoretical concepts to the groundbreaking developments that have made it indispensable. We explore the compelling need for AI, its applications across various industries, and its pivotal role in the industrial revolution. As we uncover how AI is impacting society, we begin to see the profound changes it brings to our world.

Chapter Two: Misinformation and Disinformation

In an age where information is power, the ability to create and disseminate false information at unprecedented speeds poses significant challenges. This chapter examines the dark side of AI, focusing on the creation of deepfakes and synthetic media. We explore how these technologies are used to spread misinformation, the societal impacts, and the methods to identify and prevent such deceptions.

Chapter Three: Ethical Concerns of AI

With great power comes great responsibility. AI's ethical implications are vast and complex. This chapter addresses AI bias, fairness, and transparency across industries. We delve into the ethical dilemmas that arise from AI's decision-making processes and the importance of ensuring that these systems operate fairly and transparently.

Chapter Four: Trust and Safety

The "black box" problem in AI refers to the opacity of AI decision-making processes. This chapter explores how to address this issue, build trust in AI systems, and ensure their safety and reliability. We discuss the creation of transparent algorithms and the measures needed to safeguard AI applications.

Chapter Five: Job Displacement and Economic Impact

As AI automates tasks across industries, it brings both opportunities and challenges. This chapter examines the economic impact of AI, focusing on job displacement, economic inequality, and the strategies to manage the transition to an AI-driven society. We also explore the support systems needed for affected workers.

Chapter Six: Human Rights and Privacy

AI's capabilities in data surveillance and collection raise significant human rights and privacy concerns. This chapter balances the benefits of AI with the need to protect individual rights, exploring the ethical and legal frameworks that govern AI's use in these areas.

Chapter Seven: Environmental Impact of AI

The development and deployment of AI technologies have environmental footprints. This chapter investigates the sustainability practices needed to mitigate these impacts and ensure that AI development aligns with environmental conservation goals.

Chapter Eight: Regulation and Governance of AI

Effective regulation and governance are crucial for harnessing AI's potential while mitigating risks. This chapter outlines the global, regional, national, and industrial regulations that shape AI's development and deployment. We explore the frameworks that ensure AI is used responsibly and ethically.

As we embark on this journey through the multifaceted world of AI, we invite you to explore its profound implications for our society. From the promise of innovation to the challenges of ethical dilemmas, AI stands at the frontier of human progress, beckoning us to understand and shape its future.

Chapter 1

1.0 The Genesis of Artificial Intelligence

1.1 Introduction

Artificial Intelligence (AI) stands at the forefront of technological innovation, embodying a field that is as diverse as it is profound. From its inception, AI has been envisioned to replicate and enhance human intelligence through machines. This ambition has led to many definitions and perspectives, each shedding light on different facets of AI's vast landscape.

1.1.1 The Pioneers of AI: John McCarthy (1955)

John McCarthy, often credited with coining the term "Artificial Intelligence," defined it as "the science and engineering of making intelligent machines" (Manning, 2020). This definition is significant because it highlights AI's dual nature. On one hand, AI is a scientific discipline that seeks to understand the principles of intelligence and replicate them. On the other hand, it is an engineering endeavor focused on creating machines that can perform tasks requiring intelligence. This duality underscores the interdisciplinary nature of AI, bridging fields such as computer science, cognitive psychology, neuroscience, and engineering.

Imagine a researcher observing an anthill. It may seem like chaos to a layman, but to the trained eye, there's a fascinating order to it. Ants work together in complex ways, building tunnels, finding food, and defending their colony. John McCarthy's vision was akin to understanding these intricate behaviors and creating mechanical ants that could replicate these tasks. These mechanical ants, designed with artificial intelligence, could be used for various applications, such as search and rescue missions in disaster-stricken areas where their small size and teamwork could navigate through debris more effectively than human rescuers.

1.1.2 Anticipating the Future: Nils John Nilsson

Nils John Nilsson described AI as a technology that "functions appropriately and with foresight in its environment"(Sheikh et al., 2023). This definition emphasizes the adaptive and anticipatory capabilities of AI systems. AI is not just about performing tasks; it's about doing so in a contextually appropriate and forward-thinking way.

Consider the case of self-driving cars. These vehicles are equipped with an array of sensors and cameras that constantly monitor their surroundings. They collect vast amounts of data on road conditions, traffic patterns, and pedestrian movements. With this data, AI algorithms can predict and anticipate potential hazards. For instance, if a ball rolls onto the road, the car can predict that a child might follow and slow down preemptively. This anticipatory behavior is crucial for the safety and efficiency of autonomous vehicles, ensuring they not only react to events but also foresee and mitigate potential risks.

1.1.3 The European Commission's Vision

The High-Level Expert Group on AI from the European Commission defines AI systems as those that "display intelligent behavior by analyzing their environment and taking actions – with some degree of autonomy – to achieve specific goals" (Sheikh et al., 2023). This definition underscores the autonomous decision-making aspect of AI.

Think of autonomous drones used for delivering packages in urban areas. These drones are not just following a set path; they must navigate complex city environments. They analyze their surroundings in real-time, identifying and avoiding obstacles like buildings, birds, and other drones. For example, if a drone encounters unexpected construction on its pre-planned route, it must autonomously re-route, ensuring timely and safe delivery of packages. This level of autonomy reduces the need for human intervention and enables efficient last-mile delivery solutions in congested urban spaces.

1.1.4 Cognitive Mirroring: Oxford Academic

According to Oxford Academic, AI seeks to make computers perform tasks that require psychological skills such as perception, association, prediction, planning, and motor control (Boden, 2018). This aligns AI with cognitive functions typically associated with human intelligence.

In healthcare, AI-powered diagnostic tools are revolutionizing patient care. Imagine a doctor using an AI system to diagnose diseases. The system has been trained on millions of medical records and can recognize patterns and symptoms that might be overlooked by human eyes. For example, in radiology, AI can analyze X-rays or MRI scans to detect anomalies with remarkable precision. This technology enables early detection of diseases like cancer, where early diagnosis is critical for successful treatment. The AI's ability to perceive visual data, associate it with known medical conditions, predict potential outcomes, plan treatment strategies, and assist in motor-controlled surgeries enhances the overall quality of healthcare.

1.1.5 Comprehensive AI: Winston (1992)

Patrick Winston defined AI as computations that enable perception, reasoning, and action. This definition integrates both the scientific and practical aspects of AI, focusing on its ability to solve real-world problems (Rubeis, 2024).

In the manufacturing industry, AI-driven robots are transforming production lines. These robots are equipped with advanced sensors that allow them to perceive their environment, whether it's identifying defective products or ensuring that components are precisely placed. They use reasoning to make decisions on the fly, such as adjusting their actions based on real-time feedback. For instance, a robotic arm assembling electronic devices can detect if a part is missing or misaligned and automatically correct the issue, ensuring high-quality output. This seamless integration of perception, reasoning, and action makes AI invaluable in maintaining efficiency and consistency in manufacturing processes.

These diverse perspectives on AI illustrate its multifaceted nature. AI is a field that encompasses scientific inquiry, engineering innovation, cognitive replication, and autonomous decision-making. Each definition provides a unique lens through which to view AI, highlighting different aspects of its complexity and potential. As AI continues to evolve, it will likely integrate these perspectives even further, leading to more advanced and capable systems that can transform various aspects of our lives.

1.2 Early Foundations

Mathematical Foundations: The roots of AI can be traced back to the early 20th century, with significant contributions from mathematicians like Alan Turing. In 1936, Turing introduced the concept of the Turing Machine, an abstract mathematical model that could simulate any other machine's logic. This work laid the groundwork for the idea that machines could process information in ways similar to human reasoning (Meier, 2024).

Alan Turing's creation of the Turing Machine was revolutionary. Picture a machine that could read instructions and carry out tasks based on those instructions, much like a computer program today. For example, imagine a simple machine that could solve mathematical problems by following a series of steps written on a tape. This idea was foundational because it suggested that any logical process could be encoded and executed by a machine, paving the way for modern computing.

1.3 The Birth of AI as a Field

Dartmouth Conference (1956): The formal birth of AI as a distinct field of study is often attributed to the Dartmouth Conference in 1956. Organized by John McCarthy, Marvin Minsky, Nathaniel Rochester, and Claude Shannon, this conference brought together researchers to discuss the possibility of creating intelligent machines. It was here that McCarthy coined the term "artificial intelligence" (Engelbrecht, 2023).

The Dartmouth Conference was akin to a historical summit where the greatest scientific minds of the era came together with a shared vision. It was like the founding fathers of a new nation drafting a constitution that would guide future generations. The excitement and anticipation were palpable as these pioneers laid down the theoretical foundations and ambitious goals that would shape the development of AI for decades to come.

1.3.1 Early Research and Symbolic AI

Symbolic AI: During the early years, AI research focused heavily on symbolic AI, which involved programming computers to manipulate symbols and solve problems using logical reasoning. This approach was influenced by the work of Allen Newell and Herbert A. Simon, who developed the Logic Theorist and the General Problem Solver, early AI programs that could perform tasks like proving mathematical theorems (Jones, 2023).

Symbolic AI was like teaching a machine to play chess. Chess is a game of strategy, where each move must be carefully considered based on the possible future moves of the opponent. AI researchers programmed computers to understand and manipulate the symbols representing chess pieces and the board, enabling them to predict and execute the best moves. This ability to simulate complex thought processes using symbols was a significant milestone in AI development.

1.3.2 The Rise of Machine Learning

Shift to Empirical Methods: In the 1980s and 1990s, there was a significant shift in AI research towards empirical methods, particularly machine learning. This shift was driven by the limitations of symbolic AI and the increasing availability of data and computational power. Researchers began to focus on developing algorithms that could learn from data, leading to advancements in neural networks and pattern recognition (Jones, 2023).

Imagine teaching a computer to recognize images of cats. Instead of programming specific rules for what a cat looks like, researchers fed the computer thousands of images labeled as "cat" or "not cat." The machine learning algorithm analyzed these images and learned to identify the patterns and features that distinguish cats from other objects. This process of learning from vast amounts of data revolutionized AI, making it possible for machines to handle more complex tasks with greater accuracy.

1.3.3 Modern AI and Deep Learning

Deep Learning Revolution: The 21st century has seen remarkable progress in AI, particularly with the advent of deep learning. Deep learning involves training large neural networks on vast amounts of data, enabling machines to perform tasks such as image and speech recognition with unprecedented accuracy. This approach has been fueled by advances in hardware, such as GPUs, and the availability of large datasets (Manning, 2020).

Consider the role of deep learning in revolutionizing the medical field, specifically in radiology. Traditional radiologists spend years honing their skills to interpret medical images accurately. Now, with deep learning, AI systems can be trained on thousands of images to recognize patterns indicative of various conditions, such as tumors or fractures, with astonishing precision. For example, an AI system could analyze a mammogram and highlight areas of concern, aiding radiologists in diagnosing breast cancer at an early stage when it is most treatable. This collaboration between AI and human expertise enhances diagnostic accuracy, speeds up the review process, and ultimately improves patient outcomes.

1.3.4 Ethical and Societal Implications

Ethical Considerations: As AI technology has advanced, so too have concerns about its ethical and societal implications. Issues such as bias in AI algorithms, the impact of automation on jobs, and the need for transparency and accountability in AI systems have become central topics of discussion among researchers, policymakers, and the public (Sheikh et al., 2023).

The case of facial recognition technology illustrates the ethical challenges posed by AI. While this technology has beneficial applications in security and convenience, it has also raised significant privacy concerns. In some cities, the use of facial recognition by law enforcement has sparked debates about surveillance and civil liberties. Critics argue that these systems can be prone to bias, misidentifying individuals based on race or gender. For instance, studies have shown that facial recognition algorithms often have higher error rates for people of color. These ethical concerns underscore the need for regulations and oversight to ensure that AI technologies are deployed responsibly, respecting individuals' rights and promoting fairness.

The journey of AI from its early mathematical foundations to the sophisticated deep learning systems of today is a testament to the ingenuity and perseverance of researchers across multiple disciplines. As AI continues to evolve, it will undoubtedly raise new challenges and opportunities, shaping the future in ways we are only beginning to understand.

1.4 The Need for Artificial Intelligence in Society

Artificial Intelligence (AI) is widely acknowledged as a transformative technology with the capacity to profoundly influence various facets of society. This discussion will examine the necessity of AI in societal advancement.

1.4.1 Enhancing Economic Productivity

1. Automation of Routine Tasks:

- **Manufacturing**: AI-driven automation in manufacturing processes can increase efficiency and reduce costs. For example, AI-powered robots are used in assembly lines to perform repetitive tasks with high precision, leading to increased productivity and reduced human error (West & Allen, 2018).

    In the automotive industry, companies like Tesla have integrated AI-powered robots into their assembly lines. These robots handle tasks such as welding, painting, and assembling parts with incredible accuracy and speed. This automation not only boosts production rates but also minimizes the risk of errors that can occur with human labor. Furthermore, it allows human workers to focus on more complex and creative aspects of vehicle design and development, fostering innovation and enhancing overall product quality.

- **Service Industry**: In the service sector, AI chatbots and virtual assistants handle customer inquiries, bookings, and support, freeing up human workers to focus on more complex tasks. This not only improves service efficiency but also enhances customer satisfaction (Artificial Intelligence in Society, 2024).

   Consider the hospitality industry, where hotels use AI-powered virtual assistants to manage guest interactions. For instance, AI chatbots can assist guests with booking reservations, checking in, ordering room service, and even providing local area recommendations. This technology ensures that guests receive prompt and accurate assistance, enhancing their overall experience. Meanwhile, hotel staff can concentrate on delivering personalized and high-touch services, such as event planning or catering to VIP guests, thereby improving service quality and guest satisfaction.

2. Financial Services:

- **Algorithmic Trading**: AI algorithms analyze vast amounts of market data to make trading decisions in real-time, optimizing investment strategies and improving market efficiency (Science in the Age of AI | Royal Society, 2024). This has led to the rise of high-frequency trading, where trades are executed at speeds and volumes beyond human capability.

   In the fast-paced world of stock trading, milliseconds can make a significant difference. AI-powered algorithmic trading systems are designed to execute trades at lightning speeds based on real-time market data analysis. For instance, during major market events like earnings announcements or economic reports, these algorithms can rapidly process information, identify trends, and execute trades before human traders can react. This speed and precision help investors capitalize on fleeting opportunities, optimize their portfolios, and achieve better financial outcomes.

- **Fraud Detection**: AI systems detect fraudulent activities by analyzing transaction patterns and identifying anomalies (Crompton & Burke, 2023). Banks and financial institutions use AI to monitor transactions in real-time, reducing the risk of fraud and enhancing security (Rawas, 2024).

   Imagine a bank employing AI to safeguard its customers' accounts. AI algorithms continuously analyze transaction data for unusual patterns, such as sudden large withdrawals or purchases in foreign locations. When an anomaly is detected, the system can flag the transaction for further investigation or automatically freeze the account to prevent potential fraud. For example, if a customer's credit card is used in multiple locations within a short period, the AI system can recognize this as suspicious activity and take immediate action, protecting the customer's finances and the bank's reputation.

3. Entertainment:

- **Content Recommendation**: Streaming services like Netflix and Spotify use AI to recommend movies, shows, and music based on user preferences.

  Picture a typical evening when you sit down to watch a movie on Netflix. The platform suggests a film that perfectly matches your tastes, even though you haven't actively searched for it. This personalized recommendation is the result of AI algorithms analyzing your viewing history, preferences, and even the time of day you usually watch. By understanding these patterns, the AI can predict what you might enjoy next, enhancing your viewing experience and keeping you engaged with the platform.

- **Game Development**: AI creates more realistic and challenging opponents in video games, enhancing the gaming experience.

  In the world of video games, AI is transforming how virtual opponents behave. Games like "The Last of Us Part II" use advanced AI to create enemies that react intelligently to the player's actions. For instance, if the player sneaks around and takes out one guard silently, the remaining guards may notice their colleague's absence and start searching for the intruder. This dynamic and responsive behavior makes the game more immersive and challenging, as players must constantly adapt their strategies to outsmart AI-driven opponents.

1.4.2 Advancing Healthcare

1. Diagnostics and Treatment:

- **Medical Imaging**: AI algorithms analyze medical images to detect diseases such as cancer with high accuracy (Crompton & Burke, 2023). For instance, AI systems can identify tumors in radiology scans, aiding in early diagnosis and improving treatment outcomes (Giattino et al., 2023).

  Imagine a hospital where radiologists work tirelessly to interpret hundreds of scans daily. Now, picture an AI system that assists these radiologists by rapidly and accurately analyzing each scan. One day, a middle-aged woman comes in for a routine check-up. Her mammogram is processed by an AI tool trained on millions of previous scans. The AI identifies a tiny, early-stage tumor that even the most experienced radiologist might have missed. This early detection allows for timely intervention, vastly improving her chances of successful treatment. This AI-assisted workflow not only increases diagnostic accuracy but also reduces the workload for healthcare professionals, allowing them to focus on patient care.

- **Personalized Medicine**: AI helps tailor treatments based on individual patient data, improving outcomes and reducing side effects. By analyzing genetic information and medical history, AI can recommend personalized treatment plans (Stryker & Kavlakoglu, 2024).

  Consider a patient diagnosed with a rare type of cancer. Traditional treatment plans might follow a one-size-fits-all approach, but AI offers a more nuanced solution. By analyzing the patient's genetic profile and medical history, the AI system identifies specific genetic mutations associated with the cancer. It then cross-references this data with a vast repository of clinical studies to recommend a targeted treatment plan. For example, the AI might suggest a specific drug that has shown high efficacy in patients with similar genetic profiles. This personalized approach not only increases the likelihood of successful treatment but also minimizes adverse side effects, as the treatment is tailored to the patient's unique biology.

2. Drug Discovery:

- **Accelerated Research**: AI accelerates the drug discovery process by analyzing biological data and predicting the efficacy of potential drug compounds. This reduces the time and cost associated with bringing new drugs to market.

  Picture a pharmaceutical company racing to develop a new drug for a fast-spreading virus. Traditionally, drug discovery is a lengthy process, involving years of research and billions of dollars. However, with AI, this timeline is dramatically shortened. AI algorithms sift through enormous datasets of biological information to identify promising drug candidates. One algorithm predicts that a particular molecule could inhibit the virus's ability to replicate. The company quickly synthesizes and tests this molecule, finding it to be effective. This accelerated process, driven by AI, allows the new drug to reach the market in record time, potentially saving countless lives during a public health crisis.

1.4.3 Improving Education

1. Personalized Learning:

- **Adaptive Learning Systems**: AI-powered platforms like Khan Academy adapt to individual student needs, providing customized learning experiences. These systems analyze student performance and recommend lessons tailored to their learning pace and style (Crompton & Burke, 2023).

Imagine a classroom where each student has a unique learning journey. One student excels in mathematics but struggles with reading comprehension. An AI-powered platform assesses their strengths and weaknesses through continuous interaction. The system then customizes lessons to address specific gaps in their knowledge while challenging them in areas where they excel. For instance, it might provide additional practice problems in reading and comprehension while offering advanced mathematical concepts to keep the student engaged. This personalized approach ensures that each student receives the right level of support and challenge, fostering a more effective and enjoyable learning experience.

- **Intelligent Tutoring Systems**: AI tutors provide personalized instruction and feedback, helping students understand complex concepts and improve their academic performance.

Consider a high school student struggling with algebra. Traditional tutoring sessions might not be accessible or affordable for them. An AI tutor steps in, offering interactive lessons and instant feedback. The AI identifies areas where the student makes repeated mistakes and tailors its teaching approach accordingly. For example, if the student consistently struggles with quadratic equations, the AI provides additional explanations and practice problems focused on that topic. Over time, the student's understanding improves, and their grades reflect this progress. The AI tutor's ability to offer personalized, 24/7 support makes a significant difference in the student's academic journey.

2. Administrative Efficiency:

- **Automated Grading**: AI systems automate the grading of assignments and exams, allowing educators to focus more on teaching and less on administrative tasks. This also ensures consistent and objective assessment of student work.

Imagine a university professor overwhelmed with grading hundreds of essays and exams. An AI grading system offers a solution by quickly and accurately assessing each assignment based on predefined criteria. The system provides detailed feedback to students, highlighting strengths and areas for improvement. This frees up the professor's time, allowing them to engage more deeply with students through discussions, mentorship, and personalized guidance. The consistency and objectivity of AI grading also ensure that all students are assessed fairly, regardless of subjective biases that might affect human graders.

1.4.4 Enhancing Public Services

1. Smart Cities:

- **Traffic Management**: AI systems optimize traffic flow in urban areas by analyzing real-time data from sensors and cameras. This reduces congestion, improves safety, and enhances the overall efficiency of transportation networks.

   Picture a bustling city plagued by traffic jams during rush hour. AI-driven traffic management systems come into play by continuously monitoring traffic conditions through an extensive network of sensors and cameras. These systems analyze real-time data to adjust traffic light timings, reroute vehicles, and inform drivers of alternative routes via mobile apps. For example, if a major accident causes a blockage on a key roadway, the AI system quickly detects the incident and redirects traffic to minimize delays. This dynamic response not only reduces congestion but also improves road safety by preventing secondary accidents. Over time, the city experiences smoother traffic flow and a more efficient transportation network.

- **Energy Management**: AI optimizes energy consumption in smart buildings by adjusting heating, cooling, and lighting based on occupancy and weather conditions. This leads to significant energy savings and reduces the environmental impact.

   Imagine an office building that intelligently manages its energy consumption. AI systems monitor the building's usage patterns and external weather conditions, making real-time adjustments to heating, cooling, and lighting. For instance, on a sunny winter day, the AI might reduce heating and open blinds to maximize natural warmth from the sun. At night, it dims unnecessary lights and lowers the temperature to conserve energy. These optimizations not only reduce the building's energy costs but also contribute to a smaller carbon footprint, aligning with sustainability goals. Employees also benefit from a comfortable and responsive indoor environment, enhancing their productivity and well-being.

2. Public Safety:

- **Predictive Policing**: AI analyzes crime data to predict potential criminal activities and allocate police resources more effectively. This proactive approach helps in preventing crimes and improving public safety.

   Consider a city implementing predictive policing to combat crime. AI systems analyze historical crime data, identifying patterns and trends that human analysts might miss. For example, the AI might detect a spike in burglaries in a particular neighborhood during specific times. Police departments can use this information to allocate resources more effectively, increasing patrols in vulnerable areas during high-risk periods. This proactive strategy deters criminal activities and enhances community safety. Moreover, the AI's ability to provide data-driven insights helps law enforcement agencies make informed decisions, fostering trust and cooperation between the police and the community.

1.4.5 Addressing Global Challenges

1. Climate Change:

- **Environmental Monitoring**: AI systems monitor environmental conditions and predict natural disasters, enabling timely interventions and reducing the impact of such events. For example, AI models can predict the path of hurricanes and the spread of wildfires.

  Imagine a coastal town facing the threat of hurricanes every year. Traditionally, weather forecasting relied heavily on historical data and meteorological models. With AI, the process has become far more sophisticated. AI models analyze real-time satellite imagery, atmospheric data, and historical storm paths to predict the trajectory and intensity of hurricanes with remarkable accuracy. For instance, during the 2020 hurricane season, AI-powered systems provided early warnings that allowed authorities to evacuate vulnerable populations and prepare emergency response plans more effectively. Similarly, in wildfire-prone regions, AI models assess various factors like temperature, humidity, wind patterns, and vegetation density to predict wildfire spread. This early detection enables firefighters to deploy resources strategically, containing fires before they escalate into uncontrollable infernos.

- **Sustainable Agriculture**: AI optimizes agricultural practices by analyzing soil conditions, weather patterns, and crop health. This leads to more efficient use of resources and increased crop yields, contributing to food security.

  Picture a farmer in a developing country struggling to maximize crop yields amidst unpredictable weather and limited resources. AI comes to the rescue by offering precision agriculture solutions. Using drones equipped with AI-powered sensors, the farmer can monitor soil health, moisture levels, and crop conditions in real-time. AI algorithms analyze this data to provide actionable insights, such as optimal planting times, targeted irrigation, and pest control strategies. For example, the AI might detect early signs of a pest infestation and recommend specific treatments, preventing widespread crop damage. This technology not only boosts agricultural productivity but also ensures efficient use of resources, such as water and fertilizers, ultimately enhancing food security and sustainability.

2. Healthcare Crises:

- **Pandemic Response**: During the COVID-19 pandemic, AI played a crucial role in tracking the spread of the virus, predicting outbreaks, and developing vaccines. AI models analyzed vast data to provide insights that guided public health decisions.

  The COVID-19 pandemic showcased the power of AI in managing global health crises. When the virus first emerged, AI systems rapidly processed data from numerous sources, including social media, news reports, and official health records, to identify early signs of the outbreak. One notable example is BlueDot, an AI platform that detected the outbreak in Wuhan and alerted authorities days before official announcements. Throughout the pandemic, AI models continued to predict the spread of the virus, helping governments implement targeted lockdowns and resource allocation. Furthermore, AI significantly accelerated vaccine development. By analyzing genetic sequences and previous research data, AI algorithms identified potential vaccine candidates in record time. This expedited the research and clinical trial phases, leading to the swift development and distribution of effective vaccines, which played a critical role in controlling the pandemic.

The necessity for artificial intelligence in societal development is apparent across multiple sectors. AI enhances economic productivity, advances healthcare, and improves education and public services, thereby providing many advantages that facilitate societal advancement. Furthermore, AI is integral to fostering a sustainable and resilient future by addressing significant global challenges, including climate change and healthcare crises.

1.5 Scope of Artificial Intelligence

The scope of Artificial Intelligence (AI) is vast and continually expanding, touching various domains and applications. Let's explore this in detail.

1. Technological Advancements

AI encompasses several key technologies, each contributing to its broad scope:

i. Machine Learning (ML): Machine Learning is a subset of AI that focuses on algorithms that improve through experience (Manning, 2020). There are three main types of ML:

- **Supervised Learning**: Involves training a model on labeled data. For example, a spam filter is trained on emails labeled as "spam" or "not spam" to learn how to classify new emails.

Imagine your email inbox being inundated with spam. Supervised learning algorithms can be trained on a dataset of emails that are labeled as either "spam" or "not spam." Over time, the algorithm learns to recognize patterns in the data that distinguish spam emails from legitimate ones. This process involves analyzing features such as keywords, sender information, and email structure. As a result, the spam filter becomes increasingly adept at identifying and filtering out unwanted emails, ensuring that your inbox remains clutter-free and that you receive only relevant communications.

- **Unsupervised Learning**: Deals with unlabeled data and finds hidden patterns. An example is customer segmentation in marketing, where the algorithm groups customers based on purchasing behavior without predefined labels.

   Consider a retail company wanting to better understand its customer base to improve marketing strategies. Using unsupervised learning, the company analyzes purchasing data without predefined labels. The algorithm identifies clusters of customers with similar buying habits. For example, it may discover a segment of customers who frequently purchase outdoor gear and another segment interested in high-end electronics. By recognizing these patterns, the company can tailor its marketing campaigns to target each segment more effectively, offering personalized promotions and improving customer satisfaction.

- **Reinforcement Learning**: Involves training models to make sequences of decisions by rewarding desired behaviors (Coursera, 2024). A classic example is AlphaGo, the AI that learned to play and master the game of Go by playing millions of games and learning from the outcomes.

   Reinforcement learning is like teaching a robot to play soccer. Imagine a virtual soccer environment where the AI, starting with no knowledge of the game, learns by trial and error. Initially, the robot makes random moves, but over time it learns which actions lead to goals and which do not. For every successful action (like scoring a goal), the AI receives a reward, reinforcing that behavior. Similarly, actions leading to failure (like losing possession) result in a negative reward. Through this process of continuous feedback and adjustment, the AI develops strategies to win games, eventually mastering complex moves and tactics similar to those used by human players.

ii. Natural Language Processing (NLP): NLP enables machines to understand and generate human language (Manning, 2020). This technology powers:

- **Chatbots**: Used in customer service to handle inquiries and provide support. For instance, many companies use chatbots to answer common questions, freeing up human agents for more complex issues.

Picture a telecom company receiving thousands of customer inquiries daily. Implementing an AI-powered chatbot helps manage this volume efficiently. The chatbot can handle routine questions such as "How do I check my balance?" or "How do I upgrade my plan?" by understanding and generating natural language responses. This not only speeds up response times but also ensures that human agents are available to resolve more complex issues. For instance, if a customer has a billing dispute, the chatbot can quickly transfer the conversation to a human agent, ensuring a seamless and efficient customer service experience.

a) **Language Translation**: Tools like Google Translate use NLP to translate text between languages, making communication across different languages easier (Wikipedia, 2019).

Imagine a traveler in a foreign country trying to navigate without knowing the local language. With NLP-based translation tools like Google Translate, they can simply type or speak their query in their native language, and the app provides an instant translation. For example, asking for directions or ordering food becomes much more manageable, as the traveler can communicate effectively with locals despite the language barrier. This technology also facilitates international business, where documents and communications can be accurately translated, enabling smooth and clear interactions between partners from different linguistic backgrounds.

iii. Robotics: AI-driven robots perform a wide range of tasks:

- **Industrial Automation**: Robots in manufacturing plants assemble products, perform quality checks, and handle materials. For example, car manufacturers use robotic arms to assemble vehicles.

  In a modern car manufacturing plant, robotic arms work alongside human engineers to build vehicles. These robots handle repetitive and precise tasks such as welding, painting, and assembling parts. For instance, a robotic arm equipped with AI vision systems can identify and position car components with millimeter precision, ensuring a perfect fit. This automation not only speeds up production but also maintains high quality by reducing the likelihood of human error. Additionally, robots can work around the clock without breaks, significantly increasing productivity throughout the manufacturing process.

- **Surgical Procedures**: Robots like the Da Vinci Surgical System assist surgeons in performing precise and minimally invasive surgeries (Krishna, 2021).

  Imagine a patient requiring a complex surgical procedure. The Da Vinci Surgical System, operated by a skilled surgeon, uses AI-driven robotic arms to perform the surgery with unparalleled precision. The system's robotic arms can make tiny, precise movements that would be challenging for human hands alone. For example, during a prostatectomy, the robotic system allows the surgeon to remove cancerous tissue while preserving surrounding nerves and structures. This minimally invasive approach results in shorter recovery times, reduced pain, and lower risk of complications, significantly enhancing patient outcomes.

iv. Computer Vision: This field allows machines to interpret and process visual information. Applications include:

- **Autonomous Vehicles**: Self-driving cars use computer vision to navigate roads, recognize traffic signals, and avoid obstacles. Companies like Tesla and Waymo are at the forefront of this technology.

    Picture a self-driving car navigating a busy city street. Computer vision enables the car to interpret real-time visual data from its cameras and sensors. It recognizes traffic signals, pedestrians, cyclists, and other vehicles, making split-second decisions to ensure safe travel. For example, if a pedestrian unexpectedly steps onto the crosswalk, the car's computer vision system detects the movement and automatically applies the brakes to avoid a collision. This technology, coupled with advanced AI algorithms, allows self-driving cars to operate safely and efficiently, reducing the risk of accidents and offering a glimpse into the future of transportation.

- **Facial Recognition**: This technology is used in security systems to identify individuals based on facial features. Airports and law enforcement agencies use facial recognition to enhance security (Terra, 2023).

    In a busy international airport, facial recognition technology streamlines the security process. Passengers approaching the security checkpoint have their faces scanned by AI-powered cameras. The system compares these scans with the photos on their passports to verify identities quickly and accurately. This not only enhances security by preventing unauthorized access but also speeds up the boarding process, reducing wait times for travelers. Similarly, law enforcement agencies use facial recognition to identify suspects in real-time, analyzing video footage from public spaces to detect and apprehend criminals more efficiently, thereby enhancing public safety.

2. Future Prospects

The future of AI holds even more promise:

- **Smart Cities**: AI will play a crucial role in managing urban infrastructure, optimizing traffic flow, and improving public services.

    Imagine a bustling metropolis where AI seamlessly integrates with every aspect of urban life. In this smart city, traffic congestion is a thing of the past. AI systems analyze data from thousands of sensors embedded in roads, traffic lights, and public transportation. They predict traffic flow and adjust signals in real-time to optimize vehicle movement, reducing delays and emissions. Public services are enhanced as well. For instance, waste management trucks are equipped with AI to optimize collection routes based on real-time data, ensuring efficient use of resources. Additionally, AI-powered public safety systems monitor surveillance feeds to detect and respond to emergencies swiftly, ensuring a safer environment for all residents.

- **Environmental Monitoring**: AI can analyze data from sensors and satellites to monitor environmental changes and predict natural disasters.

  Picture a vast network of AI-enabled satellites orbiting Earth, continuously gathering data on weather patterns, ocean temperatures, and forest conditions. This data is crucial for predicting natural disasters. For example, AI models analyze satellite imagery and environmental data to forecast the path of hurricanes with greater accuracy, allowing for timely evacuations and preparations. In wildfire-prone areas, AI systems detect early signs of fires by analyzing temperature anomalies and vegetation conditions. This early warning system enables firefighters to deploy resources more effectively, preventing small blazes from turning into catastrophic wildfires. Moreover, AI helps track long-term climate changes, providing valuable insights for policymakers to devise strategies for combating climate change.

- **Advanced Robotics**: Future robots will be more autonomous and capable of performing complex tasks in unstructured environments, such as disaster response and space exploration.

  Imagine an earthquake striking a densely populated city, leaving buildings collapsed and survivors trapped under rubble. Advanced robots equipped with AI are dispatched to the disaster site. These robots navigate the chaotic environment autonomously, using AI-driven sensors to identify signs of life and locate survivors. They can maneuver through tight spaces and unstable debris, delivering supplies and providing real-time data to human responders. Similarly, in the realm of space exploration, AI-powered robots play a crucial role. Picture a robot on Mars, autonomously conducting geological surveys, collecting samples, and transmitting data back to Earth. Its AI allows it to adapt to the harsh and unpredictable conditions of the Martian surface, making decisions independently to carry out its mission successfully.

AI's scope is vast and continually expanding, driven by advancements in machine learning, natural language processing, robotics, and computer vision. Its applications span various domains, from healthcare and finance to education and entertainment, with prospects promising even greater integration into our daily lives. As AI technology continues to evolve, it will undoubtedly bring about transformative changes, enhancing efficiency, solving complex challenges, and amplifying human capabilities.

1.6 Machine Learning (ML)

Machine learning, a dynamic branch of artificial intelligence, has revolutionized the way computers process data, recognize patterns, and make intelligent decisions without explicit programming. In the previous section, we briefly explored the foundational concepts of machine learning, categorizing it into supervised learning, unsupervised learning, and reinforcement learning.

Now, in this section, we will delve deeper into the principles and methodologies that drive these learning paradigms. You will gain a stronger grasp of how algorithms improve through experience, how models are trained to enhance predictive accuracy, and how various applications—from recommendation systems to autonomous machines—are powered by machine learning.

By strengthening your familiarity with this subject, you will develop a deeper understanding of how machine learning shapes technological advancements and real-world solutions. Let's embark on this insightful journey into the intricacies of machine learning.

1.6.1 Supervised Learning

Supervised learning is a fundamental method in machine learning that entails training a model with labeled data. Each training instance corresponds to a specific output label, allowing the model to learn to associate inputs with the appropriate outputs (Johnson & Wang, 2019). This concept will be explored extensively, along with several examples to demonstrate its practical applications.

How Supervised Learning Works

In supervised learning, the process typically involves the following steps:

1. **Data Collection**: Gather a dataset with input-output pairs. For example, in a spam filter, the dataset consists of emails (inputs) and labels indicating whether each email is "spam" or "not spam" (outputs).

    Imagine managing an email service with millions of users. To prevent spam emails from cluttering users' inboxes, you decide to implement a spam filter using supervised learning. You collect a vast dataset of emails, each labeled as either "spam" or "not spam." This data includes various features such as the email content, sender's address, and the presence of certain keywords. By analyzing these labeled emails, the model learns to recognize patterns that distinguish spam from legitimate emails. For instance, emails with phrases like "You've won a prize!" or from suspicious domains are more likely to be flagged as spam. As a result, the spam filter becomes increasingly accurate at keeping unwanted emails out of users' inboxes.

2. **Training**: Use the labeled data to train a machine learning model. The model learns to associate specific patterns in the input data with the corresponding labels.

   Consider a retail company that wants to predict customer churn, which refers to customers who stop using their services. The company collects a dataset with information about customers' purchase history, frequency of visits, and interactions with customer support, labeled as "churn" or "not churn." During the training phase, the model analyzes this data to identify patterns that indicate a higher likelihood of churn. For example, customers who haven't made a purchase in the past six months and frequently contacted support may be at risk of churning. By learning these associations, the model can predict which current customers are likely to churn, allowing the company to take proactive measures, such as offering discounts or personalized engagement, to retain them.

3. **Validation**: Evaluate the model's performance on a separate validation set to ensure it generalizes well to new, unseen data.

   After training a model to predict house prices based on features like location, size, and amenities, a real estate company needs to validate its performance. They use a separate set of housing data that the model hasn't seen before to evaluate its accuracy. The validation set includes various properties with known sale prices. By comparing the model's predictions to the actual sale prices, the company can assess how well the model generalizes to new data. For instance, if the model accurately predicts the prices of houses in different neighborhoods with varying features, it indicates that the model has learned the underlying patterns well and can be relied upon for future predictions.

4. **Testing**: Finally, test the model on a test set to assess its accuracy and effectiveness.

   A financial institution develops a supervised learning model to detect fraudulent transactions. After training and validating the model, they test it on a separate dataset of transactions to evaluate its performance. The test set includes both legitimate and fraudulent transactions, labeled accordingly. The model analyzes each transaction and predicts whether it is fraudulent or not. By comparing these predictions to the actual labels, the institution can measure the model's accuracy and effectiveness. For example, if the model correctly identifies the majority of fraudulent transactions while minimizing false positives (legitimate transactions flagged as fraudulent), it demonstrates its reliability. This robust testing phase ensures that the model can effectively detect and prevent fraud in real-world scenarios, protecting customers and the institution's financial assets.

Examples of Supervised Learning

1. Spam Filtering:

- **Training Data**: Emails labeled as "spam" or "not spam."
- **Model**: A classifier that learns to identify features of spam emails, such as certain keywords or patterns.
- **Application**: When a new email arrives, the model predicts whether it is spam based on the learned patterns.

Imagine an email service provider aiming to protect its users from an influx of spam emails. They collect a large dataset of emails, each tagged as "spam" or "not spam." The model is trained to recognize patterns indicative of spam, such as common phrases used in phishing attempts, suspicious links, and sender addresses. Over time, as the model processes more emails, it becomes more adept at filtering out spam, ensuring users receive only relevant and important messages.

2. Image Classification:

- **Training Data**: Images labeled with categories, such as "cat," "dog," "car," etc.
- **Model**: A convolutional neural network (CNN) that learns to recognize visual features associated with each category.
- **Application**: The model can classify new images into the correct categories, such as identifying whether a photo contains a cat or a dog.

Consider a photo-sharing app that wants to help users organize their image libraries. The app collects a vast dataset of labeled images—pictures of cats, dogs, cars, and more. A CNN is trained on this data, learning to identify the unique features of each category. When users upload new photos, the app can automatically sort them into categories, making it easy for users to find their favorite pictures of pets or vehicles.

3. Sentiment Analysis:

- **Training Data**: Text data labeled with sentiments, such as "positive," "negative," or "neutral."
- **Model**: A natural language processing (NLP) model that learns to detect sentiment based on word usage and context.
- **Application**: The model can analyze customer reviews or social media posts to determine the overall sentiment.

A company wants to understand customer feedback on its latest product. They gather thousands of reviews, each labeled as positive, negative, or neutral. The NLP model analyzes these reviews, learning to associate certain words and phrases with specific sentiments. For example, words like "excellent" and "love" are linked to positive sentiment, while words like "poor" and "disappointed" indicate negative sentiment. This analysis helps the company gauge customer satisfaction and identify areas for improvement.

4. Medical Diagnosis:

- **Training Data**: Medical records labeled with diagnoses, such as "diabetes," "heart disease," etc.
- **Model**: A predictive model that learns to identify risk factors and symptoms associated with each diagnosis.
- **Application**: The model can assist doctors by predicting the likelihood of a patient having a particular condition based on their medical data.

A hospital uses supervised learning to develop a model that predicts the risk of patients developing diabetes. They collect medical records, including patient histories, lab results, and lifestyle information, labeled with whether or not the patients developed diabetes. The model learns to identify risk factors, such as high blood sugar levels and family history. When a new patient arrives, the model analyzes their data and provides a risk assessment, helping doctors make informed decisions about preventative care.

5. Fraud Detection:

- **Training Data**: Transaction data labeled as "fraudulent" or "legitimate."
- **Model**: A classifier that learns to recognize patterns indicative of fraudulent transactions.
- **Application**: The model can flag suspicious transactions in real-time, helping to prevent fraud.

A bank aims to protect its customers from fraudulent activity. They collect transaction data, each labeled as either fraudulent or legitimate. The model learns to detect patterns that suggest fraud, such as unusual spending behaviors or transactions from unexpected locations. When a new transaction occurs, the model evaluates it in real-time and flags any suspicious activity, enabling the bank to take immediate action and protect customer accounts.

6. Speech Recognition:

- **Training Data**: Audio recordings labeled with the corresponding text.
- **Model**: A speech recognition model that learns to map audio features to text.
- **Application**: The model can transcribe spoken language into written text, which is useful in applications like virtual assistants and transcription services.

Imagine a virtual assistant like Alexa or Google Assistant. These devices rely on speech recognition models trained on vast datasets of audio recordings paired with transcriptions. The model learns to recognize the sounds of spoken words and map them to text accurately. When a user gives a voice command, the assistant transcribes it and takes appropriate action, such as setting a reminder or playing music. This technology makes interactions with devices more natural and convenient for users.

Advantages of Supervised Learning

- **Accuracy**: When trained on large, well-labelled datasets, supervised learning models can achieve high accuracy.
- **Interpretability**: The relationship between inputs and outputs is often clear, making it easier to understand how the model makes decisions.
- **Versatility**: Applicable to various tasks, from classification to regression.

Challenges of Supervised Learning

- **Data Dependency**: Requires a large amount of labelled data, which can be time-consuming and expensive to obtain.

  Consider a tech company developing a facial recognition system. To ensure high accuracy, they need a massive dataset of labelled images of diverse faces. Gathering this data involves not only taking countless photographs but also accurately labelling each one with attributes such as age, gender, and expression. This process can be both time-consuming and costly, requiring significant human effort and financial resources. Additionally, the company must address privacy concerns and obtain consent from individuals whose images are used, further complicating data collection.

- **Overfitting**: Models can become too tailored to the training data and perform poorly on new, unseen data.

  Imagine a financial institution training a model to predict loan defaults using historical data. If the model learns too much from the specific patterns in the training data, it might perform exceptionally well on that data but fail to generalize to new applicants. For example, if the training data is limited to a particular demographic or economic period, the model might struggle to predict defaults in a different demographic or during economic fluctuations. This overfitting problem means the model is highly accurate on known data but unreliable in real-world applications, potentially leading to poor decision-making and financial losses.

- **Bias**: If the training data is biased, the model's predictions will also be biased.

A healthcare organization develops an AI model to predict patient outcomes. However, if the training data primarily consists of records from one ethnic group, the model may not perform well for other groups. For instance, a model trained mostly on data from young, healthy individuals might not accurately predict outcomes for elderly or chronically ill patients. This bias can lead to unfair treatment recommendations and exacerbate existing health disparities. Addressing bias requires careful consideration of data diversity and fairness in model training and evaluation.

1.6.2 Unsupervised Learning

Unsupervised learning is a category of machine learning that focuses on unlabeled data, which lacks predefined categories or labels. The main objective of unsupervised learning is to uncover hidden patterns or intrinsic structures within the dataset. This method is especially advantageous in situations where labeling data is either impractical or unfeasible. We will examine this concept in depth, using various examples, particularly emphasizing customer segmentation in marketing.

How Unsupervised Learning Works

In unsupervised learning, the algorithm is given a dataset and must find patterns and relationships within it without any prior guidance. The two main types of unsupervised learning are clustering and association.

1. **Clustering**: This involves grouping data points into clusters based on their similarities. Common clustering algorithms include K-means, hierarchical clustering, and DBSCAN.
2. **Association**: This involves finding rules that describe large portions of the data, such as market basket analysis in retail.

Examples of Unsupervised Learning

1. Customer Segmentation in Marketing: Customer segmentation is a classic example of unsupervised learning. It involves dividing a customer base into distinct groups based on shared characteristics and behaviors. This segmentation helps businesses tailor their marketing efforts and improve customer satisfaction.

- **K-means Clustering**: One of the most popular clustering algorithms used for customer segmentation. It partitions customers into K clusters based on their purchasing behavior.

  Imagine an e-commerce company looking to understand its customer base better. They use K-means clustering to analyze purchase data, segmenting customers into groups such as "frequent buyers," "occasional buyers," and "one-time buyers"(Gomes & Meisen, 2023). This segmentation allows the company to tailor marketing campaigns to each group. For example, frequent buyers might receive loyalty rewards, occasional buyers could be targeted with special promotions, and one-time buyers might get personalized follow-up emails to encourage repeat purchases. By understanding and catering to the unique needs of each segment, the company can enhance customer satisfaction and boost sales.

- **Hierarchical Clustering**: This method builds a tree of clusters. It can be useful for understanding the hierarchical relationships between different customer segments.

  A retailer uses hierarchical clustering to delve deeper into its customer segments. This approach helps identify sub-groups within larger segments, such as "high-value frequent buyers" and "low-value frequent buyers" (Salminen et al., 2023). For instance, within the group of frequent buyers, the retailer might find that some customers consistently purchase high-end products, while others opt for more budget-friendly options. This insight enables the retailer to create more nuanced marketing strategies, such as premium product recommendations for high-value customers and discount offers for budget-conscious buyers, ultimately driving higher engagement and sales.

2. Market Basket Analysis: Market basket analysis is used to find associations between products purchased together. This technique helps retailers understand customer purchasing patterns and optimize product placement and promotions.

- **Apriori Algorithm**: This algorithm identifies frequent item sets and generates association rules.

  A supermarket employs the Apriori algorithm to analyze transaction data and uncover associations between products. They discover that customers who buy bread are also likely to buy butter (Katyayan et al., 2022). With this knowledge, the supermarket strategically places bread and butter together, increasing the likelihood of cross-selling. Additionally, they might bundle these items in promotions, encouraging customers to purchase both products. This data-driven approach not only boosts sales but also enhances the shopping experience by making it more convenient for customers to find complementary products.

3. Anomaly Detection: Unsupervised learning is also used for anomaly detection, where the goal is to identify unusual data points that do not fit the general pattern.

- **Isolation Forest**: This algorithm isolates observations by randomly selecting a feature and then selecting a split value between the maximum and minimum values of the selected feature. It is particularly effective for detecting anomalies in high-dimensional datasets.

In the realm of network security, an organization uses the Isolation Forest algorithm to monitor network traffic for anomalies. The algorithm analyzes patterns of data flow and detects deviations that may indicate a cyber attack (Saxena et al., 2024). For example, if the network experiences a sudden spike in data transfer from an unexpected location or an unusual access attempt at odd hours, the system flags these anomalies. This early detection allows the IT team to investigate and mitigate potential threats before they escalate, ensuring the security and integrity of the network.

4. Dimensionality Reduction: Dimensionality reduction techniques are used to reduce the number of random variables under consideration, simplifying the dataset while retaining its essential structure.

- **Principal Component Analysis (PCA)**: PCA transforms the data into a set of orthogonal components that capture the most variance. This technique is useful in image compression, where it reduces the number of pixels while preserving the image quality.

   In the field of digital imaging, a company aims to store high-quality images efficiently. They use PCA to compress images by reducing the number of pixels while maintaining visual integrity (Zhao et al., 2023). For example, a high-resolution image with millions of pixels can be transformed into a lower-dimensional representation that captures the most important features. When the image is displayed, it still appears clear and detailed, despite the reduced file size. This process enables the company to store and transmit images more efficiently, saving storage space and bandwidth while ensuring that image quality remains high.

Advantages of Unsupervised Learning

- **No Need for Labeled Data**: Unsupervised learning does not require labelled data, making it ideal for tasks where labelling is difficult or expensive.

   Consider a company that wants to analyze customer behavior across millions of transactions but lacks the resources to label each data point. Unsupervised learning algorithms can process this vast, unlabeled dataset to find meaningful patterns and insights without the need for manual labelling. This capability makes unsupervised learning highly valuable in situations where data labelling is impractical or impossible.

- **Discover Hidden Patterns**: It can uncover hidden patterns and structures in the data that may not be apparent through manual analysis.

   In the field of genetics, researchers use unsupervised learning to identify genetic markers associated with certain diseases. By analyzing massive datasets of genetic information, these algorithms can uncover subtle patterns and correlations that might be missed through traditional analysis. For instance, unsupervised learning might reveal a previously unknown genetic variant linked to a specific medical condition, paving the way for new research and treatments.

- **Flexibility**: Unsupervised learning algorithms can be applied to a wide range of problems and data types.

  A tech company looking to improve its recommendation system uses unsupervised learning to analyze user behavior across various platforms, including social media, streaming services, and e-commerce. The algorithms identify patterns in how users interact with different types of content, enabling the company to deliver personalized recommendations across multiple domains. This flexibility allows unsupervised learning to be leveraged in diverse fields, from entertainment to finance to healthcare.

Challenges of Unsupervised Learning

- **Interpretability**: The results of unsupervised learning can be difficult to interpret, as there are no predefined labels to guide the analysis.

  A financial analyst uses unsupervised learning to detect patterns in stock market data. While the algorithm identifies clusters of stocks that behave similarly, it does not provide explanations for these patterns. The analyst must interpret the results without clear labels, making it challenging to understand why certain stocks are grouped together and how to act on the findings. This lack of interpretability can hinder decision-making and requires additional expertise to decipher the results.

- **Evaluation**: Measuring the performance of unsupervised learning algorithms is challenging because there is no ground truth to compare against.

  A cybersecurity team deploys an unsupervised learning algorithm to detect anomalies in network traffic. While the algorithm flags unusual activities, no labelled data confirms whether these activities are genuinely malicious or benign. The team faces difficulty in evaluating the algorithm's accuracy and effectiveness, as there is no benchmark to compare against. This challenge necessitates ongoing monitoring and validation to ensure the reliability of the results.

- **Scalability**: Some unsupervised learning algorithms may struggle with large datasets or high-dimensional data.

  A retailer uses unsupervised learning to analyze customer behavior across a vast number of products and transactions. The high dimensionality of the data—considering factors like purchase frequency, product categories, and customer demographics—can overwhelm certain algorithms, leading to slow processing times and reduced accuracy. To address this, the retailer may need to implement dimensionality reduction techniques or employ more scalable algorithms, ensuring that the analysis remains efficient and effective despite the complexity of the data.

Unsupervised learning is a powerful tool for discovering hidden patterns and structures in unlabeled data. Its applications, such as customer segmentation in marketing, market basket analysis, anomaly detection, and dimensionality reduction, demonstrate its versatility and potential to provide valuable insights across various domains. As the field of machine learning continues to evolve, unsupervised learning will play an increasingly important role in helping businesses and researchers make sense of complex data.

1.6.3 Reinforcement Learning

Reinforcement Learning (RL) is a form of machine learning in which an agent learns to make decisions by taking actions within an environment to maximize a cumulative reward. In contrast to supervised learning, which depends on labelled data, RL focuses on learning through interactions with the environment. Let us explore this concept further.

How Reinforcement Learning Works

In RL, the learning process involves:

1. **Agent**: The learner or decision-maker.
2. **Environment**: The external system with which the agent interacts.
3. **State**: A representation of the current situation of the agent.
4. **Action**: The set of all possible moves the agent can make.
5. **Reward**: The feedback from the environment based on the action taken.
6. **Policy**: The strategy that the agent employs to determine the next action based on the current state.
7. **Value Function**: A function that estimates the expected cumulative reward of states or state-action pairs.

The agent's goal is to learn a policy that maximizes the cumulative reward over time. This is typically achieved through trial and error, where the agent explores different actions and learns from the outcomes.

Consider a robot vacuum cleaner learning to navigate a new home. The vacuum represents the **agent** and the home is its **environment**. At any given moment, the vacuum has a **state** that describes its current position and the layout of the room. It can take various **actions**, such as moving forward, turning left, or turning right. Each action results in a **reward**, like successfully avoiding obstacles or efficiently cleaning a dirty spot. Initially, the vacuum may bump into walls or miss dirty areas. However, through trial and error, it develops a **policy**—a strategy that helps it decide the best actions to take in different states to maximize its cleaning efficiency (the cumulative reward). Over time, the vacuum optimizes its path, learning to clean the house thoroughly and efficiently.

Examples of Reinforcement Learning

1. AlphaGo: AlphaGo, developed by DeepMind, is a prime example of RL. It learned to play and master the game of Go by playing millions of games against itself and learning from the outcomes. AlphaGo uses a combination of RL and deep learning to evaluate board positions and select moves (Adams, 2000). The success of AlphaGo demonstrated the potential of RL in solving complex problems that require strategic planning and decision-making.

AlphaGo's journey began with a significant challenge: mastering the ancient and complex game of Go, which has more possible moves than atoms in the universe. The AI started with a basic understanding of the game rules and then played against itself millions of times. Through these simulations, it learned strategies and refined its decision-making process. Each game provided feedback, with wins and losses serving as rewards and penalties. Eventually, AlphaGo defeated some of the world's best human Go players, showcasing the incredible potential of RL to handle tasks that require deep strategic thinking.

2. Robotics: RL is widely used in robotics for tasks such as navigation, manipulation, and control. For example, a robot can learn to navigate through a maze by receiving positive rewards for reaching the goal and negative rewards for hitting obstacles. Over time, the robot learns the optimal path to the goal (Lysakowski & Walberg, 1981).

Imagine a robot designed to navigate through a warehouse to transport items from one location to another. Initially, the robot moves randomly, often bumping into shelves or getting stuck. Through RL, it receives positive rewards for reaching the target location and negative rewards for collisions. The robot eventually finds the most efficient routes by continually exploring different paths and learning from their experiences. It learns to avoid obstacles, optimize its movements, and handle various challenges in the dynamic environment of the warehouse, significantly improving productivity and reducing operational costs.

3. Autonomous Vehicles: RL is crucial in developing self-driving cars. These vehicles learn to make driving decisions, such as lane changes and speed adjustments, by interacting with the driving environment. The reward signals can be based on safety metrics, efficiency, and comfort (Papers with Code - Reinforcement Learning (RL), n.d.).

Think of a self-driving car navigating busy city streets. Through RL, the car learns to make real-time decisions by interacting with its environment. It receives rewards for safe driving behaviors, such as maintaining a safe distance from other vehicles, stopping at red lights, and smooth lane changes. Negative rewards come from near misses or abrupt braking. Over time, the car's AI refines its driving policy, learning to anticipate and react to complex traffic scenarios. This continuous learning process enhances the car's ability to navigate safely and efficiently, contributing to the development of reliable autonomous vehicles.

4. Game Playing: Beyond AlphaGo, RL has been used to develop agents that play various video games. For instance, the RL algorithm DQN (Deep Q-Network) was used to achieve human-level performance in several Atari games by learning from raw pixel inputs and game scores (Fahad Mon et al., 2023).

Imagine an AI playing the classic Atari game Breakout. At first, the AI randomly moves the paddle, missing many balls. Through RL, the AI receives positive rewards for successfully hitting the ball and negative rewards for missing it. Over thousands of games, the DQN algorithm learns the optimal strategies to keep the ball in play, break more bricks, and achieve higher scores. This process involves recognizing patterns in the game's visual input and responding with precise actions. The result is an AI that can master the game and achieve scores comparable to or surpass human players, demonstrating the power of RL in gaming.

5. Finance: In finance, RL is used for portfolio management and trading strategies. An RL agent can learn to allocate assets in a portfolio by maximizing returns and minimizing risks based on historical market data (Li, 2017).

Consider an investment firm using RL to manage a portfolio of stocks. The RL agent is trained on historical market data, learning to balance the portfolio by buying and selling assets. It receives rewards for positive returns and penalizations for losses or high volatility. Over time, the agent refines its strategies, learning to anticipate market trends and react to changes. For example, the agent might recognize patterns indicating an economic downturn and adjust the portfolio to minimize losses. This continuous learning and adaptation process helps the firm optimize its investment strategies, aiming for consistent and robust financial performance.

1.6.4 Natural Language Processing (NLP)

Natural Language Processing (NLP) is an AI field that focuses on the interaction between computers and human language. It enables machines to understand, interpret, and generate human language. NLP combines computational linguistics with machine learning and deep learning models.

How NLP Works

NLP involves several key tasks:

1. **Tokenization**: Splitting text into words or sentences.

    Imagine a digital assistant that helps you write emails. The first step in understanding your input is tokenization, where the assistant breaks down your sentence into individual words or tokens. For example, if you say, "Send an email to John," the assistant splits this into tokens: ["Send", "an", "email", "to", "John"]. This process helps the assistant analyze each component of the sentence to understand your command.

2. **Part-of-Speech Tagging**: Identifying the grammatical parts of speech in a sentence.

   Consider a grammar-checking tool integrated into your word processor. When you type, "The quick brown fox jumps over the lazy dog," the tool identifies the parts of speech for each word: ["The" (Determiner), "quick" (Adjective), "brown" (Adjective), "fox" (Noun), "jumps" (Verb), "over" (Preposition), "the" (Determiner), "lazy" (Adjective), "dog" (Noun)]. By understanding the grammatical structure, the tool can suggest improvements and corrections to enhance your writing.

3. **Named Entity Recognition (NER)**: Identifying entities such as names, dates, and locations in text.

   Imagine a news aggregator app that summarizes daily news articles for you. To provide relevant updates, the app uses NER to identify key entities in the text. For example, in the sentence, "The President of the United States, Joe Biden, visited New York on September 20th," the app recognizes "Joe Biden" as a person, "United States" and "New York" as locations, and "September 20th" as a date. This allows the app to generate concise summaries and highlight important information.

4. **Sentiment Analysis**: Determining the sentiment expressed in a piece of text.

   A company monitors social media to gauge public opinion about its brand. They use sentiment analysis to evaluate tweets, reviews, and comments. For instance, the tweet "I love the new product, it's amazing!" is analyzed as positive, while "The customer service was terrible" is labeled as negative. By aggregating these sentiments, the company can track overall customer satisfaction and identify areas for improvement.

5. **Machine Translation**: Translating text from one language to another.

   A travel enthusiast plans a trip to Japan and uses a translation app to communicate with locals. When they input "How do I get to the nearest train station?" the app translates it to Japanese: "最寄りの駅への行き方は？". The accuracy and fluency of the translation enable effective communication despite the language barrier, enhancing the travel experience.

6. **Text Summarization**: Creating a concise summary of a longer text.

Consider a busy professional who needs to stay informed but doesn't have time to read lengthy reports. He uses a text summarization tool that condenses comprehensive documents into summaries. For example, a 10-page report on market trends is summarized into a few key points: "Market growth driven by technology sector. Increased investment in AI and cybersecurity. Forecasted expansion in emerging markets." This allows the professional to quickly grasp essential information and make informed decisions.

7. **Question Answering**: Building systems that can answer questions posed in natural language.

A student uses an AI-powered educational app to study for exams. They type in a question like, "What are the main causes of climate change?" The app processes this question and provides a concise, accurate answer: "The main causes of climate change are greenhouse gas emissions from human activities, deforestation, and industrial processes." This capability helps the student efficiently find information and enhance their learning experience.

Examples of NLP in Action

Artificial Intelligence has infiltrated many aspects of our daily lives, often in ways we might not even notice. Let's delve into some examples of Natural Language Processing (NLP) at work, demonstrating its versatility and impact.

1. Chatbots: Your Virtual Customer Service Agent

Imagine this: you're frustrated with a product, and instead of waiting on hold for ages, you type your concern into a chat window. Within seconds, you're greeted by a chatbot that understands your issue and provides a solution, saving you time and reducing your stress.

For instance, companies like Amazon and banks employ chatbots to handle customer inquiries efficiently. These virtual agents use NLP to comprehend and respond to user questions, enabling seamless customer support (Sawicki et al., 2023).

2. Language Translation: Bridging the Gap

Remember that time you were traveling abroad and couldn't understand the local language? Tools like Google Translate come to the rescue by instantly translating your text. This magic happens through NLP, which utilizes vast datasets and sophisticated models to break down language barriers (Khurana et al., 2022).

Imagine a businessman in Tokyo using Google Translate to negotiate with a partner in Lagos, making international business smoother than ever.

3. Sentiment Analysis: Gauging the Mood

Have you ever wondered how businesses know what people are saying about them online? Through sentiment analysis, NLP scans customer reviews, social media posts, and other text data to determine the overall sentiment—whether it's positive, negative, or neutral (Siddharth et al., 2022).

For example, a restaurant chain might use sentiment analysis to identify unhappy customers and address their concerns, improving overall customer satisfaction.

4. Speech Recognition: Conversing with Technology

"Hey Siri, what's the weather like today?" Speech recognition systems like Siri and Alexa are prime examples of NLP in action. These systems convert spoken language into text and process it to generate appropriate responses (Sheetal Kusal et al., 2023).

Think about how this technology can assist visually impaired individuals, enabling them to interact with their devices using voice commands, thereby enhancing accessibility.

5. Text Summarization: Digesting Information Quickly

Ever felt overwhelmed by the sheer amount of information available online? NLP techniques are used to create concise summaries of long documents, helping you grasp the key points quickly. This is particularly useful in fields like news aggregation and academic research (Adams, 2000).

Imagine a journalist needing to stay updated with numerous articles daily—text summarization tools can make this task manageable by providing quick overviews.

1.7 The AI Revolution and Impact on Society

1.7.1 Industrial Automation

AI-driven robots are transforming industrial automation, making manufacturing processes more efficient, precise, and safe. Here are some notable examples:

1. Automobile Manufacturing: Precision on the Assembly Line

Picture a bustling car assembly line, where robots and humans work in perfect harmony. Car manufacturers like Ford and BMW use robotic arms to build vehicles with unparalleled precision (Daley, 2019). These arms weld, paint, and assemble parts flawlessly, reducing human error and speeding up production (Khanna, 2024).

In one instance, a Ford plant adopted robotic arms to streamline its operations. Within months, the plant saw a significant drop in defects and a spike in production rates, proving the immense potential of AI in manufacturing.

Collaborative robots, or cobots, are another marvel of AI. These robots work alongside human workers, handling repetitive tasks such as sanding car bodies or applying adhesives. This collaboration not only boosts productivity but also allows human workers to tackle more complex and creative tasks (Web, 2024).

2. Quality Control: Ensuring Perfection

Imagine robots with hawk-like vision, scanning products for defects. Companies like Intel use AI-powered computer vision systems to inspect products, ensuring high-quality output. These systems can detect even the tiniest flaws in semiconductor manufacturing, guaranteeing excellence (Daley, 2019).

In addition to quality control, predictive maintenance is a game-changer. Siemens employs AI-driven robots to monitor equipment health and predict maintenance needs. This proactive approach minimizes downtime and extends the lifespan of machinery, saving companies significant costs (Daley, 2019).

A semiconductor manufacturing plant once struggled with frequent equipment failures. After implementing AI for predictive maintenance, the plant's efficiency soared, with a drastic reduction in unplanned downtimes.

3. Material Handling: Seamless Logistics

Envision a warehouse where autonomous mobile robots (AMRs) navigate seamlessly, transporting materials and products. Amazon utilizes these robots to streamline its logistics operations, drastically reducing the time required to fulfil orders (Web, 2024).

The introduction of AMRs revolutionized logistics at one of Amazon's largest fulfilment centers. Robots carried products across vast warehouse floors, ensuring timely deliveries and enhancing overall efficiency.

Both **Reinforcement Learning (RL)** and **Natural Language Processing (NLP)** continue to push the boundaries of technology. RL focuses on training models to make sequences of decisions by rewarding desired behaviors, epitomized by systems like AlphaGo. NLP, on the other hand, enables machines to understand and generate human language, facilitating applications such as chatbots, language translation, and sentiment analysis.

The interplay between RL and NLP is propelling AI advancements, expanding its capabilities and impact across various industries.

1.7.2 Surgical Procedures

AI-driven robots have significantly advanced the field of surgery, offering unprecedented precision, control, and outcomes. Let's explore some key examples that highlight their transformative impact:

1. Da Vinci Surgical System: Precision in the Operating Room

Imagine a surgeon sitting at a console, manipulating robotic arms that translate their hand movements into precise actions inside a patient's body. The Da Vinci Surgical System allows surgeons to perform complex procedures with remarkable accuracy (Patel, 2024). This system is commonly used for surgeries such as prostatectomies, hysterectomies, and cardiac valve repairs. The robotic arms, equipped with advanced instruments, provide greater dexterity and stability than human hands alone, reducing the risk of complications and promoting faster recovery times (Godwin Ugwua, 2023).

Consider Dr. Patel, a leading cardiac surgeon, who once faced a challenging valve repair surgery. Using the Da Vinci system, he was able to navigate the delicate tissues and blood vessels with exceptional precision, avoiding any damage to surrounding structures. The patient's recovery was swift, with minimal post-operative pain and a shorter hospital stay, showcasing the benefits of robotic-assisted surgery.

2. Orthopedic Surgery: Personalized Implants and Better Outcomes

In orthopedic surgery, AI-assisted robots are making significant strides in procedures like knee and hip replacements. These robots use advanced imaging and AI algorithms to analyze the patient's biomechanics and create personalized surgical plans. This ensures that implants are placed with high accuracy, leading to better alignment, longevity, and patient outcomes (RAIA, 2024).

Imagine Mary, an active retiree, needed a knee replacement due to severe arthritis. Her surgeon utilized an AI-assisted robotic system to plan the surgery meticulously. The robot analyzed Mary's unique knee structure and movement patterns, allowing for a custom-fit implant. Post-surgery, Mary experienced a dramatic improvement in mobility and reduced pain, enabling her to resume her favorite activities like hiking and dancing.

3. Spinal Surgery: Enhanced Precision and Safety

AI technologies are also revolutionizing spinal surgeries, where precision is critical. AI algorithms assist surgeons by analyzing preoperative imaging to plan and execute procedures with high accuracy. This reduces the likelihood of complications, such as nerve damage, and improves patient outcomes (Han et al., 2024).

Consider John, who had been suffering from chronic back pain, underwent a spinal fusion surgery assisted by AI technology. The AI system provided detailed insights from John's MRI scans, guiding the surgeon to the exact spots needing intervention. The surgery was a success, with John experiencing significant pain relief and regaining his ability to perform daily tasks without discomfort.

4. Real-Time Assistance: Hugo™ Robotic-Assisted Surgery System

Developed by Medtronic, the Hugo™ Robotic-Assisted Surgery System leverages AI to provide real-time assistance to surgeons during procedures. This system offers insights by identifying anatomical structures and predicting potential complications, thereby enhancing surgical accuracy and safety (Dam, 2023).

Example: The Hugo system played a crucial role during a complex abdominal surgery. It continuously analyzed the surgical site and provided real-time alerts to the surgeon about critical areas and potential complications. This allowed the surgical team to adjust their approach dynamically, ultimately leading to a successful operation with no unexpected issues.

AI-driven robots are transforming various industries by performing a wide range of tasks with increased efficiency, precision, and safety. In industrial automation, they streamline manufacturing processes, improve quality control, and optimize material handling. In the medical field, they enhance the precision and outcomes of surgical procedures, making surgeries safer and less invasive. These advancements underscore the profound impact of AI and robotics on modern society, paving the way for continued innovation and improvement in numerous fields.

1.7.3 Autonomous Vehicles

Computer vision is a critical component in the development of autonomous vehicles, enabling them to perceive and interpret their surroundings. Let's explore some key applications and examples that showcase their impact:

1. Navigation and Path Planning: The Road Ahead

Autonomous vehicles rely on sophisticated systems to navigate roads, recognize traffic signals, and avoid obstacles. Tesla's Autopilot system is a prime example, using a combination of cameras, radar, and ultrasonic sensors to process visual data and make real-time driving decisions (Efe, 2024).

Imagine driving through a bustling city with Teslas around you, smoothly navigating traffic without human intervention. Tesla's Autopilot uses computer vision algorithms to interpret the environment, allowing the car to adjust its speed, change lanes, and even stop at red lights, ensuring a safe and efficient journey.

Waymo, a subsidiary of Alphabet Inc., takes this a step further with advanced computer vision techniques to create detailed 3D maps of the environment. These maps help the vehicle understand its surroundings and navigate safely (Efe, 2024).

Waymo's self-driving cars offer a glimpse into the future in Phoenix, Arizona. Equipped with lidar and cameras, these cars create high-definition maps, allowing them to navigate complex urban environments with precision and ease.

2. Object Detection and Recognition: Seeing is Believing

For autonomous vehicles to operate safely, they must accurately detect and recognize objects such as pedestrians, cyclists, and other vehicles. Mobileye's EyeQ system, for example, uses deep learning algorithms to ensure safe interactions on the road (Efe, 2024).

Picture a busy crosswalk with pedestrians and cyclists. An autonomous vehicle equipped with Mobileye's EyeQ system can identify each person and vehicle, predicting their movements and adjusting its path to avoid collisions.

Traffic sign recognition is another critical aspect, with systems developed by Bosch and Continental using computer vision to recognize and interpret traffic signs. This allows autonomous vehicles to obey traffic laws and navigate complex road environments (Efe, 2024).

On a highway, an autonomous vehicle encounters various traffic signs, including speed limits and construction warnings. Thanks to advanced computer vision, the vehicle accurately interprets these signs and adjusts its driving behavior accordingly.

3. Lane Detection and Keeping: Staying on Track

Lane detection and keeping are vital for highway driving. NVIDIA's Drive PX platform uses convolutional neural networks (CNNs) to detect lane markings and keep the vehicle centered in its lane (Efe, 2024).

Imagine cruising on a highway with an autonomous vehicle that effortlessly stays within its lane, even during sharp curves or heavy traffic. NVIDIA's Drive PX platform ensures this by continuously analyzing lane markings and adjusting the vehicle's trajectory.

1.7.4 Facial Recognition

Facial recognition technology leverages computer vision to identify individuals based on their facial features. Here are some notable applications and examples that highlight its significance:

1. Security and Surveillance: Enhancing Safety

Many airports worldwide use facial recognition systems to enhance security and streamline passenger processing. The U.S. Transportation Security Administration (TSA), for instance, employs facial recognition at various airports to verify passenger identities and expedite boarding (Adjabi et al., 2020).

At a busy airport, facial recognition technology scans passengers' faces, quickly matching them with their travel documents. This not only speeds up the boarding process but also enhances security by accurately identifying individuals.

Law enforcement agencies also use facial recognition to identify suspects and solve crimes. The New York Police Department (NYPD) has implemented this technology to match surveillance footage with criminal databases, aiding in the identification and apprehension of suspects (Adjabi et al., 2020).

During an investigation, the NYPD uses facial recognition to analyze footage from a crime scene. The system quickly identifies a suspect by matching the facial features with those in the criminal database, leading to a swift arrest.

2. Access Control: Secure and Convenient

Facial recognition is widely used in smartphones for secure access. Apple's Face ID technology uses a combination of infrared sensors and machine learning algorithms to accurately recognize users' faces, providing a secure and convenient authentication method (Adjabi et al., 2020).

With a simple glance, a smartphone owner can unlock their device, thanks to Apple's Face ID technology. This combination of security and convenience has become a standard feature in modern smartphones.

Companies like NEC and Hikvision provide facial recognition solutions for corporate security, allowing businesses to control access to sensitive areas and monitor employee attendance (Adjabi et al., 2020).

In a high-security office building, employees use facial recognition to access restricted areas. The system ensures that only authorized personnel can enter, enhancing security and streamlining attendance monitoring.

3. Retail and Marketing: Enhancing Customer Engagement

Retailers are leveraging facial recognition to analyze customer behavior and preferences, transforming the shopping experience.

Customer Analytics: Alibaba's "Smile to Pay" system allows customers to make payments using facial recognition, offering a seamless and convenient checkout process. This system not only enhances the shopping experience but also provides valuable data for personalized marketing (Adjabi et al., 2020).

In an Alibaba store, a customer simply smiles at a camera to complete their purchase. This innovative payment method is quick and secure, and it also collects data on customer preferences, enabling personalized marketing strategies.

Personalized Advertising: Digital billboards equipped with facial recognition can display targeted advertisements based on the demographics and emotions of passersby. This technology enables more effective and engaging advertising campaigns (Adjabi et al., 2020).

While walking through a shopping mall, a passerby notices a digital billboard that displays an advertisement for a product they've been interested in. The billboard uses facial recognition to gauge the person's age and mood, tailoring the ad to be more relevant and appealing.

Computer vision is transforming various industries by enabling machines to interpret and process visual information. In autonomous vehicles, it enhances navigation, object detection, and lane-keeping capabilities, making self-driving cars safer and more efficient. In facial recognition, it improves security, access control, and customer engagement, offering numerous benefits across different sectors. These advancements highlight the profound impact of computer vision on modern technology and its potential for future innovations.

1.7.5 AI Fraud Detection

Artificial Intelligence (AI) has become a crucial tool in detecting and preventing fraudulent activities in the financial sector. By analyzing transaction patterns and monitoring activities in real-time, AI systems can identify suspicious behavior and mitigate fraud risks. Here are some key applications and examples:

Real-Time Transaction Monitoring

Pattern Recognition: Spotting the Anomalies AI systems use machine learning algorithms to analyze vast amounts of transaction data and identify patterns indicative of fraud. For example, neural networks can detect anomalies in transaction sequences that may suggest fraudulent activity. These systems continuously learn from new data, improving their accuracy over time (Sood et al., 2023).

Imagine a bank that processes millions of transactions daily. The AI system in place analyzes these transactions in real time, looking for unusual patterns. One day, the system flags a series of small but rapid transactions from multiple accounts, all linked to a single point of sale. This anomaly raises a red flag for potential fraudulent activity. The bank's fraud investigation team is immediately alerted and can freeze the suspicious accounts, preventing further losses. Over time, the AI learns from this incident and becomes more adept at recognizing similar fraudulent patterns in the future.

Credit Card Fraud: Vigilant Monitoring Companies like Visa and Mastercard employ AI to monitor credit card transactions in real time. AI models analyze spending patterns and flag transactions that deviate from the norm, such as unusually large purchases or transactions in different geographic locations (Bao et al., 2020).

Consider Sarah, a frequent traveler, who receives a notification from her credit card company while she's on a business trip. The AI system noticed a large purchase made in a city she recently visited, which seemed out of character compared to her usual spending habits. The system temporarily holds the transaction and alerts Sarah to verify it. Sarah confirms that she did make the purchase, and the transaction proceeds smoothly. This prompt detection not only protects Sarah's account from potential fraud but also gives her peace of mind while travelling.

Behavioral Analysis: Understanding User Actions

User Behavior Analytics (UBA): Anomalies in Actions AI systems track user behavior to detect deviations that may indicate fraud. For instance, if a user's login patterns suddenly change, such as logging in from a new device or location, the system can flag this as suspicious. Banks use UBA to protect online banking platforms from unauthorized access (Bao et al., 2020).

Imagine John, a long-term customer of a major bank, suddenly starts logging into his account from a new device and a different city. The AI system, which tracks user behavior, identifies this change as unusual and flags it. John receives a notification asking him to verify his identity. It turns out that John was travelling for work and using a new company laptop. This quick verification process ensures that John's account is secure while accommodating his new login circumstances.

Insider Threat Detection: Monitoring from Within AI can also monitor employee behavior to detect potential insider threats. By analyzing access patterns and data usage, AI systems can identify employees who may be engaging in fraudulent activities (Bao et al., 2020).

Imagine that the AI system in a financial firm monitors employees' access to sensitive information. One day, it detects unusual activity from an employee who is accessing large volumes of confidential data during non-working hours. The system flags this behavior as potentially suspicious and alerts the security team. An investigation reveals that the employee was attempting to steal proprietary information. Thanks to the AI system's vigilance, the firm can prevent data theft and take appropriate action against the employee.

AI-driven fraud detection systems play a vital role in safeguarding the financial sector. By monitoring transactions in real-time and analyzing user behavior, these systems can quickly identify and mitigate fraud risks, protecting both institutions and customers. The continuous learning capabilities of AI ensure that these systems remain adaptive and effective in the ever-evolving landscape of financial fraud.

1.7.6 Algorithmic Trading

Algorithmic trading involves using computer algorithms to execute trades at high speeds and volumes, optimizing investment strategies based on market data. AI has significantly enhanced this process by enabling more sophisticated analysis and decision-making. Here are some key applications and examples:

High-Frequency Trading (HFT)

Speed and Efficiency: Executing with Lightning Speed. High-Frequency Trading (HFT) firms leverage AI to execute trades within fractions of a second, capitalizing on fleeting opportunities in the market. Citadel Securities, a leading firm in HFT, uses AI to perform thousands of trades per second. Their algorithms analyze real-time market data to identify and exploit short-term price discrepancies, generating consistent profits from small price movements (Ligon, 2024).

Imagine that at Citadel Securities, the trading floor is abuzz with activity as AI algorithms continuously scan global markets for arbitrage opportunities. One day, an unexpected announcement caused a temporary dip in the stock prices of a major tech company. The AI system detects this anomaly in milliseconds and initiates a series of rapid trades to buy the stock at a lower price. Moments later, as the market corrects itself, the AI sells the stock at a higher price, securing a profit. This high-speed trading, driven by AI, allows Citadel Securities to stay ahead of market fluctuations and maximize their gains.

Virtu Financial, another prominent HFT firm, employs AI-driven algorithms to assess risks and adjust trading strategies instantaneously. These algorithms process vast amounts of data in microseconds, enabling Virtu to capitalize on fleeting market opportunities (Team DigitalDefynd, 2024).

Virtu Financial's AI system monitors global financial news, economic indicators, and market sentiment in real-time. During a volatile trading session, news of a geopolitical event breaks, causing sudden market swings. The AI system quickly analyzes the situation, adjusts risk parameters, and executes trades that hedge against potential losses while taking advantage of the market's rapid movements. Virtu's ability to swiftly respond to market dynamics showcases the power of AI in high-frequency trading.

Market Making: Balancing Supply and Demand AI-powered market-making algorithms dynamically adjust bid and ask prices based on real-time market conditions. This helps maintain liquidity in the market and ensures that trades are executed efficiently. Firms like Jane Street use AI to optimize their market-making strategies, improving their ability to provide liquidity and manage risk (CP, 2024).

Imagine Jane Street, a leading market-making firm, relies on AI to maintain liquidity in various financial markets. Their AI system continuously analyzes market trends, order flows, and price movements to set optimal bid and ask prices. During a period of high volatility, the AI detects a surge in trading activity for a particular stock. It quickly adjusts the bid and asks prices to accommodate the increased demand while ensuring minimal spread between them. This dynamic adjustment ensures that traders can buy and sell the stock without significant price gaps, maintaining market stability. Jane Street's use of AI in market-making exemplifies how advanced algorithms can enhance market efficiency and liquidity.

Algorithmic trading, powered by AI, has revolutionized the financial markets by enabling high-speed, high-volume trading with unparalleled precision. The continuous advancements in AI technology further enhance the capabilities of HFT and market-making strategies, driving innovation and efficiency in the financial sector.

1.7.7 Personalized Learning

Personalized learning involves tailoring educational experiences to meet each student's unique needs, preferences, and abilities. AI-powered platforms have significantly advanced this approach by providing customized learning experiences. Here are some key applications:

Adaptive Learning Systems

Khan Academy: Personalized Lesson Recommendations Khan Academy uses AI to analyze student performance and recommend personalized lessons. The platform adapts to each student's learning pace, providing additional practice for concepts they struggle with and advancing them to new topics when ready (K. Bayly-Castaneda et al., 2024). This personalized approach helps students master subjects more effectively.

Imagine Emma, a high school sophomore, struggles with algebra. She logs into Khan Academy, where the AI system analyzes her previous performance and identifies areas of difficulty. The system recommends targeted lessons and practice exercises to help Emma improve her understanding of algebraic equations. As she progresses, the AI adapts, offering more challenging problems when she is ready. This personalized approach allows Emma to build confidence in her math skills and excel in her coursework.

DreamBox Learning: Adaptive Mathematics Education DreamBox Learning is an adaptive learning platform that focuses on mathematics education for K-8 students. It uses AI to assess students' understanding in real-time and adjust the difficulty of problems accordingly. The system provides immediate feedback and hints, helping students build a strong foundation in math (Laak, 2024).

Consider Jake, a third-grader, who uses DreamBox Learning for his math homework. The AI system monitors his progress as he solves math problems, adjusting the difficulty based on his performance. When Jake struggles with a particular concept, the platform offers hints and additional practice problems to reinforce his understanding. Conversely, when he excels, the AI introduces more complex challenges to keep him engaged. This dynamic and responsive approach ensures that Jake continuously builds his math skills at an appropriate pace.

Smart Sparrow: Interactive and Personalized Courseware Smart Sparrow offers adaptive learning technology that allows educators to create interactive and personalized courseware. The platform uses AI to track student interactions and performance, adapting the content to meet individual learning needs. This approach enhances student engagement and improves learning outcomes (Kam Cheong Li & Billy Tak-Ming Wong, 2023).

In a college biology course, Professor Smith uses Smart Sparrow to create an interactive module on genetics. As students engage with the module, the AI system tracks their progress and identifies areas where they may need additional support. For instance, when a student struggles with understanding Mendelian inheritance patterns, the AI provides supplementary materials and interactive simulations to clarify the concept. This personalized approach keeps students engaged and helps them master complex topics more effectively.

AI-powered personalized learning platforms are revolutionizing education by providing tailored experiences that cater to individual student needs. These adaptive learning systems enhance student engagement, improve learning outcomes, and help students master subjects more effectively. The continuous advancements in AI technology ensure that personalized learning remains dynamic and responsive to the evolving needs of students.

The infographics below show an estimate of the application of AI across different industries and the percentages of their application.

Industry	AI Application	Percentage
Healthcare	Medical imaging analysis	35%
Finance	Fraud detection	30%
Retail	Personalized recommendations	25%
Manufacturing	Predictive maintenance	20%
Transportation	Autonomous vehicles	15%
Customer Service	Chatbots and virtual assistants	40%
Marketing	Targeted advertising	30%
Entertainment	Content recommendation	25%
Agriculture	Crop monitoring and management	10%
Education	Personalized learning	15%

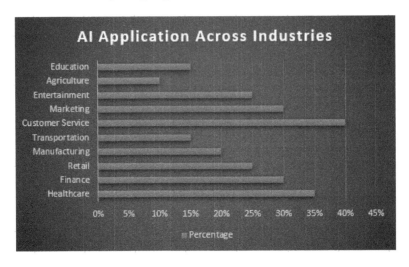

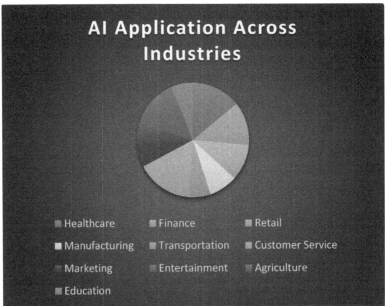

These percentages are approximate and can vary based on different studies and reports. The impact and adoption rates might differ slightly across regions and specific companies within each industry.

1.8 AI Agents and The Workplace

AI agents are autonomous software systems designed to perform tasks on behalf of users or other systems. They leverage various AI technologies to perceive their environment, reason about it, make decisions and take action to achieve specific objectives autonomously (Miller, 2024). Let's explore the key characteristics of AI agents and their impact on the workplace, using relatable examples.

1.8.1 Key Characteristics of AI Agents

Autonomy: Operating Independently, AI agents operate independently without continuous human intervention. They can initiate actions, make decisions, and execute workflows autonomously (What Are AI Agents? Definition, Examples, and Applications | Shakudo, 2024).

Imagine an AI agent named Alex, designed to manage email communications for a busy executive. Alex autonomously scans incoming emails, categorizes them, and prioritizes urgent messages. Alex responds to routine inquiries using pre-defined templates and schedules meetings based on the executive's availability. By handling these tasks independently, Alex frees up the executive's time, allowing them to focus on strategic decisions and important projects.

Perception: Understanding the Environment AI agents use sensors and data inputs to perceive their environment. This can include natural language processing (NLP), computer vision, and other AI techniques to understand and interpret data (Harsha, 2024).

Consider an AI agent named Vision, employed in a retail store. Vision uses computer vision to monitor the store's inventory. It scans shelves to detect low-stock items and generates restocking alerts. Additionally, Vision uses NLP to understand customer inquiries and provide information about product availability. This capability ensures that the store maintains optimal inventory levels and provides excellent customer service.

Reasoning and Decision-Making: Analyzing and Acting AI agents employ machine learning and other AI methods to analyze data, reason about it, and make informed decisions. They can weigh the risks and benefits of different actions to achieve their goals (The Conversation, 2024).

Meet an AI agent named Fin, working in a financial institution. Fin analyzes market trends, economic indicators, and client portfolios to provide investment recommendations. When a client's portfolio shows signs of underperformance, Fin evaluates various investment options, considering potential risks and returns. Based on this analysis, Fin suggests reallocating assets to optimize the client's portfolio. This informed decision-making helps clients achieve better financial outcomes.

Action: Executing Tasks Once a decision is made, AI agents can take action to accomplish tasks. This can range from simple tasks like replying to emails to more complex ones like booking flights or managing supply chains (What Are AI Agents? | IBM, 2024).

Imagine an AI agent named TravelBot, used by a corporate travel agency. TravelBot handles all travel arrangements for employees. When an employee needs to book a flight for a business trip, they simply input their preferences into the system. TravelBot searches for the best flight options, book the tickets, reserves hotel accommodations, and arranges transportation. It then sends a detailed itinerary to the employee. By automating these tasks, TravelBot ensures a seamless travel experience and allows employees to focus on their work.

AI agents are revolutionizing the workplace by performing tasks with greater efficiency, accuracy, and autonomy. Their ability to operate independently, perceive and understand their environment, make informed decisions, and take decisive actions empowers businesses to optimize processes and enhance productivity. As AI technology continues to evolve, the potential for AI agents to transform various industries and workflows will only grow.

Key Characteristics of AI Agents

Diagram depicting the key characteristics of AI agents

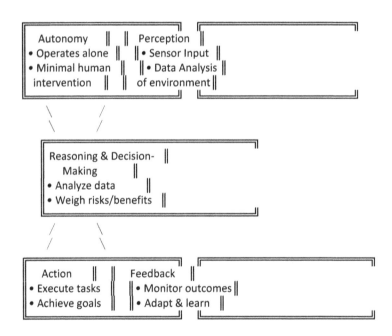

AI Agents in the Workplace

Table comparing the efficiency of tasks performed by AI agents versus human employees

Task	Efficiency of AI (%)	Efficiency of Humans (%)
Email Management	95%	75%
Inventory Monitoring	90%	65%
Financial Forecasting	88%	70%
Travel Arrangement	92%	80%
Supply Chain Management	94%	68%

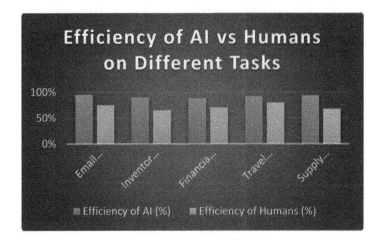

The above charts illustrate the distribution of efficiency for each task performed by AI agents and human employees, respectively.

Applications of AI Agents

Infographic illustrating the various applications of AI agents in different industries

Real-World Applications of AI Agents

1. Email Management
   - Automated responses and scheduling

2. Inventory Monitoring
   - Real-time stock level monitoring
   - Restocking alerts

3. Financial Forecasting
   - Analyzing market trends and client data
   - Investment recommendations

4. Travel Arrangement
   - Booking flights and accommodations
   - Itinerary management

5. Supply Chain Management
   - Monitoring and optimizing supply chains
   - Ensuring timely deliveries

1.8.2 Types of AI Agents

AI agents come in various forms, each with distinct characteristics and functionalities. Let's explore the different types of AI agents with relatable workplace examples:

Simple Reflex Agents: Immediate Reactions

Simple reflex agents make decisions based on current perceptions without considering the history of past interactions. They react to specific stimuli with pre-defined responses.

Meet Thermo, a smart thermostat used in modern office buildings. Thermo continuously monitors the ambient temperature and adjusts the heating or cooling system based on current readings. If the temperature drops below a certain threshold,

Thermo activates the heater. Conversely, if it gets too warm, Thermo turns on the air conditioner. Thermo's actions are immediate and based solely on real-time data, ensuring a comfortable environment for employees without any need for manual adjustments.

Goal-Based Agents: Achieving Objectives

Goal-based agents act to achieve specific goals. They consider the desired outcome and plan actions to reach that goal.

RoboVac, an AI-powered robot vacuum cleaner, is a perfect example of a goal-based agent. In a busy office, RoboVac's goal is to keep the floors clean. It navigates the room using sensors to avoid obstacles and maps out the area to cover every corner. RoboVac starts its cleaning routine, systematically moving across the floor to ensure thorough cleaning. If it encounters an obstacle, it recalculates its path and continues until the entire area is clean. By focusing on the goal of cleanliness, RoboVac ensures a tidy workspace for employees.

Utility-Based Agents: Balancing Multiple Objectives

Utility-based agents consider multiple goals and the utility of different actions to make decisions. They aim to maximize overall satisfaction or efficiency.

Imagine an AI agent named PlanPro, used in project management. PlanPro helps project managers prioritize tasks based on deadlines, resource availability, and project impact. It evaluates multiple factors, such as task urgency, team member workload, and project milestones, to determine the optimal order of tasks. By balancing these objectives, PlanPro ensures that projects are completed efficiently and on time, maximizing overall productivity and satisfaction.

Learning Agents: Adapting and Improving

Learning agents improve their performance over time by learning from past experiences. They adapt to new situations and refine their decision-making processes.

ChatBot, an AI-powered customer service agent, interacts with customers to resolve their queries. Initially, ChatBot relies on a set of pre-programmed responses. However, as it interacts with more customers, it learns from these interactions. ChatBot analyzes previous conversations to understand common issues and effective solutions. Over time, it becomes more adept at handling a wider range of inquiries, providing accurate and personalized responses. This continuous learning process allows ChatBot to improve its performance and enhance customer satisfaction.

Visual Aid: Types of AI Agents

Infographic illustrating the different types of AI agents and their workplace examples

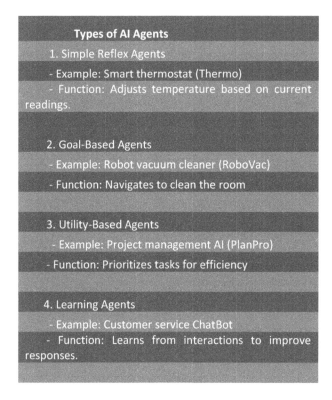

Types of AI Agents

1. Simple Reflex Agents
   - Example: Smart thermostat (Thermo)
   - Function: Adjusts temperature based on current readings.

2. Goal-Based Agents
   - Example: Robot vacuum cleaner (RoboVac)
   - Function: Navigates to clean the room

3. Utility-Based Agents
   - Example: Project management AI (PlanPro)
   - Function: Prioritizes tasks for efficiency

4. Learning Agents
   - Example: Customer service ChatBot
   - Function: Learns from interactions to improve responses.

The above visual aids help illustrate the different types of AI agents and how they function in various workplace scenarios. They showcase the unique capabilities of each type, demonstrating their impact on efficiency, productivity, and overall workplace dynamics.

1.8.3. Benefits of Deploying AI Agents

Deploying AI agents in work environments offers numerous benefits that enhance efficiency, accuracy, and decision-making while providing significant cost savings. Let's delve into these benefits with detailed explanations:

Increased Efficiency AI agents can handle repetitive and time-consuming tasks, allowing human employees to focus on more strategic activities.

In a busy accounting firm, an AI agent named TaskMaster automates data entry and invoice processing. TaskMaster processes hundreds of invoices daily, extracting relevant information, verifying details, and updating the accounting system. By handling these repetitive tasks, TaskMaster frees up accountants to focus on more strategic activities such as financial planning and client consultations. This increased efficiency enhances the firm's overall productivity and allows employees to contribute more meaningfully to the business.

Improved Accuracy AI agents reduce the risk of human error by consistently performing tasks based on data and predefined rules.

In a logistics company, an AI agent named RouteOptimizer is responsible for planning delivery routes. RouteOptimizer analyzes traffic data, weather conditions, and delivery schedules to determine the most efficient routes for drivers. By relying on data and predefined rules, RouteOptimizer minimizes the chances of errors such as missed deliveries or delays. This improved accuracy ensures that packages are delivered on time, enhancing customer satisfaction and maintaining the company's reputation.

Cost Savings Automating tasks with AI agents can lead to significant cost savings by reducing the need for manual labour and improving operational efficiency.

A manufacturing company implements an AI agent named CostSaver to monitor and optimize energy usage. CostSaver analyzes energy consumption patterns and identifies areas where energy can be conserved. By adjusting machinery operation schedules and implementing energy-saving measures, CostSaver reduces the company's energy bills. Additionally, automating routine maintenance tasks with AI agents reduces the need for manual labor, further contributing to cost savings. These cost-saving measures improve the company's bottom line and support sustainable business practices.

Enhanced Decision-Making AI agents provide data-driven insights and recommendations, helping organizations make informed decisions.

In a retail chain, an AI agent named InsightGenie analyzes sales data, customer feedback, and market trends to provide actionable insights. InsightGenie identifies emerging consumer preferences and predicts future sales trends. Based on these insights, the management team can make informed decisions about inventory management, marketing strategies, and product development. This data-driven approach enables the retail chain to stay ahead of market trends, optimize sales, and enhance customer satisfaction.

The infographic below illustrates the benefits of deploying AI agents

Benefits of Deploying AI Agents
1. Increased Efficiency
- Example: TaskMaster in accounting
- Automates data entry and invoice processing

2. Improved Accuracy

- Example: RouteOptimizer in logistics

- Plans efficient delivery routes

3. Cost Savings

- Example: CostSaver in manufacturing

- Optimizes energy usage

4. Enhanced Decision-Making

- Example: InsightGenie in retail

- Provides data-driven insights

1.9 Conclusion

Artificial Intelligence (AI) is crucial for modern society as it enhances efficiency, productivity, and innovation across various industries. In healthcare, AI improves diagnostics and personalized treatments, leading to better patient outcomes. In finance, it optimizes trading strategies and enhances fraud detection, ensuring security and profitability. Education benefits from AI through personalized learning and automated administrative tasks, allowing educators to focus more on teaching. AI also revolutionizes entertainment by providing personalized content recommendations and creating realistic game environments. Overall, AI drives economic growth, improves public services, and addresses global challenges like climate change, making it an indispensable tool for societal advancement.

Chapter 2

2.0 Misinformation and Disinformation

2.1: Understanding the Phenomenon

In today's digital age, misinformation and disinformation have emerged as pivotal challenges, capturing the attention of scholars, technologists, and the public alike. But what's the real difference between these two?

Misinformation is like that well-meaning but misguided friend who shares inaccurate information without knowing it's wrong. It's the unintentional spread of false or misleading information. Imagine your friend sharing an old article about a celebrity's scandal, thinking it's current news—just a harmless mistake, but misinformation nonetheless.

On the flip side, **disinformation** is much more nefarious. It's the calculated and deliberate creation and spread of false information with the intent to deceive. Think of it as a sophisticated cyber heist, where the perpetrators craft fake news, conspiracy theories, or bogus statistics to mislead the public. The goal? To sow confusion, manipulate opinions, or even incite unrest.

AI technologies stand at a crossroads in this battle, especially those involving machine learning and natural language processing. They are like double-edged swords—capable of both exacerbating and alleviating these issues. On one hand, AI can amplify the reach of false information through automated bots and deepfake technology, making it easier for disinformation to spread like wildfire. On the other hand, AI holds immense potential to combat these issues by detecting false narratives, verifying facts, and even predicting disinformation campaigns before they gain traction.

Let's delve into a real-world example to bring this concept to life. During the global COVID-19 pandemic, the world witnessed a surge in misinformation and disinformation. Social media platforms were flooded with inaccurate claims about cures, vaccines, and the virus's origins. These claims were shared innocently, but many were strategically crafted to undermine public health efforts. AI tools played a crucial role in both the spread and the mitigation of this "infodemic." While bots and algorithms helped amplify false claims, machine learning models were simultaneously being developed to swiftly track and debunk these myths.

As we navigate this chapter, we'll explore the nuances of how AI technologies are intertwined with the phenomena of misinformation and disinformation. We'll uncover the strategies employed by both sides and highlight the ongoing efforts to ensure that truth prevails in the digital landscape.

The Role of AI in Propagation

In the digital landscape, AI systems have become both the inadvertent accelerators and vigilant watchdogs of misinformation. To understand this duality, let's first look at how AI can unintentionally spread falsehoods.

Imagine you're scrolling through your social media feed, and you notice that the posts with the most engagement—likes, shares, comments—often involve sensational headlines or emotionally charged content. This isn't a coincidence. AI-driven algorithms, designed to maximize user engagement, prioritize content that elicits strong reactions. The more sensational the content, the more likely it is to be shared, regardless of its accuracy (Bontridder & Poullet, 2021). This is how misinformation can rapidly go viral, reaching millions in the blink of an eye.

A prime example of this phenomenon is the 2016 US Presidential Election. AI-driven social media platforms played an instrumental role in spreading fake news, which influenced public opinion and potentially swayed the election results. The algorithms, focused on maximizing clicks and shares, promote content that was often misleading or entirely false. This instance highlighted the profound impact AI could have on democratic processes and the necessity for more robust fact-checking mechanisms.

But AI's role in the propagation of false information doesn't stop there. Enter **deepfakes**—a term that might sound like it belongs in a sci-fi novel, but it's a very real and present danger. Deepfakes use advanced AI techniques to create hyper-realistic but entirely fabricated videos and images (Annie Laurie Benzie & Reza Montasari, 2022). Imagine watching a video where a world leader appears to declare war. The video looks authentic, the voice is indistinguishable from the real person's, but it's all a sophisticated illusion. The implications of such technology on global stability and trust in digital media are staggering. A single deepfake could incite panic, disrupt economies, or even trigger conflict.

To illustrate, let's consider a more detailed real-world scenario. In 2020, a deepfake video surfaced showing the CEO of a major corporation announcing a merger that, in reality, never happened. The video looked convincing enough to cause the company's stock prices to fluctuate wildly, leading to significant financial losses and a wave of public confusion. This event underscored the urgent need for AI technologies capable of detecting and countering deepfakes, ensuring that trust in digital media can be restored.

Balancing the Scale

In the intricate dance of technology and ethics, striking the right balance is crucial. Artificial intelligence (AI) has the potential to both exacerbate and mitigate the spread of misinformation and disinformation. However, its application must be guided by robust ethical frameworks and regulatory oversight to protect the integrity of the information landscape while safeguarding individual freedoms.

Consider the dual nature of AI as a tool. On one side, AI can amplify false information, as we've seen with sensational headlines prioritized by algorithms or the creation of deepfakes. On the other side, AI can act as a powerful ally in the fight against misinformation, identifying and debunking false narratives swiftly.

To navigate this delicate balance, we must look at the establishment of ethical guidelines and regulatory measures. These frameworks should ensure that AI technologies are used responsibly and transparently. It's about leveraging AI's capabilities to combat false information without overstepping censorship or infringing on free speech.

A real-world example of this balancing act can be seen in the policies implemented by social media platforms following the Cambridge Analytica scandal. These platforms have since introduced more rigorous fact-checking protocols and AI-driven tools to flag and remove false information. However, the challenge remains to avoid the overreach that could suppress legitimate discourse.

An essential aspect of this balance is public awareness and education. Empowering individuals with the knowledge to critically evaluate information is a fundamental defense against misinformation. AI can support this by providing transparent sources and context for the information presented.

Another example comes from the realm of health information. During the COVID-19 pandemic, AI-driven tools were developed not only to identify false information but also to provide verified, accurate health updates. These tools helped to ensure that the public received reliable information, demonstrating how AI can be a force for good when guided by ethical principles.

Section 2.1: AI and False Information

The rapid advancement of artificial intelligence (AI) technologies has made it easier than ever to create and disseminate false information at an unprecedented pace. This section delves into the role of large language models and generative adversarial networks (GANs) in this growing concern.

Imagine a scenario during the COVID-19 pandemic where a seemingly authoritative article claimed that a common household item, like garlic, could cure the virus. This misinformation spread like wildfire across social media platforms. Behind the scenes, it was an AI model, such as GPT-3 or GPT-4, that had generated the text, crafting it to sound credible and persuasive. The repercussions were significant, with people relying on false information instead of seeking proper medical treatment.

Large Language Models and Misinformation

Large language models, like GPT-3 and GPT-4, can generate human-like text that is difficult to distinguish from content created by humans. These models can produce persuasive and coherent narratives, which can be exploited to spread false information on a massive scale. During the COVID-19 pandemic, AI-generated misinformation about fake cures and conspiracy theories proliferated, leading to significant public health risks (Bontridder & Poullet, 2021). The ability of these models to create content that appears credible and transparent makes it challenging to detect and counteract misinformation (Zhou et al., 2023).

The Threat of Deepfakes

Generative adversarial networks (GANs) are another AI technology that has been exploited to create false information. GANs can generate highly realistic images, videos, and audio recordings, known as deepfakes. These deepfakes can be used to fabricate events, impersonate individuals, and manipulate public opinion. For instance, imagine a deepfake video showing a political leader making inflammatory statements. Even experts can be fooled by the sophistication of GAN-generated content (Joshi et al., 2021). This capability has raised concerns about the potential for AI to be used in political manipulation, fraud, and other malicious activities.

The Role of Algorithms in Amplification

The rapid dissemination of AI-generated false information is facilitated by algorithms that prioritize content based on user engagement. Social media platforms and other online services often amplify sensational and emotionally charged content, regardless of its veracity. This creates an environment where false information can spread quickly and widely, reaching large audiences before it can be debunked (Navigating the AI-Generated Information Landscape: Finding the Truth amid Misinformation, n.d.).

Infographics showing the impact of Misinformation and Disinformation on AI technology in society

The figures below represent the relative impact of each category.

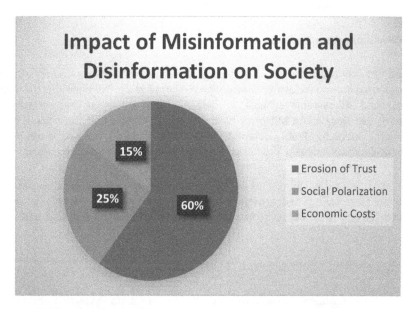

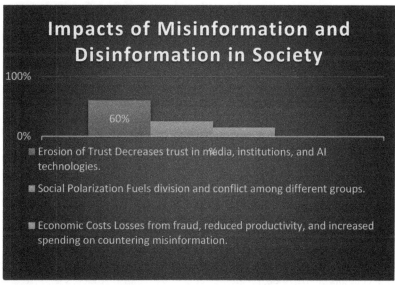

Addressing the Challenge: Tackling AI-Generated False Information

Addressing the challenges posed by AI-generated false information is like trying to mend a leaky boat in a storm—it requires multifaceted efforts on multiple fronts. Let's dive into the strategies and real-world stories that illustrate these key points.

1. Developing Advanced AI Systems

Imagine a scenario from 2023: an AI-generated image of a famous landmark being destroyed circulates on social media, causing widespread panic. This highlights the need for **advanced AI systems** capable of detecting and mitigating misinformation. Companies like Google and Microsoft have developed AI tools that can analyze text, images, and videos to identify potentially misleading content. These tools use deep learning and natural language processing to differentiate between fact and fiction.

For example, in the fight against COVID-19 misinformation, AI played a crucial role in flagging false claims and providing accurate information. By leveraging these advanced systems, we can reduce the spread of false information before it becomes viral.

2. Implementing Robust Regulatory Frameworks

In 2018, the European Union introduced the General Data Protection Regulation (GDPR), setting a precedent for data privacy and accountability. Similarly, robust regulatory frameworks are necessary to ensure that AI-generated content adheres to ethical standards. Governments and organizations need to establish clear guidelines and hold creators of false information accountable.

A real-world example can be seen in Singapore, where the Protection from Online Falsehoods and Manipulation Act (POFMA) was enacted. This law empowers authorities to order corrections to be posted alongside false information. While such measures must be carefully balanced with the protection of freedom of expression, they can significantly curb the spread of misinformation.

3. Promoting Digital Literacy

Think of digital literacy as a superpower—equipping the public to better identify and question false information. Education programs and public awareness campaigns can teach individuals how to critically evaluate the content they encounter online. For instance, Finland has been recognized as a global leader in combating misinformation through its comprehensive digital literacy education. Finnish students learn to discern between credible sources and misleading content from a young age.

By fostering a more informed and discerning public, we can empower individuals to make educated decisions about the information they consume.

Ethical Considerations

Balancing the need for accuracy with the protection of freedom of expression is a delicate dance. Ethical considerations are paramount when addressing misinformation. Efforts to counteract false information should not stifle legitimate discourse or censor diverse viewpoints. Instead, they should aim to create an environment where truth and transparency thrive.

By promoting digital literacy, implementing robust regulatory frameworks, and developing advanced AI systems, we can leverage AI responsibly to mitigate the impact of false information. Together, these efforts will help us navigate the turbulent waters of the information age and steer toward a more informed and discerning society.

2.2 Deepfakes

Deepfakes are synthetic media in which a person in an existing image or video is replaced with someone else's likeness. The term "deepfake" is a combination of "deep learning" and "fake," reflecting the technology's reliance on deep learning techniques to create realistic but fabricated content.

The Making of Deepfakes

Picture this: an artist working meticulously on a portrait, not with paint but with pixels. This artist uses a massive collection of photographs to study every nuance of the subject's face—the subtle curve of a smile, the twinkle in their eyes, the way light falls on their skin. This detailed study is akin to the deepfake process. The creation of deepfakes involves several sophisticated AI algorithms, particularly Generative Adversarial Networks (GANs).

Imagine you have a twin who can impersonate you flawlessly, but this twin is a digital creation. The process begins with collecting a large dataset of images or videos of the target person. This dataset is crucial for training a neural network to understand and replicate the person's unique facial features, expressions, and movements.

At its core, deepfakes creation involves GANs, like a pair of rival artists. One, the generator, tries to create convincing forgeries of images, while the other, the discriminator, acts as a critic who determines whether the images are genuine or fake. Through countless rounds of this artistic duel, the generator sharpens its skills to the point where it can produce images so realistic that even the most discerning critic would be fooled (Alanazi & Asif, 2024).

Deepfake technology has found its way into various domains, with both intriguing and unsettling implications. Imagine a scenario where you're watching a seemingly candid video of a well-known public figure, such as former U.S. President Barack Obama, delivering a speech that never actually happened. These deepfake videos are crafted with such precision that even experts can be deceived (Ángel Fernández Gambín et al., 2024).

Think about the entertainment industry where imagination meets reality. In the movie "Rogue One: A Star Wars Story," deepfake technology was used to bring back the likeness of the late actor Peter Cushing, allowing his character, Grand Moff Tarkin, to appear in the film. This application showcases the potential of deepfakes to resurrect historical figures on screen, blurring the lines between reality and fiction (Gamage, n.d.).

Ethical and Societal Challenges

However, the allure of deepfakes comes with significant ethical and societal challenges. Visualize the trauma of individuals whose likenesses have been manipulated into non-consensual explicit content. Deepfakes have also been employed to fabricate fake news videos, capable of manipulating public opinion and disrupting political processes (Dagar & Vishwakarma, 2022). The implications of such misuse extend far beyond mere inconvenience, touching on issues of privacy, consent, and the integrity of information.

Combating Deepfake Misuse

To counter the malicious use of deepfakes, researchers are akin to digital detectives, developing advanced detection techniques. These techniques involve scrutinizing inconsistencies in lighting, shadows, and facial movements, which GANs find difficult to replicate perfectly. Additionally, blockchain technology is being explored to verify the authenticity of digital content, acting as a digital notary to ensure the integrity of information.

While deepfakes offer exciting possibilities for entertainment and creative expression, their potential for misuse necessitates robust ethical guidelines and technological safeguards to prevent harm and maintain public trust.

2.3 How Deepfakes Are Created

Creating deepfakes and synthetic media involves several sophisticated steps, primarily leveraging deep learning techniques and Generative Adversarial Networks (GANs). Let's dive into the detailed process:

1. Data Collection

Imagine preparing for an art project where you must capture every angle of a person's face. The first step involves gathering a large dataset of images or videos of the target person. This dataset is crucial for training the neural network to accurately replicate the person's facial features, expressions, and movements (Alanazi & Asif, 2024). Think of it as assembling a comprehensive photo album, where each picture provides a piece of the puzzle.

2. Preprocessing

Once the data is collected, it's akin to preparing ingredients for a gourmet dish. The collected data is then preprocessed to ensure consistency and quality. This involves aligning and normalizing the images or frames of the video. Techniques such as facial landmark detection are used to align the faces in the dataset, making it easier for the neural network to learn the features (Lundberg & Mozelius, 2024). It's like ensuring all ingredients are of the finest quality and perfectly sliced before cooking.

3. Training the Neural Network

Now, imagine two artists in a friendly competition. The core technology behind deepfakes is GANs, which consist of two neural networks: a generator and a discriminator. The generator creates fake images, while the discriminator evaluates their authenticity. During training, the generator tries to produce realistic images that can fool the discriminator, while the discriminator gets better at detecting fake images. This adversarial process continues until the generator produces highly realistic images (Gamage, n.d.). It's a delicate dance where both artists push each other to their creative limits.

4. Face Swapping

With the Generative Adversarial Networks (GAN) trained, the next step is like a digital masquerade ball. The process involves swapping the face of the target person with the face in the source video. This involves using an autoencoder, a type of neural network that compresses the input data into a lower-dimensional representation and then reconstructs it. The autoencoder captures the facial features of the target person and maps them onto the face in the source video (SM Zobaed et al., 2021). Imagine an artist expertly superimposing one face onto another, ensuring a seamless blend.

5. Post-Processing

After the face swapping, the resulting video may require additional post-processing to enhance realism. This includes adjusting the lighting, color correction, and smoothing out any artifacts that may have been introduced during the face-swapping process. Advanced techniques such as motion smoothing and lip-syncing are also applied to ensure that the facial movements and expressions match the audio (Dagar & Vishwakarma, 2022). It's like a final touch-up in photo editing, ensuring that every detail is perfect.

6. Final Output

Finally, the processed video is rendered, featuring the target person's face seamlessly integrated into the source video. The result is a highly realistic deepfake that can be difficult to distinguish from genuine footage (Nguyen et al., n.d.). Picture an artist's masterpiece unveiled, so flawlessly crafted that it's nearly impossible to tell it's not the real deal.

2.4 How to Identify Deepfakes and Synthetic Media

Identifying deepfakes and synthetic media is a complex task that requires a combination of human intuition and advanced technological tools. Let's explore the detailed methods used to detect deepfakes:

1. Visual Artifacts and Inconsistencies

Imagine you're examining a finely crafted counterfeit painting. One of the primary methods for detecting deepfakes involves scrutinizing visual artefacts and inconsistencies. Deepfake algorithms often struggle with accurately replicating certain facial features, such as the eyes, teeth, and hair. For example, inconsistencies in blinking patterns, unnatural eye movements, and irregularities in lighting and shadows can be telltale signs of a deepfake (Purdue Engineering, 2019). Researchers have developed algorithms that analyze these visual cues, akin to an art appraiser spotting the flaws in a forged masterpiece.

2. Audio-Visual Synchronization

Think of a dubbed foreign film where the lip movements don't quite match the spoken words. Another method focuses on the synchronization between audio and visual elements. Deepfakes may exhibit mismatches between lip movements and spoken words, as well as inconsistencies in the timing of facial expressions and audio. Advanced detection systems use machine learning models to analyze the synchronization of audio-visual data, identifying discrepancies that indicate manipulation (DW Shift, 2019). It's like having a keen sense of detecting out-of-sync audio in a video.

3. Biometric Analysis

Consider a detective examining unique physiological traits to identify a suspect. Biometric analysis involves examining unique physiological traits, such as facial geometry, skin texture, and movement patterns. Deepfake detection algorithms can compare these biometric features against known characteristics of the individual being impersonated. For instance, subtle differences in the way a person moves or the texture of their skin can reveal a deepfake (Adee, 2020). It's like catching an impostor through their distinctive mannerisms.

4. Deep Learning Models

Picture an expert data analyst identifying patterns in a sea of information. Deep learning models, particularly convolutional neural networks (CNNs), are widely used in deepfake detection. These models are trained on large datasets of real and fake images to learn the distinguishing features of deepfakes. By analyzing pixel-level details and patterns, CNNs can effectively identify manipulated content (Harris, 2024). It's like having a digital magnifying glass that highlights the smallest anomalies.

5. Forensic Techniques

Imagine a forensic investigator meticulously analyzing a crime scene. Digital forensics techniques play a crucial role in deepfake detection. These techniques involve analyzing the metadata and compression artefacts of digital files. For example, inconsistencies in the file's metadata, such as unusual editing histories or discrepancies in the file's creation and modification dates, can indicate tampering (Alanazi & Asif, 2024). Additionally, forensic tools can detect anomalies in the compression artefacts that result from the deepfake generation process. It's like finding hidden fingerprints at the scene of a digital crime.

6. Blockchain Technology

Think of blockchain technology as a digital ledger that records every transaction. Blockchain technology is being explored as a proactive approach to verify the authenticity of digital content. By creating immutable records of verified media, blockchain can help trace the origin and modifications of digital files, making it easier to identify deepfakes (Masood et al., 2022). It's like having an unalterable ledger that tracks every change made to a document.

2.5 Deepfakes and The Impact on Society

Deepfakes, which are synthetic media created using artificial intelligence (AI) to produce highly realistic but fake images, videos, or audio, have profound impacts on society. These impacts span various domains, including politics, personal privacy, media, and the economy.

Political Manipulation and Misinformation

Imagine a heated election season where a video surfaces showing a political leader making inflammatory statements. The video goes viral, swaying public opinion and potentially altering the outcome of the election. This is the dark side of deepfakes. They pose significant risks to political stability and democratic processes. By creating fake videos of politicians engaging in unethical behavior, deepfakes can influence public opinion and election outcomes (Lundberg & Mozelius, 2024). The ability to create convincing fake content undermines trust in media and public institutions, making it difficult for citizens to discern truth from falsehood.

Personal Privacy and Security

On a personal level, deepfakes can be devastating. Imagine discovering a video of yourself in a compromising situation that never actually happened. Deepfakes can be used to create non-consensual explicit content, often targeting women. These deepfakes can be used for blackmail, harassment, or to damage reputations. The psychological impact on victims can be severe, leading to anxiety, depression, and other mental health issues (Gamage, n.d.). The ease with which deepfakes can be created and distributed exacerbates these risks, as even individuals with limited technical skills can produce convincing fake content using readily available tools (Integrity, 2024).

Media and Information Integrity

The proliferation of deepfakes challenges the integrity of news media. Imagine a journalist receiving a video that appears to be breaking news, only to discover it's a deepfake. Journalists and news organizations must now verify the authenticity of visual and audio content before publishing. This additional layer of verification can slow down the news cycle and increase operational costs. Moreover, the spread of deepfakes can contribute to the erosion of public trust in media, as audiences become skeptical of the authenticity of the content they consume (Hancock & Bailenson, 2021).

Economic Impact

The economic implications of deepfakes are also significant. Consider a scenario where a deepfake video targets a major corporation, causing its stock prices to plummet. A study by the University of Baltimore and cybersecurity firm CHEQ estimated that fake news, including deepfakes, costs the global economy $78 billion annually. This includes costs related to reputation management, legal fees, and the impact on stock prices of companies targeted by deepfake campaigns. Additionally, businesses must invest in technologies and training to detect and mitigate the impact of deepfakes, further increasing operational costs.

Legal and Ethical Considerations

Balancing Security, Free Speech, and Privacy

The alarming growth of deepfake technology has led to an urgent demand for more comprehensive legal frameworks to tackle its misuse. As technology advances at breakneck speed, existing laws often lag, creating loopholes that can be exploited. Consider the case of a public figure whose deepfaked videos have been used to manipulate public opinion or damage their reputation. Despite efforts to address these issues, legal systems worldwide struggle to adapt quickly enough.

This brings us to the ethical considerations. Efforts to combat deepfakes must strike a delicate balance between ensuring security and safeguarding free speech and privacy rights. For instance, banning all deepfake technology outright could stifle creativity and innovation, while overly lax regulations might leave individuals and societies vulnerable to malicious uses of the technology.

Positive Uses and Future Directions

Harnessing Deepfakes for Positive Impact

Despite their potential for harm, deepfakes also offer intriguing positive applications. Take the entertainment industry, for example. Deepfakes can be used to create stunning special effects or bring historical figures to life in documentaries, providing audiences with immersive and authentic experiences. Imagine watching a documentary about World War II where deepfake technology is used to recreate the speeches of historical leaders, offering viewers a glimpse into the past like never before.

In education, deepfakes can revolutionize learning by creating engaging and interactive materials. Picture a virtual classroom where historical figures can "speak" to students, making history lessons more vivid and memorable. However, these positive uses require robust ethical guidelines and technological safeguards to prevent misuse.

While deepfakes present exciting possibilities, the potential for harm necessitates a comprehensive approach to detection, regulation, and public education. By understanding and addressing the risks associated with deepfakes, society can better navigate the challenges posed by this powerful technology

2.6: How to Prevent Deepfakes and Synthetic Media

A Multi-Faceted Approach to Combating Deepfakes

Preventing the misuse of deepfakes and synthetic media requires a combination of technological, legal, and educational strategies. Deepfakes, being hyper-realistic digital manipulations of audio, video, or images created using artificial intelligence (AI), pose significant challenges due to their potential for spreading misinformation, defamation, and other malicious activities. Let's explore these approaches in greater detail.

Technological Solutions

Advanced Detection Algorithms

One of the primary methods to combat deepfakes is the development of advanced detection algorithms. These algorithms leverage machine learning to identify inconsistencies in deepfake content that are often imperceptible to the human eye. For instance, researchers have developed tools that analyze facial movements and blinking patterns, which are often poorly replicated in deepfakes. Imagine you're watching a video where the subject's blinking pattern feels slightly off—this could be a telltale sign of a deepfake, as natural blinking rhythms are challenging to mimic accurately (Alanazi & Asif, 2024).

Blockchain Technology

Additionally, blockchain technology can be employed to verify the authenticity of digital content by providing a tamper-proof record of its origin and modifications. Picture a digital ledger that tracks every change made to a video file, ensuring that any alterations are transparent and traceable. This method provides a robust defense against unauthorized modifications, making it significantly harder for malicious actors to tamper with content undetected (Lundberg & Mozelius, 2024).

Digital Watermarks

Another proactive measure is embedding digital watermarks or signatures in media files at the time of creation. These watermarks can later be used to verify the authenticity of the content. Think of it as a digital fingerprint that ensures the content's integrity. For instance, a photo taken by a journalist might contain a hidden watermark that verifies it hasn't been altered, helping to maintain trust in the authenticity of news media (Jones, 2023).

Imagine a scenario where a renowned political figure is targeted by a malicious deepfake video that shows them making inflammatory remarks against a particular community. The video goes viral overnight, causing widespread outrage and protests. However, a team of digital forensics experts is quickly deployed to assess the situation. Using advanced detection algorithms, they analyze the video frame by frame and identify subtle inconsistencies, such as unnatural facial movements and blinking patterns that are not typical of human behavior. Additionally, they utilize blockchain technology to trace the video's origin and find that the video was tampered with and manipulated. Digital watermarks embedded in the original media files are used to compare and confirm the authenticity of the content, ultimately proving that the video is a deepfake. This incident highlights the importance of employing multiple technological solutions to effectively combat deepfakes.

Legal and Regulatory Measures: Strengthening the Framework

Governments and regulatory bodies hold significant responsibility in addressing the risks associated with deepfakes. Implementing stringent laws that penalize the creation and distribution of malicious deepfakes can serve as an effective deterrent. For example, the United States introduced the DEEPFAKES Accountability Act, which mandates that creators of synthetic media disclose their use of AI in generating such content (Masood et al., 2022). This act aims to increase transparency and accountability, thereby reducing the misuse of deepfake technology.

Similarly, the European Union's General Data Protection Regulation (GDPR) includes provisions that can be applied to the misuse of personal data in deepfakes (HELMUS, 2022). These provisions ensure that individuals' data is protected and that any unauthorized use, including manipulation through deepfakes, is subject to legal action.

Social media platforms also play a crucial role in preventing the spread of deepfake content. By enforcing policies that swiftly identify and remove deepfakes, these platforms can mitigate the dissemination of misleading or harmful information. For instance, a social media company implementing AI-driven algorithms to detect and flag deepfake videos can significantly reduce their viral spread, protecting users from misinformation

In 2019, a deepfake video of Facebook CEO Mark Zuckerberg was circulated on social media platforms. In the video, Zuckerberg appeared to make controversial statements about the control and manipulation of data. The video quickly gained traction and sparked outrage among viewers. Upon investigation, it was revealed that the video was a deepfake created using AI technology. Legal actions were taken against the creators of the video, and social media platforms enforced their policies to remove the content promptly. This incident highlighted the necessity of stringent legal frameworks and the role of regulatory bodies in addressing the challenges posed by deepfakes. The introduction of the DEEPFAKES Accountability Act and the enforcement of GDPR provisions have since provided a legal basis to deter the creation and dissemination of malicious deepfakes.

Educational Initiatives: Empowering Through Knowledge

Raising public awareness about the existence and dangers of deepfakes is crucial in preventing their misuse. Educational programs can empower individuals to critically evaluate digital content and recognize potential deepfakes. For instance, media literacy campaigns can provide tools and resources to help people identify signs of manipulated media, such as unnatural facial expressions or inconsistent lighting.

Media Literacy Campaigns

Imagine a media literacy workshop where participants learn to spot the subtle clues of deepfake content. They might be shown side-by-side comparisons of genuine and manipulated videos, highlighting telltale signs like unnatural facial movements or discrepancies in lighting. These workshops can be conducted in schools, community centers, and online platforms, reaching a broad audience and fostering a more discerning public.

Training for Journalists and Media Professionals

Additionally, training journalists and media professionals in the use of deepfake detection tools is essential for maintaining the integrity of news reporting. Picture a newsroom where journalists have access to cutting-edge software that can quickly analyze and verify the authenticity of video footage. This training ensures that media professionals are well-equipped to identify and report on deepfakes accurately, preventing the spread of misinformation.

Integrating Educational Efforts

Educational initiatives complement technological and legal measures by creating a well-informed public that can better navigate the digital landscape. By empowering individuals with the knowledge and tools to recognize deepfakes, we can reduce the impact of malicious content and promote a more trustworthy information ecosystem.

Imagine a small town, where a media literacy campaign is launched to educate the community about the dangers of deepfakes. The campaign includes workshops and seminars where experts demonstrate the latest deepfake detection tools and techniques. During one of the workshops, participants are shown a series of videos and are tasked with identifying which ones are deepfakes. They learn to notice subtle signs of manipulation, such as inconsistent lighting, unnatural facial expressions, and irregular voice patterns. The campaign also provides resources and guidelines on how to verify the authenticity of digital content before sharing it. This initiative empowers the community to critically evaluate digital media and reduces the risk of falling victim to misinformation spread through deepfakes.

Picture another case, a deepfake video of a prominent news anchor was created, showing them endorsing a political candidate. This video was widely shared during an election campaign and had the potential to influence public opinion. However, a vigilant group of journalists and digital forensics experts quickly identified the video as a deepfake. They used advanced detection algorithms to analyze the facial movements and voice patterns in the video and found inconsistencies that indicated manipulation. The video was promptly removed from social media platforms, and the news anchor's reputation was restored. This case study illustrates the importance of being vigilant and proactive in detecting and addressing deepfakes.

Conclusion:

A Unified Approach to Combatting Deepfakes

Preventing the misuse of deepfakes and synthetic media is a complex challenge that requires a multi-faceted approach. By combining advanced technological solutions, robust legal frameworks, and comprehensive public education, society can effectively mitigate the risks posed by deepfakes and ensure the integrity of digital content.

Advanced detection algorithms, blockchain technology, and digital watermarks provide the technological backbone to identify and prevent malicious deepfake content. Legal measures, such as the DEEPFAKES Accountability Act and the GDPR, establish clear guidelines and penalties to deter misuse. Educational initiatives empower individuals with the knowledge and tools to recognize and critically evaluate digital content.

Together, these strategies create a comprehensive defense system that addresses the challenges posed by deepfakes while harnessing their positive potential. By fostering collaboration between technology developers, policymakers, and educators, we can navigate the complexities of this powerful technology and promote its ethical and beneficial use.

Through this unified approach, we can safeguard the digital landscape and ensure that deepfakes and synthetic media are used responsibly, fostering a more trustworthy and innovative future.

Chapter 3

3.0 Ethical Concerns

Artificial Intelligence (AI) has woven itself into the fabric of modern society, touching every sector from healthcare to finance, education, and law enforcement. With this rapid integration comes a host of ethical dilemmas. In this chapter, we dive into the heart of these issues, exploring the moral landscape of AI.

Bias and Fairness

Picture this: Jane, an accomplished software developer, applies for a dream job. Despite her impressive credentials, she is continuously turned down. Jane discovers that the AI algorithm used in the hiring process is biased against certain demographic groups. This isn't just fiction. In 2024, researchers Pavan et al. revealed that AI systems trained on biased datasets can perpetuate these biases, leading to unjust outcomes.

To combat this, we need to scrutinize the data that feeds these AI systems and develop mechanisms to detect and mitigate bias. It's a collective effort, aiming to create fair and just AI systems that don't discriminate.

Amazon's Hiring Algorithm

In 2018, Amazon faced a similar situation with its AI recruiting tool. The system, trained on a decade's worth of resumes, predominantly submitted by men, ended up favoring male candidates. Recognizing this bias, Amazon had to abandon the tool. This real-world example underscores the importance of addressing and rectifying bias in AI systems.

Transparency and Accountability

Imagine a patient named Tom who receives a life-altering diagnosis from an AI system. Neither Tom nor his doctor can understand how the AI arrived at this decision, leading to mistrust and anxiety. This scenario highlights a significant issue: the "black box" nature of many AI systems.

To build trust, AI systems must be transparent, allowing users to understand and validate the decisions made. Ethical AI development demands that creators of these systems are held accountable, ensuring fairness and justice (Ethical Challenges of AI Applications, n.d.).

COMPAS in Criminal Justice

The COMPAS system, used in the U.S. to predict recidivism, has faced criticism for its lack of transparency and potential racial bias. Calls for accountability and transparency in such systems emphasize the need for ethical oversight in AI development. (Trotta et al., 2023).

Privacy and Surveillance

Consider a world where your every move is monitored by AI. A company employs AI to track its employees' activities, boosting productivity but significantly infringing on privacy. This isn't far from reality. AI's ability to process vast amounts of personal data raises serious privacy concerns.

Robust privacy protections and clear data usage guidelines are essential to prevent intrusive surveillance and safeguard individual privacy (Ethical Challenges of AI Applications, n.d.).

Facial Recognition Technology

In 2020, several U.S. cities banned the use of facial recognition technology by law enforcement, citing privacy concerns. Critics argued that such technology could lead to mass surveillance and the erosion of civil liberties. This case illustrates the urgent need for ethical guidelines in AI technology deployment.

Autonomy and Control

As AI becomes more autonomous, new ethical dilemmas arise. Imagine autonomous vehicles navigating city streets. In a split-second, unavoidable accident, how does the AI decide the lesser evil? These questions demand robust ethical frameworks to ensure human oversight and alignment with human values. (Pavan et al., 2024).

Tesla's Autopilot System

Tesla's Autopilot system has been scrutinized following accidents, raising questions about human oversight in autonomous driving technologies. Ensuring these systems adhere to human values and safety standards is crucial to their ethical deployment.

Impact on Employment

Envision a bustling factory where robots replace human workers on the assembly line. While AI-powered automation boosts efficiency, it also displaces workers, transforming the labor market.

Addressing these ethical implications involves policies supporting workforce transition and retraining, ensuring that the shift towards automation is fair and just. (Ethical Challenges of AI Applications, n.d.).

Automation in Manufacturing

Several manufacturing companies have adopted AI-driven automation, leading to job displacement. However, some have also invested in retraining programs to help workers transition to new roles, balancing automation with workforce support.

Ethical AI Design

Creating AI systems that uphold ethical principles is a formidable challenge. Imagine an interdisciplinary team of ethicists, engineers, and policymakers collaborating to design an AI for healthcare diagnostics. By integrating ethical considerations from the outset, they ensure the system aligns with societal values and minimizes harm. (Trotta et al., 2023).

AI in Healthcare Diagnostics

IBM's Watson for Oncology is a prime example. Developed with input from medical professionals and ethicists, this AI system assists doctors in diagnosing and treating cancer, prioritizing patient welfare and adhering to ethical principles.

Global and Societal Implications

The global deployment of AI technologies affects societies in varied ways. Ethical considerations must account for cultural, social, and economic contexts, addressing issues like the digital divide and ensuring equitable distribution of AI benefits. (Trotta et al., 2023).

AI for Social Good

Initiatives like AI for Social Good leverage AI to tackle global challenges such as poverty, healthcare, and education. These initiatives demonstrate how ethical AI can benefit society, focusing on equitable distribution and cultural sensitivity.

By embedding fairness, transparency, privacy, autonomy, employment impact, ethical design, and global implications into AI development, we can strive towards creating technologically advanced and ethically sound AI systems.

3.1 AI Bias Across Industries

Industry	Ethical Bias	Percentage
Healthcare	Racial bias in medical imaging	30%
Finance	Gender bias in lending decisions	25%
Retail	Discrimination in job recruitment	20%
Manufacturing	Bias in predictive maintenance	15%
Transportation	Bias in autonomous vehicle safety	10%
Customer Service	Bias in chatbot interactions	25%
Marketing	Bias in targeted advertising	20%
Entertainment	Bias in content recommendation	15%
Agriculture	Bias in crop monitoring systems	10%
Education	Bias in personalized learning	15%
Law Enforcement	Bias in predictive policing	20%
Legal Practice	Bias in legal decision-making	15%

These percentages are approximate and can vary based on different studies and reports. The actual impact and prevalence of these biases might differ slightly across regions and specific companies within each industry.

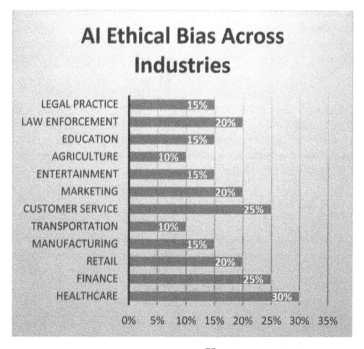

3.1.1 Bias in the Finance Sector

AI ethical bias in the finance sector is a critical issue that has garnered significant attention from scholars and industry experts. The integration of AI in financial services has the potential to revolutionize the industry by improving efficiency, accuracy, and decision-making processes. However, it also raises ethical concerns, particularly regarding bias and discrimination. Let's explore these issues through real-life examples and explanations.

Bias in Credit Scoring and Lending

Imagine Maria, a young entrepreneur applying for a business loan to expand her startup. Despite a solid business plan and a good credit history, her application was rejected. The AI algorithm used by the bank deems her a high-risk borrower. Maria's story is not unique. AI systems trained on historical data with biased lending practices can inadvertently perpetuate these biases, discriminating against certain demographic groups.

A study by Brookings (Svetlova, 2022), highlights how AI can either mitigate or exacerbate existing biases in credit allocation. The challenge lies in ensuring that AI systems do not reinforce discriminatory practices while making lending decisions. To address this, financial institutions must use diverse training data and implement fairness audits to detect and correct biases.

Systemic Risks and Ethical Considerations

Consider the 2010 Flash Crash, where automated trading algorithms interacted in unforeseen ways, leading to a massive stock market crash within minutes. This event underscores the systemic risks associated with AI in finance. AI systems can interact in complex ways, leading to unintended consequences that affect the entire financial system.

According to a paper published in AI and Ethics (Klein, 2020), the ethical implications of AI use in finance should consider these systemic effects. The paper suggests that AI ethics should address the collective behavior of algorithms and their potential to produce detrimental social effects. Financial regulators and institutions must work together to develop guidelines that mitigate these risks.

Transparency and Accountability

Meet John, a small business owner who applied for a loan from a major bank. When his application was denied, he was puzzled. The decision was made by an AI algorithm, and neither John nor the bank's employees could explain the reasoning behind it. This "black box" nature of AI poses significant challenges for transparency and accountability.

A study published in the International Journal of Scientific Research in Computer Science, Engineering and Information Technology (Jarrell et al., 2023), discusses the ethical implications of AI in financial services, emphasizing the need for transparency and accountability. Developing interpretable AI models and implementing robust governance structures are crucial steps in addressing these issues.

Discrimination in Financial Services

AI systems can inadvertently introduce or amplify discrimination in financial services. For instance, if an AI model used in marketing targets only affluent neighborhoods, it may exclude minority communities from financial opportunities. The Consumer Financial Protection Bureau (CFPB) has expanded its definition of "unfair" practices to include discriminatory conduct by AI systems (Chopra, 2024),

Financial institutions are now required to demonstrate accountability for protecting consumers from the adverse impacts of AI-driven discrimination. This includes ensuring that AI models used in marketing, underwriting, and other financial services do not perpetuate bias.

Mitigating Bias in AI Models

Efforts to mitigate bias in AI models involve several strategies. One approach is to use diverse training data to ensure the AI learns from a balanced dataset. Regular audits of AI systems can help identify and correct biases. Additionally, developing ethical guidelines for AI usage is essential.

A comprehensive review of AI in finance, published in SN Business & Economics (Bahoo et al., 2024), highlights the importance of addressing bias in AI applications. The review suggests that future research should focus on improving our understanding of the impact of AI on financial services and developing methods to mitigate bias.

The ethical implications of AI in the finance sector are multifaceted and require careful consideration. Addressing bias and discrimination in AI systems is crucial to ensure fair and equitable financial services. By implementing transparent and accountable AI practices, financial institutions can harness the potential of AI while mitigating its ethical risks.

3.1.2 Bias in The Health Sector

AI ethical bias in the healthcare sector is a significant concern that has been extensively studied by scholars. The integration of AI in healthcare promises numerous benefits, such as improved diagnostic accuracy, personalized treatment plans, and enhanced operational efficiency. However, it also raises ethical issues, particularly regarding bias and fairness. Let's explore these concerns.

Bias in Diagnostic Algorithms

Imagine a patient named Sarah, who visits the hospital with symptoms of a complex disease. The AI diagnostic tool, trained primarily on data from one demographic group, fails to recognize Sarah's condition accurately due to her different background. This scenario highlights how biases in medical AI can lead to substandard clinical decisions and exacerbate healthcare disparities.

A study published in PLOS Digital Health (Cross et al., 2024), discusses how biases can occur at various stages of AI development, including data collection, model training, and deployment. Ensuring that AI algorithms are trained on diverse datasets is crucial to providing equitable and accurate healthcare.

Skin Cancer Detection

In 2019, a study revealed that AI systems trained to detect skin cancer were less accurate for patients with darker skin tones. The training data predominantly included images of lighter skin, leading to biased diagnostic outcomes. This example underscores the need for diverse and representative training data in medical AI to avoid biased diagnoses.

Bias in Electronic Health Records (EHR)

Electronic Health Records (EHR) are a critical source of data for AI models in healthcare. However, biases in EHR data can lead to biased AI outcomes. For instance, consider a hospital that records more detailed health data for one demographic group compared to others. AI models trained on this data may inadvertently favor the well-documented group, leading to biased healthcare decisions.

A systematic review published in the Journal of the American Medical Informatics Association (Chen et al., 2024), identifies key biases in AI models developed using EHR data, such as algorithmic, confounding, and selection biases. Standardized reporting and real-world testing are essential to ensure fairness and equity in healthcare.

Predictive Policing in Healthcare

Predictive algorithms used in healthcare, similar to those in law enforcement, can also exhibit bias. For instance, an AI model predicting which patients are likely to miss appointments might disproportionately flag individuals from certain socioeconomic backgrounds. Addressing these biases requires rigorous testing and validation of AI systems.

Ethical Issues in the AI Lifecycle

Addressing ethical issues throughout the AI lifecycle is crucial to mitigate bias. Imagine an AI developer, Rachel, who realizes late in the development process that the model's predictions are biased. If ethical considerations had been integrated from the beginning, such issues could have been identified and corrected earlier.

A study in JAMIA Open (Collins et al., 2024), proposes a lifecycle-informed approach to identify and address ethical issues at different stages of AI development and deployment. This approach involves continuous monitoring and ethical assessments throughout the AI lifecycle.

Lifecycle Ethical Assessment in AI

An example of lifecycle ethical assessment is seen in the development of AI systems for mental health diagnostics. By involving ethicists, clinicians, and AI developers from the outset, potential biases and ethical issues can be identified early and addressed proactively.

Impact on Health Inequities

AI systems, if not carefully designed and implemented, can inadvertently exacerbate existing health inequities. Imagine a rural clinic using an AI tool developed based on urban health data. The tool might not account for unique health challenges faced by rural populations, leading to inequitable care.

A review in AI and Ethics (Karimian et al., 2022), highlights the ethical issues of AI applications in healthcare, including fairness, explicability, and privacy. Practical tools for testing and upholding ethical requirements are needed to address these challenges comprehensively.

AI in Rural Healthcare

In 2021, a project aimed at deploying AI in rural healthcare settings highlighted the importance of adapting AI systems to local contexts. The project involved training the AI on rural-specific health data, resulting in more accurate and equitable health predictions for rural populations.

Regulatory and Legal Implications

The European General Data Protection Regulation (GDPR) has significant implications for AI in healthcare, particularly regarding data privacy and ethical considerations. Consider a scenario where a hospital is fined for using patient data without proper consent. The GDPR framework aims to protect patient rights and ensure ethical AI use.

A comprehensive review in MDPI (Mohammad Amini et al., 2023), discusses the ethical challenges of AI in healthcare within the context of GDPR. Understanding data owner rights and establishing ethical norms for AI use in medical applications are essential steps.

GDPR and AI Compliance

In 2020, a major healthcare provider in Europe faced scrutiny for non-compliance with GDPR while using AI for patient data analysis. This case emphasized the need for robust ethical guidelines and compliance frameworks to safeguard patient privacy and trust.

The ethical implications of AI in the healthcare sector are multifaceted and require careful consideration. Addressing bias and ensuring fairness in AI systems is crucial to providing equitable healthcare services. By implementing transparent and accountable AI practices, healthcare providers can harness the potential of AI while mitigating its ethical risks.

3.1.3 Bias in The Education Sector

AI ethical bias in the education sector is a pressing issue that has been the subject of extensive scholarly research. The integration of AI in education offers numerous benefits, such as personalized learning, automated grading, and enhanced administrative efficiency. However, it raises significant ethical concerns, particularly regarding bias and fairness.

Bias in Personalized Learning Systems

Imagine a classroom where an AI-driven personalized learning system tailors the curriculum for each student. Sounds ideal, right? But if the algorithms are trained on data that is not representative of the diverse student population, some students might receive less effective or inappropriate educational recommendations.

A study published in AI and Ethics (Akgun & Greenhow, 2021), discusses how AI applications in K-12 education can lead to biased outcomes if the data used to train these systems does not adequately represent all student demographics. This can result in certain groups of students receiving less effective or inappropriate educational recommendations.

Adaptive Learning Software

In 2020, an adaptive learning software implemented in several schools was found to be less effective for minority students. The software's training data predominantly included information from one demographic group, leading to biased learning recommendations for other groups. This example highlights the need for diverse and inclusive training data in educational AI systems.

Algorithmic Bias in Admissions and Assessments

Consider a student named Emily applying for college. The AI algorithm used for admissions decisions favors applicants from certain backgrounds due to biases in the training data. This perpetuates existing inequalities and affects fair access to education.

A review in AI & Society (Dieterle et al., 2022), highlights the cyclical ethical effects of using AI in education, including how biases in algorithms can affect decisions related to student admissions and assessments. Continuous monitoring and adjustment of AI systems are essential to ensure fairness and equity.

College Admissions Algorithms

In 2019, several universities faced backlash for using AI algorithms that disproportionately favored applicants from affluent backgrounds. These algorithms were trained on historical admissions data, which reflected existing biases. The controversy sparked a broader conversation about fairness in AI-driven admissions processes.

Ethical Challenges in AI-Driven Educational Tools

The ethical implications of AI-driven educational tools extend beyond bias to include issues of transparency, accountability, and privacy. Imagine a scenario where an AI system uses a student's performance data to predict their future success, but neither the student nor the teachers understand how these predictions are made.

An article in the International Journal of Artificial Intelligence in Education (Holmes et al., 2021), discusses the need for a community-wide framework to address these ethical challenges. Integrating ethical considerations into designing and deploying AI systems in education is crucial to prevent unintended consequences.

Predictive Analytics in Education

In 2021, a school district implemented predictive analytics to identify students at risk of dropping out. While the tool helped in early intervention, it also raised concerns about data privacy and the transparency of the predictive models. Ensuring that such tools are used ethically and transparently is vital for maintaining trust.

Impact on Teacher-Student Dynamics

AI systems can also impact the dynamics between teachers and students. For example, using AI for automated grading and feedback can reduce meaningful interactions between teachers and students, potentially diminishing the quality of education.

A study published in Education and Information Technologies (Nguyen et al., 2022), explores the ethical principles for AI in education and highlights the potential negative effects on teacher-student relationships. The study calls for a balanced approach that leverages AI's benefits while maintaining the human element in education.

Automated Grading Systems

In 2020, an AI-powered automated grading system was introduced in several schools to ease the workload of teachers. However, teachers reported that the system's feedback lacked the nuanced understanding that only a human teacher could provide. This example underscores the importance of maintaining human involvement in educational processes.

Mitigating Bias in Educational AI Systems

Efforts to mitigate bias in educational AI systems involve several strategies. These include using diverse training data, conducting regular audits of AI systems, and developing ethical guidelines.

A comprehensive review of AI and Ethics (Akgun & Greenhow, 2021), outlines the ethical challenges and dilemmas of using AI in education and provides recommendations for addressing these issues. The review suggests that educators and policymakers should collaborate to develop ethical standards and practices for AI in education.

Ethical AI Practices in Education

In 2022, a coalition of educators, policymakers, and AI developers launched an initiative to develop ethical guidelines for AI in education. The initiative focused on creating fair and inclusive AI systems that respect student privacy and promote transparency. This collaborative effort highlights the importance of ethical practices in the educational use of AI.

The ethical implications of AI in the education sector are multifaceted and require careful consideration. Addressing bias and ensuring fairness in AI systems is crucial to providing equitable educational opportunities. By implementing transparent and accountable AI practices, educational institutions can harness the potential of AI while mitigating its ethical risks.

3.1.4 Bias in The Legal Sector

AI ethical bias in the legal sector is a critical issue that has been extensively studied by scholars. The integration of AI in legal services offers numerous benefits, such as increased efficiency, improved accuracy, and enhanced decision-making processes. However, it also raises significant ethical concerns, particularly regarding bias and fairness. Here are some key points to illustrate these issues.

Bias in Judicial Decision-Making

Imagine a defendant named Michael, who is up for parole. The decision is influenced by an AI algorithm designed to assess the likelihood of reoffending. However, this algorithm is trained on historical data that may reflect societal biases. Michael, who belongs to a minority group, faces a higher risk of an unfair decision due to these biases.

A study published in AI & Society (Gordon, 2021), discusses how AI can influence parole decisions in the United States. The study highlights that biases in historical data can lead to discriminatory outcomes, particularly against minority groups. This can result in unfair sentencing and parole decisions that perpetuate existing inequalities in the legal system.

COMPAS and Recidivism Predictions

The COMPAS system, used in the U.S. to predict recidivism, has faced scrutiny for its biased outcomes. Research has shown that the system is more likely to falsely predict higher risks of reoffending for minority defendants compared to white defendants. This example underscores the need for unbiased and fair AI systems in judicial decision-making.

Algorithmic Bias in Legal Research and Document Review

Consider a law firm that relies on AI-powered tools for legal research and document review. These tools can expedite the process, but if the training data is biased, the outcomes can be skewed. For example, an AI system might prioritize certain legal precedents over others based on biased training data, affecting the quality and fairness of legal advice.

A review in the International Journal of Law and Information Technology (Henz, 2021), highlights the ethical implications of using AI in legal research. Biases in the data used to train these systems can lead to biased legal research outcomes, which can affect the quality and fairness of legal advice and representation.

AI in Legal Document Review

In 2020, a major law firm implemented an AI-powered document review system. While the system improved efficiency, it was found to favor documents from certain jurisdictions over others, reflecting biases in the training data. This case highlights the importance of diverse and representative training data in legal AI systems.

Ethical Challenges in AI-Driven Legal Services

The ethical implications of AI-driven legal services extend beyond bias to include issues of transparency, accountability, and privacy. Imagine a client whose legal case is influenced by an AI recommendation, but neither the client nor the lawyer understands how the AI arrived at its conclusion.

An article in the Journal of Legal Ethics (Barabas, 2020), discusses the need for a comprehensive framework to address these ethical challenges. Integrating ethical considerations into the design and deployment of AI systems in legal services is crucial to prevent unintended consequences.

AI in Legal Advice

In 2019, an AI system used to provide legal advice was found to lack transparency in its decision-making process. Clients and lawyers alike were unable to understand the reasoning behind the AI's recommendations, leading to mistrust. This example underscores the need for transparency and accountability in AI-driven legal services.

Impact on Legal Education and Practice

AI systems can also impact legal education and practice. For example, using AI for automated legal research and document review can lead to a reduction in the need for junior lawyers and paralegals. This shift can affect career opportunities and the traditional path of gaining experience in the legal profession.

A study published in the Journal of Legal Education (Alvarez et al., 2024), explores the ethical principles for AI in legal education and highlights the potential negative effects on the legal profession. The study calls for a balanced approach that leverages AI's benefits while maintaining the human element in legal practice.

Automation in Legal Practice

In 2021, a large law firm reduced its hiring of junior associates due to the implementation of AI-powered legal research tools. While the technology improved efficiency, it also impacted the traditional career path for young lawyers. This example highlights the need for a balanced approach that preserves opportunities for human involvement in legal practice.

Mitigating Bias in Legal AI Systems

Efforts to mitigate bias in legal AI systems involve several strategies. These include using diverse training data, conducting regular audits of AI systems, and developing ethical guidelines.

A comprehensive review of AI and Ethics (Gordon, 2021) outlines the ethical challenges and dilemmas of using AI in legal services and provides recommendations for addressing these issues. The review suggests that legal professionals and policymakers should work together to develop ethical standards and practices for AI in the legal sector.

Ethical AI Practices in Law

In 2022, a group of legal professionals and AI developers collaborated to establish ethical guidelines for AI in legal services. The initiative focused on creating fair and inclusive AI systems that promote transparency and accountability. This collaborative effort underscores the importance of ethical practices in the legal use of AI.

The ethical implications of AI in the legal sector are multifaceted and require careful consideration. Addressing bias and ensuring fairness in AI systems is crucial to providing equitable legal services. By implementing transparent and accountable AI practices, legal professionals can harness the potential of AI while mitigating its ethical risks.

3.1.5 Bias in Law Enforcement

AI ethical bias in law enforcement is a significant concern that has been extensively studied. The integration of AI in law enforcement offers numerous benefits, such as improved efficiency, predictive policing, and enhanced decision-making processes. However, it also raises critical ethical issues, particularly regarding bias and fairness. Here are some key points and real-world examples to illustrate these issues.

Bias in Predictive Policing

Imagine a neighborhood where predictive policing algorithms forecast high crime rates. Police presence is increased based on these predictions, and individuals in the community feel scrutinized and targeted. These algorithms can perpetuate existing biases present in historical crime data, leading to unjust outcomes.

A study published in AI and Ethics (Almasoud & Jamiu Adekunle Idowu, 2024), discusses how predictive policing can amplify societal biases, particularly racial biases. The study highlights that police actions are a major contributor to model discrimination in predictive policing and introduces techniques like Conditional Score Recalibration (CSR) to mitigate these biases.

Predictive Policing in Chicago

In Chicago, the predictive policing program aimed to reduce crime by predicting hotspots and potential offenders. However, it faced criticism for disproportionately targeting minority communities. The algorithm, trained on historical crime data, reflected existing biases, resulting in over-policing certain neighborhoods. This example underscores the need for fairness and accountability in predictive policing algorithms.

Algorithmic Fairness and Transparency

Consider a police department that uses AI to determine patrol routes and allocate resources. The lack of transparency in these AI algorithms poses significant ethical challenges. Officers and the public may not understand how decisions are made, leading to mistrust and potential bias.

A review in the International Journal of Law and Information Technology (Malek, 2022) emphasizes the need for transparency and accountability in AI systems to ensure fairness. Biases in the data used to train these systems can lead to biased outcomes, affecting the quality and fairness of law enforcement practices.

AI in Law Enforcement Transparency

In 2020, a city implemented AI to optimize police patrol routes. However, when questioned about the decision-making process, officials could not explain how the AI arrived at its conclusions. This lack of transparency led to public outcry and demands for more accountable AI systems in law enforcement.

Impact on Minority Communities

AI systems in law enforcement can disproportionately target minority communities. An article in MIT Technology Review (Heaven, 2020) highlights how predictive policing algorithms can reinforce systemic racism. The study discusses the long history of data being weaponized against Black communities and calls for the dismantling of biased predictive policing tools.

Discriminatory Policing Practices

In several cities across the United States, predictive policing tools have been criticized for disproportionately targeting Black and Hispanic communities. These tools, relying on biased historical data, have been shown to exacerbate existing inequalities, leading to increased scrutiny and arrests in these communities.

Ethical Challenges in AI-Driven Law Enforcement

The ethical implications of AI-driven law enforcement extend beyond bias to include issues of privacy and accountability. Imagine a scenario where an AI system identifies an individual as a potential suspect based on data analysis, but the individual has no prior criminal record. This raises significant privacy concerns and ethical dilemmas.

An article in the Journal of Legal Ethics (Barabas, 2020) discusses the need for a comprehensive framework to address these ethical challenges. Integrating ethical considerations into the design and deployment of AI systems in law enforcement is crucial to prevent unintended consequences.

Facial Recognition and Privacy

In 2019, the use of facial recognition technology by law enforcement agencies sparked debates about privacy and civil liberties. Cases of misidentification and wrongful arrests highlighted the ethical challenges of using AI in law enforcement, emphasizing the need for robust privacy protections and accountability measures.

Mitigating Bias in Law Enforcement AI Systems

Efforts to mitigate bias in law enforcement AI systems involve several strategies. These include using diverse training data, conducting regular audits of AI systems, and developing ethical guidelines.

A comprehensive review of AI and Ethics (Alvarez et al., 2024) outlines the ethical challenges and dilemmas of using AI in law enforcement and provides recommendations for addressing these issues. The review suggests that law enforcement agencies and policymakers should work together to develop ethical standards and practices for AI in law enforcement.

Ethical AI Practices in Law Enforcement

In 2022, a task force was established to develop ethical guidelines for the use of AI in law enforcement. The task force focused on creating fair and transparent AI systems that respect civil rights and promote accountability. This collaborative effort highlights the importance of ethical practices in the use of AI in law enforcement.

The ethical implications of AI in law enforcement are multifaceted and require careful consideration. Addressing bias and ensuring fairness in AI systems is crucial to providing equitable law enforcement services. By implementing transparent and accountable AI practices, law enforcement agencies can harness the potential of AI while mitigating its ethical risks.

3.1.6 Bias in The Media Sector

AI ethical bias in the media sector is a significant concern that has raised several debates. The integration of AI in media offers numerous benefits, such as personalized content recommendations, automated journalism, and enhanced data analytics. However, it also raises critical ethical issues, particularly regarding bias and fairness. Here are some examples to illustrate these issues.

Bias in Content Recommendation Systems

Imagine you're watching your favorite streaming service, and the AI-driven content recommendation system suggests shows and movies. If these algorithms are trained on data that is not representative of diverse audiences, they may favor certain types of content while ignoring others. This can result in a lack of diversity in the content you see.

A study published in AI and Ethics (Trattner et al., 2021) discusses how algorithmic content selection and user personalization can introduce risks and societal threats. The study highlights the need for responsible media technology to balance these opportunities and benefits against their potential for negative impacts.

Content Recommendation Bias

In 2020, several streaming platforms faced criticism for their content recommendation algorithms, which were found to prioritize content appealing to specific demographic groups. This led to the underrepresentation of diverse voices and stories, highlighting the need for inclusive training data in AI-driven content recommendation systems.

Algorithmic Bias in News Production

Consider a newsroom where AI algorithms generate news stories. If the training data is biased, these algorithms can perpetuate existing biases. For example, if the data predominantly includes news from certain sources, the AI might produce biased news coverage.

A review in the Handbook of Global Media Ethics (Chen & Chekam, 2021) explores how algorithms are redefining news production and distribution processes, giving rise to automated journalism. The study emphasizes that biases in the data used to train these systems can lead to biased news coverage, affecting the quality and fairness of journalism.

Automated Journalism Bias

In 2019, a news organization implemented AI-generated news stories. However, the AI system was found to favor certain topics and perspectives, reflecting the biases in its training data. This example underscores the importance of diverse and balanced training data in AI-driven news production.

Ethical Challenges in AI-Driven Media

The ethical implications of AI-driven media extend beyond bias to include issues of transparency, accountability, and privacy. Imagine a scenario where an AI system determines which news articles to promote, but the criteria are not transparent.

An article in AI & Society (Ouchchy et al., 2020) discusses the media's portrayal of AI ethics. The study suggests that media coverage of AI ethics can shape public debate and influence the development and regulation of AI technologies.

Media Transparency

The Hidden Algorithms Behind Our Newsfeeds

In 2020, millions of users woke up to a subtle yet profound change in their social media experience. Sophia, a freelance journalist, noticed that her carefully curated newsfeed was suddenly flooded with sensationalist content, overshadowing the independent news sources she trusted. Confused by the sudden shift, she tried tweaking her settings, but the algorithm seemed impervious to her preferences. Frustrations like Sophia's echoed globally, as users realized they had little insight into the opaque algorithmic decisions dictating their digital environments.

This incident sparked widespread demands for transparency from both users and regulators. The lack of clarity on how content was selected and prioritized raised concerns about manipulation, misinformation, and the erosion of user autonomy. It became evident that in AI-driven media systems, transparency isn't just a technical preference—it's a necessity for maintaining trust and safeguarding democratic discourse.

Impact on Minority Representation

Silenced Stories: When Algorithms Overlook Voices

Alex, an indie musician from an underrepresented community, tirelessly uploaded his music to streaming platforms, hoping to share his culture's rich soundscapes with the world. Despite positive feedback from listeners who stumbled upon his work, Alex noticed his music rarely appeared in recommended playlists. Meanwhile, mainstream artists dominated the suggestions. His experience wasn't isolated.

In 2023, a UNESCO study highlighted how biased AI algorithms in media often marginalize minority voices, leading to a homogenized cultural landscape. The study revealed that AI systems, trained on data reflecting existing societal biases, could amplify gender and racial stereotypes while sidelining diverse perspectives. This not only affects artists like Alex but also deprives audiences of the rich tapestry of global cultures. (Artificial Intelligence: Examples of Ethical Dilemmas | UNESCO, 2023).

Stereotyping in Media

The Ripple Effect of Biased Advertising

Consider Maya, a young professional exploring career opportunities online. She noticed that advertisements for leadership roles and STEM careers rarely appeared on her social media feeds. Instead, she was bombarded with ads for beauty products and home decor. Investigative reports uncovered that AI-driven advertising platforms were segmenting audiences based on entrenched gender norms, reinforcing outdated stereotypes.

These practices have far-reaching implications. By perpetuating narrow representations of roles and interests, AI systems influence individual choices and societal expectations. The reinforcement of such stereotypes not only undermines progress toward equality but also limits the potential of countless individuals like Maya.

Mitigating Bias in Media AI Systems

Building a Fairer Digital World

Addressing these ethical concerns requires a multifaceted approach:

- **Diverse Training Data:** Curating datasets that encompass a wide range of voices and experiences helps AI systems provide more balanced outcomes. This diversity reduces the risk of bias by ensuring that minority groups are adequately represented.
- **Regular Audits and Transparency:** Implementing routine checks on AI algorithms can identify biases that may have been introduced during system updates or as a result of evolving data patterns. Transparency in these processes builds trust with users.
- **Ethical Guidelines and Collaboration:** In 2024, Almasoud & Jamiu Adekunle Idowu conducted a comprehensive review addressing the ethical challenges of AI in media. They emphasized the importance of collaboration between media organizations, AI developers, and policymakers to establish ethical standards. Their recommendations include the adoption of clear policies that prioritize fairness, accountability, and inclusivity.

Ethical Guidelines in Media

A Unified Front for Responsible AI

Recognizing the urgency, a coalition of forward-thinking media organizations and AI developers convened in 2022 to draft ethical guidelines for AI use in media. These guidelines focus on:

- **Fair Representation:** Ensuring content algorithms do not discriminate against or marginalize any group.
- **Algorithmic Transparency:** Making the decision-making processes of AI systems understandable to users, granting them more control over their content consumption.
- **Accountability Measures:** Establishing protocols for addressing grievances related to AI biases, including corrective actions and public reporting.

This collective effort signifies a pivotal step toward responsible AI integration in media. By adhering to these guidelines, companies can foster a more inclusive digital environment that respects and amplifies diverse voices.

Conclusion

Charting the Path Forward

The ethical implications of AI in the media sector are profound and multifaceted. As AI continues to shape our information ecosystems, it's imperative to proactively address the challenges of bias and representation. By implementing strategies such as utilizing diverse training data, conducting regular audits, and adhering to collaboratively developed ethical guidelines, we can steer AI systems toward promoting equity and inclusivity.

These efforts are not just technical adjustments but foundational shifts that prioritize humanity at the core of technological advancement. In doing so, media organizations can harness the transformative potential of AI while safeguarding against its risks, ultimately contributing to a more just and vibrant society where every voice has the opportunity to be heard.

Chapter 4

4.0 Trust and Safety

The world of artificial intelligence (AI) has brought incredible advancements but also significant challenges, particularly in terms of trust and safety. One of the major issues is the "black box" problem, which refers to AI systems whose internal workings are not transparent or understandable. Let's explore this concept and its real-world implications.

4.1 The Black Box Problem

Imagine you have a magical box. You put in some information and out comes a result, but what happens inside the box remains a mystery. This is the essence of the black box problem in AI. Users, developers, and even the creators of these systems often can't see or understand how decisions are being made inside these complex models. This opacity leads to significant issues related to trust, accountability, and fairness.

4.1.1 What is Black Box AI?

Black box AI systems show you the input and the output, but the internal decision-making process is a mystery (Kosinski, 2024). This lack of transparency can be due to the intricate nature of the algorithms, proprietary constraints, or the sheer complexity of the machine learning models involved. It's like trying to understand the recipe for a dish just by tasting it—without seeing any of the ingredients or the cooking process.

In simple terms, think of it as a highly sophisticated recipe that a chef uses to create a dish. You can taste the final product (the output) and know what ingredients went in (the input), but the exact steps the chef took to combine and cook those ingredients are hidden from you. (What Is Black Box AI?, n.d.).

4.1.2 How Does Black Box AI Work?

To grasp how black box AI functions, let's delve into the world of deep learning. Deep learning models, which are a subset of machine learning, use artificial neural networks composed of multiple layers. These layers process data through interconnected nodes (neurons), performing complex calculations to identify patterns and make predictions.

When you feed data into a deep learning model, it traverses through these layers, each adding its own set of calculations. The model tweaks the connections between neurons based on the data it processes, learning to make accurate predictions. However, these internal adjustments and the precise paths taken within the model are opaque, even to the developers who created it.

To make this more relatable, think of a deep learning model as a massive maze. You can see the entrance (input) and the exit (output), but the winding paths taken inside the maze to reach the exit remain hidden. This opacity is what makes black box AI both powerful and problematic. (What Is Black Box AI?, n.d.).

Examples of Black Box AI

1. **Facial Recognition Systems**: These systems utilize deep learning to identify individuals based on their facial features. Trained on vast datasets of images, they learn to recognize patterns and distinguish one face from another. However, the specific features and patterns the model uses to make these distinctions remain hidden, raising questions about transparency and accuracy.

2. **Predictive Policing**: Algorithms in predictive policing analyze historical crime data to forecast where crimes are likely to occur and who might commit them. These systems can perpetuate biases present in the training data, leading to discriminatory outcomes. For instance, if historical data reflects biased policing, the AI might unfairly target certain demographic groups. (Blouin, 2023).

3. **Credit Scoring**: AI algorithms in credit scoring evaluate an individual's creditworthiness based on numerous data points. These systems can be opaque, making it hard for people to understand why they were denied credit. This lack of transparency can lead to unfair treatment, particularly if the model exhibits bias against certain demographics. (Kosinski, 2024).

4. **Autonomous Vehicles**: Self-driving cars rely on AI to make real-time driving decisions, such as braking or lane changes. These decisions stem from complex calculations within deep learning models. However, the rationale behind these decisions is often not transparent, which can pose significant safety concerns in the event of an accident. (Blouin, 2023).

To drive home these points, let's consider the real-world story of a young woman named Lisa who applied for a loan to start her small business. Despite having a good credit history, her loan application was rejected. When Lisa sought an explanation, she was given none—the decision had been made by an opaque AI system. This left her frustrated and distrustful of the system, illustrating the tangible impacts of black box AI on people's lives.

By understanding and addressing the black box problem, we can work towards more transparent, accountable, and fair AI systems. The journey is complex, but the goal is clear: to build AI that not only advances technology but also earns and maintains the trust of its users.

4.2 Addressing the Black Box Problem

The black box problem in AI can be quite daunting, but there are ways to make AI systems more transparent, understandable, and trustworthy. Let's break it down.

1. Explainable AI (XAI)

Imagine you're a detective trying to solve a mystery. Explainable AI (XAI) helps you by showing clues and explaining how each clue leads to solving the case.

- **Local Interpretable Model-agnostic Explanations (LIME)**: Think of LIME as a magnifying glass that helps you see the small details. For instance, doctors use LIME to understand how an AI diagnoses diseases from X-rays. It highlights parts of the X-ray that influenced the AI's decision, making it easier for doctors to trust and use the AI's insights. (Keita, 2023).
- **SHapley Additive exPlanations (SHAP)**: SHAP is like breaking down a recipe to see how each ingredient contributes to the final dish. In banking, SHAP helps explain why an AI approved or denied a loan by showing the role of each factor (like income and credit history) in the decision. This transparency builds trust with customers. (Keita, 2023).

2. Model Transparency and Interpretability

Imagine reading a "choose your own adventure" book where each choice is mapped out. Transparent and interpretable AI models work similarly.

- **Decision Trees**: These models are like flowcharts that show each decision and its outcomes. In farming, a decision tree-based AI helps farmers decide when to plant crops by considering factors like weather and soil. Farmers can follow the AI's reasoning step-by-step, making the advice easy to understand and trust. (IBM, 2024).
- **Rule-based Systems**: These systems use simple "if-then" rules, much like following a recipe. In law, a rule-based AI helps lawyers analyze contracts by highlighting potential risks based on predefined rules. This clarity makes the AI's recommendations easy to follow and reliable. (IBM, 2024).

3. Regular Audits and Bias Detection

Think of regular audits like routine check-ups at the doctor to make sure everything is running smoothly.

- **Fairness Metrics**: These metrics check if the AI is fair to everyone. For example, a social media company uses fairness metrics to ensure their content recommendation AI treats all user groups equally, promoting a diverse and inclusive experience. (Jagati, 2023).
- **Bias Correction Algorithms**: These algorithms fix biases, like adjusting a recipe to suit everyone's taste. A tech company uses them to ensure their AI doesn't favor certain genders or ethnicities during the hiring process, promoting diversity and fairness. (Jagati, 2023).

4. Robust Governance Structures

Imagine playing a board game with clear rules and a referee to ensure fair play. Strong governance structures in AI work the same way (ScaDS PubRel, 2023).

- **Example**: An automaker set up an AI ethics board to oversee its self-driving car technology. This board reviews AI decisions, conducts audits, and ensures ethical guidelines are followed. Their oversight builds public trust in the safety of autonomous vehicles.

5. Transparency in AI Decision-Making

Think of transparency in AI like watching a cooking show where the chef explains every step.

- **Example**: A government agency uses an AI system to allocate public resources more efficiently. They provide detailed explanations of how the AI makes decisions, allowing citizens to understand and give feedback. This openness fosters trust and accountability.

By using these strategies, we can make AI systems more transparent, accountable, and trustworthy. Picture a world where AI serves humanity with clarity and fairness (Blouin, 2023).

4.3 Building Trust in The AI Decision-Making Processes

To ensure widespread adoption and acceptance of AI technologies, it's vital to build trust in the AI decision-making process. This can be achieved through several key principles: transparency, accountability, fairness, robustness, and privacy. Let's explore these principles.

1. Transparency

Imagine watching a magic trick. Transparency in AI means understanding the magician's moves instead of just marveling at the trick. By using Explainable AI (XAI) techniques like LIME and SHAP, we can make AI decisions more understandable (IBM, 2015).

- **Example**: In healthcare, doctors use AI to diagnose diseases. With XAI techniques, doctors can see which symptoms and data points the AI used to make a diagnosis. This transparency helps doctors trust the AI's recommendations, just like knowing the magician's secret builds confidence in the trick (Kovari, 2024).

2. Accountability

Think of accountability as having a team captain who takes responsibility for the team's actions. In AI, establishing clear lines of responsibility and robust governance structures ensures that there are mechanisms to hold AI systems and their developers accountable.

- **Example**: In finance, AI algorithms determine credit scores. Regular audits ensure that these algorithms do not discriminate against certain demographic groups. Financial institutions can set up committees to oversee these processes, ensuring they follow ethical standards. This accountability is like having a referee who ensures fair play in a game. (Lukyanenko et al., 2022).

3. Fairness

Fairness in AI is about making sure everyone gets a fair shot, much like a referee ensuring both teams play by the rules. This involves using diverse training data, implementing fairness metrics, and applying bias correction algorithms.

- **Example**: In hiring, AI systems screen job applicants. If the AI is trained on biased historical data, it might favor certain groups unfairly. By using diverse training data and testing the AI for fairness, companies can ensure their hiring processes are equitable. It's like revising the game's rules to ensure everyone has a fair chance to win. (Building Trust in AI: 3 Key Principles for Responsible AI Development, 2024).

4. Robustness

Robustness means the AI can perform well under various conditions, like a car that drives smoothly on different terrains. Ensuring robustness involves making AI systems resilient to adversarial attacks and capable of handling unexpected inputs.

- **Example**: Autonomous vehicles rely on AI to make driving decisions. To ensure safety, these AI systems undergo extensive testing under different conditions, from rainy days to busy city streets. Implementing fail-safes helps the AI handle unexpected situations, much like a car equipped with airbags for sudden impacts. (Building Trust in Automated Decision-Making – AI Ethics and Leadership, 2024).

5. Privacy

Privacy in AI is about protecting personal data, like keeping your diary safe from prying eyes. This involves data anonymization techniques and adhering to data protection regulations such as the GDPR.

- **Example**: In personalized marketing, AI uses customer data to tailor advertisements. By anonymizing this data and allowing customers to control their information, companies build trust in their AI systems. It's like assuring your diary is locked and only you have the key. (Intellias, 2024).

Building trust in AI decision-making requires a multi-faceted approach, embracing transparency, accountability, fairness, robustness, and privacy. By adopting these principles, organizations can ensure their AI systems are trustworthy and reliable, fostering greater acceptance and adoption of AI technologies. Imagine a world where AI serves humanity with integrity and clarity, much like a well-played game where everyone knows the rules and trusts the referee.

Industry	Trust and Safety Area	Percentage
Healthcare	Data privacy and security	35%
Finance	Fraud detection and prevention	30%
Retail	Customer data protection	25%
Manufacturing	Equipment safety and reliability	20%
Transportation	Autonomous vehicle safety	15%
Customer Service	Accuracy and reliability of responses	40%
Marketing	Ethical advertising practices	30%
Entertainment	Content moderation	25%
Agriculture	Environmental impact monitoring	10%
Education	Student data privacy	15%
Law Enforcement	Fairness in predictive policing	20%
Legal Practice	Transparency in decision-making	15%

These are the infographics on AI trust and safety across industries.

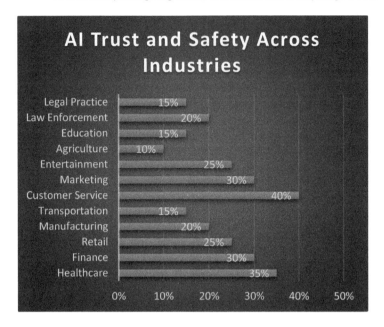

These percentages are approximate and can vary based on different studies and reports. The impact and adoption rates might differ slightly across regions and specific companies within each industry.

4.4 Creating Transparency in The AI Decision-Making Process

Creating transparency in the AI decision-making process is crucial for building trust, ensuring accountability, and promoting fairness. Let's explore some real-world examples.

Examples of Transparency in AI Decision-Making

1. Healthcare

Sepsis Detection at Johns Hopkins: Imagine a hospital using an advanced AI system called TREWS (Targeted, Real-time Early-Warning System) to detect sepsis early. Sepsis is a life-threatening condition, and early detection is vital. TREWS sends real-time alerts to healthcare providers, explaining why it flagged a patient as high-risk. For example, it might highlight a sudden drop in blood pressure and an increase in white blood cell count as critical factors. By providing these explanations, healthcare providers can understand and trust the system, ensuring timely intervention and better patient outcomes (Intellias, 2024).

2. Finance

Credit Risk Assessment: Picture a FinTech company that developed a SaaS lending platform using AI to assess credit risk. When a person applies for a loan, the platform not only gives a credit score but also provides transparent explanations. For instance, it might explain that a high debt-to-income ratio or a recent late payment affected the score. This transparency helps borrowers understand the reasons behind their approval or denial, building trust in the system and allowing them to take steps to improve their creditworthiness. (Intellias, 2024).

3. Law Enforcement

Predictive Policing: Imagine law enforcement agencies using predictive policing algorithms to analyze historical crime data and predict where crimes might occur. To build trust with the community, these agencies use explainable AI techniques to provide transparent explanations. For example, the AI might indicate that increased burglaries in a specific area are due to a recent rise in unemployment. By sharing these insights, the community understands the logic behind the predictions, fostering trust and cooperation between law enforcement and residents. (Intellias, 2024).

Achieving Transparency in AI Decision-Making

To achieve transparency in AI decision-making, organizations need a comprehensive strategy that includes:

1. **Explainable AI Methodologies**: Developing AI systems that can explain their decision-making processes, much like a teacher explaining a math problem step-by-step.
2. **Transparent and Interpretable Models**: Using models that stakeholders can easily understand, such as decision trees or rule-based systems.
3. **Regular Auditing Practices**: Conducting routine checks to ensure AI systems are functioning correctly and fairly, similar to regular health check-ups.
4. **Strong Governance Frameworks**: Establishing clear rules and oversight committees to ensure AI systems are developed and used ethically.
5. **Enhanced Transparency in Decision-Making**: Providing detailed explanations of how AI systems make decisions, akin to a chef explaining a complex recipe.

By integrating these approaches, organizations can create AI systems that are not only transparent but also accountable and reliable. This comprehensive strategy helps build trust, ensuring that AI serves humanity clearly and fairly.

4.5 Ensuring the Safety and Reliability of AI Application

Ensuring the safety and reliability of AI applications is crucial for their successful deployment and acceptance across various sectors. Let's explore how to achieve this with some relatable examples.

1. Robustness and Resilience

Imagine a tightrope walker maintaining balance despite strong winds and unpredictable shifts. Similarly, AI systems must be robust and resilient to handle unexpected inputs and adversarial attacks. Techniques such as adversarial training help AI models maintain their performance even under challenging conditions.

Example: In autonomous vehicles, robustness is critical for safety. These AI systems must handle various driving conditions, from bad weather to sudden obstacles. Researchers have developed techniques to test and improve the robustness of these systems, ensuring they can operate safely in real-world scenarios (Nguyen et al., 2024). It's like ensuring the tightrope walker has the skills and tools to stay balanced no matter what.

2. Explainability and Transparency

Transparency in AI decision-making processes is essential for building trust and ensuring accountability. Explainable AI (XAI) techniques provide insights into how AI models make decisions, making it easier to identify and address potential issues.

Example: In healthcare, doctors use AI to diagnose diseases. To trust the AI's recommendations, they need transparency. Techniques like LIME and SHAP explain the predictions of complex models, helping medical professionals understand how the AI arrived at a diagnosis. It's like a detective explaining the clues and logic behind solving a mystery. (Establishing and Evaluating Trustworthy AI: Overview and Research Challenges, 2020).

3. Ethical Guidelines and Regulatory Compliance

Adhering to ethical guidelines and regulatory requirements is crucial for ensuring the safety and reliability of AI applications. This includes following industry-specific standards and complying with data protection regulations like the GDPR.

Example: In the finance sector, AI algorithms used for credit scoring must comply with regulations to prevent discrimination against certain demographic groups. Financial institutions regularly audit these algorithms to ensure they adhere to ethical standards and regulations. It's like ensuring a referee enforces fair play rules in a game. (Ryan, 2020).

4. Regular Audits and Monitoring

Conducting regular audits and continuous monitoring of AI systems is essential to identify and address potential issues. This involves testing AI models for fairness, accuracy, and robustness, and making necessary adjustments to mitigate any identified biases.

Example: In predictive policing, AI systems analyze crime data to predict potential incidents. Regular audits ensure these systems do not perpetuate biases in law enforcement. By continuously monitoring, agencies can identify and address biases, ensuring fair and equitable policing practices. It's like a quality control team ensuring products meet high standards (Herrera, 2023).

5. Human-in-the-Loop (HITL) Systems

Incorporating human oversight in AI decision-making processes can help ensure safety and reliability. Human-in-the-loop (HITL) systems involve human intervention at critical points in the AI decision-making process, allowing for manual review and correction of AI outputs.

Example: In healthcare, HITL systems ensure AI recommendations for treatment plans are reviewed by medical professionals before being implemented (vzhuk, 2023). This oversight helps prevent critical errors that could harm patients. It's like having a pilot take control during turbulence to ensure a safe flight.

6. Robust Governance Structures

Establishing robust governance structures ensures accountability in AI systems. This includes setting up committees or boards to oversee AI development and deployment, conducting regular audits, and ensuring compliance with ethical guidelines.

Example: In the finance sector, financial institutions can establish governance frameworks to oversee AI algorithms for trading and investment decisions. These frameworks help ensure AI systems operate safely and reliably (Nguyen et al., 2024). It's like having a board of directors ensure a company follows ethical and legal standards.

4.6 Conclusion

Guaranteeing the safety and reliability of AI applications requires a holistic strategy that encompasses robustness and resilience, explainability and transparency, compliance with ethical standards and regulations, ongoing audits and monitoring, human-in-the-loop mechanisms, and strong governance frameworks. By implementing these measures, organizations can ensure their AI systems are secure, dependable, and credible. This multifaceted approach fosters trust and facilitates the successful deployment of AI across various sectors, much like a well-coordinated team working towards a common goal.

Chapter 5

5.0 Job Displacement and Economic Impact

Artificial intelligence (AI) has the potential to significantly impact the job market, leading to large-scale job displacement in various sectors. This phenomenon is driven by AI's ability to automate tasks previously performed by humans, often with greater efficiency and accuracy.

Below are the areas that may be severely affected as a result of the introduction of artificial industries across various industries.

The below percentages are approximate and can vary based on different studies and reports. The impact and prevalence of these areas might differ slightly across regions and specific companies within each industry.

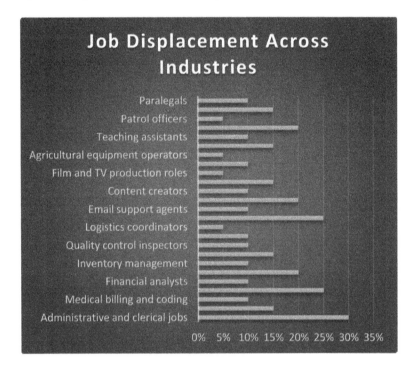

Industry	Affected Area	Percentage
Healthcare	Administrative and clerical jobs	30%
Healthcare	Medical transcriptionists	15%
Healthcare	Medical billing and coding	10%
Finance	Bank tellers and clerical staff	25%
Finance	Financial analysts	10%
Retail	Cashiers and customer service reps	20%
Retail	Inventory management	10%
Manufacturing	Assembly line workers	15%
Manufacturing	Quality control inspectors	10%

Transportation	Drivers (e.g., truck, taxi drivers)	10%
Transportation	Logistics coordinators	5%
Customer Service	Call center agents	25%
Customer Service	Email support agents	10%
Marketing	Marketing analysts	20%
Marketing	Content creators	10%
Entertainment	Content moderation	15%
Entertainment	Film and TV production roles	5%
Agriculture	Manual labourers	10%
Agriculture	Agricultural equipment operators	5%
Education	Administrative Staff	15%

Education	Teaching assistants	10%
Law Enforcement	Routine administrative tasks	20%
Law Enforcement	Patrol officers	5%
Legal Practice	Legal researchers	15%
Legal Practice	Paralegals	10%

5.1 Job Displacement in The Banking Sector

AI is transforming the banking sector, leading to significant job displacement in various roles. Here's how AI is making waves in employment:

5.1.1 Customer Service and Support

Picture this: It's 2 AM and you have a pressing banking issue. Instead of waiting until morning for a human representative, an AI-powered chatbot or virtual assistant is ready to help. These AI systems can provide 24/7 service, handle multiple queries simultaneously, and offer personalized responses based on customer data. This reduces the need for human customer service representatives. A real-world example is Bank of America's AI-driven virtual assistant named Erica, which assists customers with their banking needs (Kreps & Fletcher, 2017). Since its launch, Erica has handled millions of customer interactions, offering solutions instantly and efficiently.

5.1.2 Fraud Detection and Risk Management

Imagine being able to sift through millions of transactions in seconds to detect fraud. AI algorithms excel at this by analyzing large volumes of transaction data and identifying patterns that may indicate fraudulent activity (AI Is in Banking Is the Talent Ready?, 2024). This automation reduces the need for human analysts to manually review transactions. Additionally, AI systems can assess credit risk more accurately, leading to more efficient and reliable risk management processes. For instance, some banks use advanced AI models to monitor transactions for signs of fraud in real-time, flagging suspicious activities before they can escalate.

5.1.3 Loan Processing and Underwriting

Consider the traditional loan application process, which involves a significant amount of paperwork and manual evaluation. AI is streamlining this by automating the evaluation of loan applications. AI algorithms can quickly analyze an applicant's financial history, credit score, and other relevant data to determine their creditworthiness (Fares et al., 2022). This reduces the need for human underwriters and speeds up the loan approval process. For example, some banks now offer instant loan approvals thanks to AI-powered underwriting systems, making the process faster and more efficient for both the bank and the customer.

5.1.4 Trading and Investment Management

Imagine the bustling world of stock markets, where every second counts. In the past, human traders would spend hours analyzing market trends, making calls, and executing trades. Today, AI has revolutionized this process. AI-driven trading algorithms can analyze massive amounts of market data in real-time and execute trades at lightning speed. These algorithms can identify patterns and trends that might elude human traders, making decisions in microseconds that can significantly impact profitability.

For instance, high-frequency trading firms use AI to gain a competitive edge. These firms employ sophisticated algorithms that can process information from various sources, such as news reports, financial statements, and market signals, to make informed trading decisions. This capability often results in AI outperforming human traders in terms of speed and accuracy.

Additionally, robo-advisors are changing the landscape of investment management. These AI-powered tools provide automated investment advice and portfolio management services (Batiz-Lazo et al., 2022). They assess an individual's financial situation, risk tolerance, and investment goals to offer personalized recommendations. Robo-advisors continuously monitor and adjust portfolios to optimize returns, reducing the need for human financial advisors for routine investment management tasks. This allows human advisors to focus on more complex financial planning and strategy development.

5.1.5 Back Office Operations

In the realm of back-office operations, AI is bringing about a silent revolution. These operations, often unseen by customers, are crucial for the smooth functioning of banks. Tasks like data entry, compliance checks, and reporting are essential but can be repetitive and time-consuming when done manually. AI steps in to automate these processes, ensuring efficiency and accuracy.

Consider the example of data reconciliation. AI systems can process and match large volumes of financial transactions with unprecedented speed and precision. They ensure that all records are accurate and comply with regulatory requirements, minimizing errors that could have significant financial implications. This automation reduces the reliance on human employees for these repetitive tasks, freeing them to engage in more strategic activities.

Moreover, AI-powered compliance tools can monitor transactions in real-time to ensure they meet regulatory standards. These systems can detect anomalies or potential compliance breaches, allowing banks to address issues proactively. By automating these back-office functions, banks can reduce operational costs, improve accuracy, and maintain compliance with evolving regulations.

5.2 Job Displacement in The Manufacturing Sector

AI is revolutionizing the manufacturing sector, bringing about significant changes in various roles. Here's a deeper look at how AI is transforming the landscape:

5.2.1 Assembly Line Jobs

Imagine walking into a modern automotive factory. The sight that greets you is likely one filled with robots tirelessly working on assembly lines. These robots handle tasks such as welding, painting, and assembling components with remarkable precision and efficiency. For instance, companies like Tesla and Ford utilize advanced robotics to ensure their assembly lines run smoothly and efficiently.

In the past, these tasks required a substantial human workforce, but today, robots perform them more efficiently and without the need for breaks. This shift has led to significant job displacement, as fewer human workers are needed on the assembly line (Putman, 2024). While this change increases productivity and consistency in production, it also raises concerns about the future of jobs traditionally held by human workers.

5.2.2 Quality Control

Quality control is a critical aspect of manufacturing, ensuring that products meet high standards before reaching consumers. Traditionally, human inspectors carried out this task, meticulously checking for defects. However, AI-powered systems are now taking over. These systems use advanced vision technologies to inspect products with incredible accuracy and speed (Putman, 2024).

For example, in electronics manufacturing, AI-driven vision systems can detect even the smallest defects in components, ensuring that only top-quality products move forward in the production process. This automation not only enhances the quality of products but also reduces the need for human inspectors, leading to job displacement in quality control roles.

5.2.3 Predictive Maintenance

Maintenance is another area where AI is making a significant impact. Traditionally, maintenance workers performed routine checks and repairs to keep machinery running smoothly. However, AI is changing this through predictive maintenance. By analyzing data from sensors on machinery, AI algorithms can predict when maintenance is needed, preventing breakdowns and reducing downtime.

This approach means that maintenance can be carried out only when necessary, rather than on a fixed schedule, saving time and resources. As a result, the need for human maintenance workers to perform routine checks and repairs diminishes, leading to job displacement in this area (Espina-Romero et al., 2024). AI ensures that equipment runs optimally, increasing overall efficiency in manufacturing processes.

5.2.4 Warehouse Operations

Now, let's move into the heart of distribution: the warehouse. Warehouses are buzzing hives of activity, with items being picked, packed, and sorted continuously. Traditionally, these tasks required a large workforce. However, AI and robotics are taking over these operations, bringing about a silent revolution.

Consider Amazon's fulfillment centers, where AI-powered robots handle picking, packing, and sorting tasks (Putman, 2024). These robots navigate vast warehouses with precision, selecting items and preparing them for shipment. This automation has significantly reduced the need for human workers in these roles. While robots work tirelessly without breaks, human workers are freed from repetitive tasks, but this also means fewer jobs in warehouse operations.

5.3 Job Displacement in The Transport and Logistics Sector

AI is making waves in the transport and logistics sector, bringing about significant changes in various roles. Let's delve into how AI is transforming this industry:

5.3.1 Autonomous Vehicles

Picture a world where trucks drive themselves and drones deliver packages to your doorstep. Autonomous vehicles, including self-driving trucks and delivery drones, are set to revolutionize the logistics industry. Companies like Aurora are at the forefront of developing self-driving trucks that can operate without human intervention. Imagine a long-haul truck that navigates highways on its own, reducing the need for human truck drivers.

Similarly, delivery drones are taking over last-mile deliveries. These drones can zip through the skies, dropping off packages at customers' doorsteps efficiently (The AI Revolution in Transportation, 2024). This reduces the need for human couriers, who traditionally handled these deliveries. The convenience and efficiency of autonomous vehicles are undeniable, but they also lead to job displacement for truck drivers and couriers.

5.3.2 Traffic Management

Let's navigate the bustling streets of a modern city. Traffic jams are a common headache for many urban areas, but AI is stepping in to smooth out the chaos. Intelligent traffic management systems use real-time data from sensors, cameras, and connected vehicles to dynamically adjust traffic signals. This means traffic lights can change in response to actual traffic conditions, reducing congestion and improving traffic flow (Abduljabbar et al., 2019).

Imagine driving through a city where traffic lights are synchronized perfectly to get you to your destination faster. AI analyzes data from various sources, such as traffic cameras and connected vehicles, to understand traffic patterns and make real-time adjustments. This reduces the need for human traffic controllers, who traditionally managed traffic flow manually. For instance, cities like Los Angeles and London have implemented AI-driven traffic management systems to improve efficiency and reduce traffic jams.

5.3.3 Supply Chain Optimization

Supply chains are the backbone of any manufacturing and retail operation, ensuring that products move smoothly from production to consumers. AI is transforming supply chain management by automating tasks such as inventory management, demand forecasting, and logistics planning.

Imagine a system that predicts demand for products with remarkable accuracy, adjusting inventory levels to minimize stockouts and overstock situations. AI algorithms analyze vast amounts of data, including sales trends, market conditions, and consumer behavior, to optimize supply chain operations. This reduces the need for human workers to manually track and manage these processes (Espina-Romero et al., 2024).

For example, a major retailer might use AI to predict a spike in demand for winter coats before the cold season hits. The system adjusts inventory levels across different regions, ensuring stores are well-stocked without overloading warehouses. This level of precision helps in maintaining a balance between supply and demand, reducing waste and improving efficiency.

5.4 Job Displacement in The Clerical and Administrative Sector

AI is significantly transforming the clerical and administrative sector, bringing about notable changes in various roles. Let's explore how AI is reshaping this field:

5.4.1 Data Entry and Processing

Imagine a bustling office where stacks of documents need to be entered into digital systems. Traditionally, clerical workers performed this meticulous task, spending hours on data entry. However, AI-powered systems are now stepping in to automate these tasks. For example, optical character recognition (OCR) technology can convert scanned documents into editable text, eliminating the need for manual data entry.

AI algorithms can process large volumes of data quickly and accurately, reducing the need for human intervention (Georgieff & Hyee, 2022). This means that data entry tasks that once took days can now be completed in a matter of minutes. While this automation enhances efficiency, it also leads to job displacement for clerical workers who previously handled these tasks.

5.4.2 Customer Service and Support

Think about the times you've contacted customer support for help. Increasingly, AI-driven chatbots and virtual assistants are taking over these interactions. These AI systems can provide 24/7 service, handle multiple queries simultaneously, and offer personalized responses based on customer data (Shine & Whiting, 2023). For example, many companies use AI chatbots to manage customer interactions, providing quick and efficient responses to common inquiries.

This shift reduces the need for human customer service representatives, leading to job displacement for clerical staff in customer service roles. While AI handles routine queries, human representatives are freed up to handle more complex issues that require a personal touch.

5.4.3 Scheduling and Administrative Tasks

Managing schedules, booking appointments, and organizing meetings are essential tasks in any office setting. AI can automate these administrative tasks, streamlining operations and increasing efficiency. AI-powered virtual assistants like Microsoft's Cortana and Google's Assistant can manage calendars, send reminders, and even reschedule meetings when conflicts arise.

Imagine having an AI assistant that can seamlessly handle all your scheduling needs, ensuring that you never miss an appointment. This automation reduces the need for human administrative assistants, who traditionally performed these tasks. While it streamlines operations, it also leads to job displacement for clerical workers in administrative roles.

5.4.4 Document Management

Imagine the piles of paperwork that accumulate in any office, making it a challenge to find and organize important documents. Traditionally, clerical workers would spend hours sorting, filing, and retrieving these documents. However, AI is transforming document management by automating these processes.

AI-powered systems can categorize and tag documents based on their content. For instance, a scanned contract can be automatically tagged with relevant keywords, making it easy to retrieve later. This automation significantly reduces the need for human workers to manually organize and manage documents, leading to job displacement in clerical roles. AI can also analyze documents, extracting key information and even summarizing content, which further enhances efficiency.

5.4.5 Financial and Accounting Tasks

Consider the traditional roles of accountants and clerical staff in handling financial data. Tasks such as invoice processing, expense management, and financial reporting required meticulous attention to detail and significant manual effort. AI is now stepping in to automate these financial and accounting tasks.

AI algorithms can analyze financial data, detect anomalies, and generate reports with high accuracy. For example, an AI system can automatically process invoices, check for discrepancies, and update financial records without human intervention. This reduces the need for human accountants and clerical staff, leading to job displacement in the financial sector.

Imagine a scenario where a company receives hundreds of invoices daily. Instead of having a team of clerks manually entering data and verifying information, an AI system can handle this volume effortlessly. It can process each invoice, flag any inconsistencies, and ensure that all records are accurate. This automation not only saves time but also reduces the risk of human error.

5.5 Job Displacement in The Health Sector

AI is significantly transforming the healthcare sector, bringing about notable changes in various roles. Here's a closer look at how AI is reshaping this field:

5.5.1 Diagnostics and Imaging

Imagine the world of medical imaging—X-rays, MRIs, and CT scans. Traditionally, radiologists would analyze these images, spending hours meticulously examining them for signs of abnormalities. However, AI algorithms are increasingly stepping in to perform these tasks. These algorithms can detect abnormalities with remarkable accuracy, often surpassing human radiologists in speed and precision (Ariyo, 2024). For instance, AI systems have been developed to identify early signs of diseases like cancer, potentially reducing the need for human radiologists. This automation can lead to job displacement for radiologists and other diagnostic professionals.

Imagine an AI system that can quickly and accurately analyze thousands of X-rays, spotting early signs of lung cancer that might be missed by the human eye. This not only speeds up the diagnostic process but also improves accuracy, leading to better patient outcomes. However, it also means that fewer radiologists are needed to perform these tasks.

5.5.2 Administrative Tasks

The administrative side of healthcare is often bogged down by data entry, appointment scheduling, and medical coding. AI-powered tools are now streamlining these tasks. These tools can handle large volumes of data quickly and accurately, reducing the need for human administrative staff. For example, AI systems can automate the process of medical billing and coding, which traditionally requires significant human labor.

Imagine a hospital where an AI system manages appointment scheduling, ensuring that there are no overlaps or missed slots. It can also handle medical billing, accurately coding and processing invoices without human intervention (Reddy, 2024). This automation leads to significant efficiency gains but also results in job displacement for medical coders and administrative assistants.

5.5.3 Patient Monitoring and Care

Patient monitoring is another area where AI is making a significant impact. AI-powered wearables and remote monitoring systems can provide continuous data on vital signs and other health metrics. These systems can alert healthcare providers to potential issues before they become critical, reducing the need for constant human supervision.

Imagine a wearable device that continuously monitors a patient's heart rate and oxygen levels, sending real-time data to healthcare providers. If the system detects any anomalies, it can alert the medical staff immediately, allowing for prompt intervention. This reduces the need for roles such as nursing assistants and home health aides, who traditionally performed these monitoring tasks (Gimbel, 2024).

5.5.4 Telemedicine and Virtual Health Assistants

Imagine a world where visiting the doctor's office is as simple as picking up your phone. AI-driven chatbots and virtual health assistants are making this a reality by triaging patients, providing basic health information, and assisting in remote consultations. These AI systems can handle a large number of patient interactions simultaneously, reducing the need for human healthcare providers in initial consultations and follow-ups (Reddy, 2024).

Picture an AI virtual assistant that can ask you about your symptoms, provide preliminary advice, and even schedule a follow-up appointment with a doctor if necessary. This technology ensures that patients receive timely responses, especially in cases where immediate medical attention is not required. While this enhances accessibility and efficiency, it also leads to job displacement for roles traditionally involved in patient intake and preliminary assessments.

For example, instead of waiting for a nurse or a medical assistant to assess your symptoms and record your medical history, an AI-driven chatbot can do this in minutes. It can also provide basic health advice and direct you to the appropriate level of care. This reduces the workload for healthcare professionals but also means fewer positions for those who would typically perform these tasks.

5.5.5 Pharmaceutical Research and Development

The world of drug discovery is often a lengthy and complex process, involving extensive human-led laboratory work. AI is now accelerating this process by analyzing vast amounts of data to identify potential drug candidates and predict their efficacy. AI algorithms can simulate how different compounds interact with biological targets, drastically reducing the time and resources needed for experimentation.

Imagine AI systems sifting through millions of chemical compounds to identify those that are most likely to be effective against a particular disease. This capability allows researchers to focus on the most promising candidates, speeding up the development process. For example, AI can predict how a new drug will interact with human cells, potentially reducing the need for extensive laboratory testing.

However, this also means job displacement for researchers and laboratory technicians who previously performed these tasks (Daley, 2023). While AI can significantly speed up drug discovery and development, it also reduces the need for manual labor in the initial phases of research.

5.6 Job Displacement in The Retail Sector

AI is significantly transforming the retail sector, bringing notable changes to various roles. Let's explore how AI is reshaping this field:

5.6.1 Cashier and Checkout Roles

Imagine walking into a store, picking up the items you need, and simply walking out without stopping at a checkout counter. AI-powered self-checkout systems and cashier-less stores are making this a reality. For example, Amazon Go stores use AI to track items customers pick up and automatically charge their accounts. This technology streamlines the shopping experience but can lead to job displacement for cashiers (Wu Yili, 2023).

Picture yourself in an Amazon Go store: you grab a sandwich, a drink, and some snacks, and simply walk out. Sensors and cameras track what you take, and your account is billed automatically. This convenience is made possible by AI, which eliminates the need for human cashiers, reducing the number of cashier roles in retail.

5.6.2 Inventory Management

Managing inventory is a critical task in retail, ensuring that products are always available when customers need them. AI is revolutionizing inventory management by automating tasks such as stock monitoring, replenishment, and demand forecasting.

Imagine AI algorithms that can predict future product demand based on historical sales data and market trends. These systems help retailers optimize stock levels and reduce waste. For instance, if data shows a spike in demand for winter coats as the cold season approaches, AI can ensure that stores are well-stocked without overloading warehouses (Shopify, 2024). This reduces the need for human workers to manually manage inventory, leading to job displacement.

5.6.3 Personalized Shopping Experiences

Imagine walking into a store, and the shelves seem to know exactly what you need. AI is making personalized shopping experiences possible by analyzing customer data to provide tailored recommendations and promotions. AI algorithms can study a customer's purchase history and browsing behavior to suggest products they might be interested in.

For instance, if you've recently bought running shoes, AI might suggest sportswear or fitness trackers that complement your purchase. This personalization not only improves customer satisfaction but also boosts sales for retailers. While this enhances the shopping experience, it also reduces the need for human sales associates who traditionally provided personalized recommendations.

Imagine an online store where AI algorithms analyze your browsing history, purchase patterns, and even time spent on product pages to tailor recommendations. You receive personalized emails with suggestions and promotions that match your preferences, making shopping more convenient and enjoyable (Thomas, 2023). This level of personalization reduces the role of human sales associates, leading to job displacement.

5.6.4 Supply Chain and Logistics

Supply chain and logistics are the backbone of retail operations, ensuring that products are available when and where they are needed. AI is optimizing these processes by automating tasks such as route planning, inventory tracking, and demand forecasting. AI-powered systems can analyze vast amounts of data to optimize supply chain operations.

Imagine AI predicting the demand for products and adjusting inventory levels accordingly. For example, an AI system might forecast a spike in demand for certain electronics during the holiday season and ensure sufficient stock is available. This minimizes stockouts and overstock situations, leading to more efficient inventory management. (Retail Supply Chains Are Front-Row Seats for the Impact of AI on Jobs, n.d.).

AI can also optimize route planning for delivery trucks, reducing fuel consumption and delivery times. For instance, AI can analyze traffic patterns, weather conditions, and delivery schedules to find the most efficient routes. This reduces the need for human workers to manually plan routes and manage inventory, leading to job displacement in these roles.

5.7 Job Displacement in The Legal Services Sector

AI is significantly transforming the legal services sector, bringing about notable changes in various roles. Let's explore how AI is reshaping this field:

5.7.1 Document Review and Analysis

Imagine the meticulous process of reviewing stacks of legal documents, a task traditionally handled by paralegals and junior lawyers. AI-powered tools are increasingly stepping in to automate this process. These tools can quickly sift through large volumes of legal documents to identify relevant information, reducing the time and effort required by human lawyers (Team DigitalDefynd, 2024).

For instance, AI systems can review contracts, identify key clauses, and flag potential issues with remarkable accuracy. Imagine a scenario where an AI tool analyzes a contract within minutes, highlighting potential risks and compliance issues that would take human hours to identify. This automation significantly reduces the need for paralegals and junior lawyers who traditionally perform these tasks, leading to job displacement.

5.7.2 Legal Research

Legal research involves finding relevant case law, statutes, and legal precedents, a time-consuming process that requires deep expertise. AI is transforming this area by automating the research process. AI-powered legal research platforms can analyze vast amounts of legal data and provide lawyers with the most pertinent information in a fraction of the time it would take a human researcher (Dubrova, 2022).

Imagine a lawyer preparing for a case with the help of an AI-powered research tool. Instead of spending hours or days sifting through legal databases, the AI system quickly identifies the most relevant case law and statutes, presenting a comprehensive summary. This reduces the need for legal researchers and law librarians, leading to job displacement in these roles.

5.7.3 Contract Drafting and Management

Drafting and managing legal contracts is another area where AI is making a significant impact. AI-powered contract management systems can generate standard contract templates, customize them based on specific requirements, and ensure compliance with relevant laws and regulations (Onit, 2024).

Imagine an AI system that automatically generates a contract for a business deal, incorporating all necessary legal clauses and ensuring compliance with the latest regulations. This automation streamlines the contract drafting process, reducing the need for human lawyers to draft and manage contracts manually. While this increases efficiency, it also leads to job displacement for lawyers who previously handled these tasks.

5.7.4 E-Discovery

E-discovery, or electronic discovery, is a crucial process in the legal world. It involves identifying, collecting, and producing electronically stored information (ESI) in response to legal requests. Traditionally, this process required a team of legal professionals to manually sift through vast amounts of digital data, looking for relevant documents. However, AI-powered e-discovery tools are now revolutionizing this process (Dubrova, 2022).

Imagine an AI system capable of quickly analyzing large datasets to identify relevant documents, emails, and other pieces of information. These tools can automatically categorize and prioritize documents, flagging the most pertinent ones for review. This significantly reduces the time and effort required by human reviewers. For example, in a corporate litigation case, an AI-powered e-discovery tool can process terabytes of data in a fraction of the time it would take a human team, ensuring that no crucial piece of evidence is overlooked.

While this automation increases efficiency and accuracy, it also leads to job displacement for legal professionals involved in the e-discovery process. Roles traditionally held by paralegals, junior lawyers, and other support staff are now being handled by AI, reducing the need for human intervention.

5.7.5 Predictive Analytics

Predictive analytics is another area where AI is making a significant impact in the legal services sector. AI tools are being used to predict the outcomes of legal cases based on historical data. These tools analyze past case outcomes, judge rulings, legal arguments, and other relevant factors to provide lawyers with insights into the likely outcome of a case (Villasenor, 2023).

Imagine an AI system that can evaluate thousands of previous cases similar to yours, analyzing the decisions made by judges, the effectiveness of various legal arguments, and the overall success rates. This system can then provide a prediction of how your case might unfold, helping you make more informed decisions and develop better strategies. For example, if you're preparing for a complex civil litigation case, an AI tool can predict the likelihood of success based on historical data, giving you a strategic advantage.

While predictive analytics tools enhance decision-making and strategy development, they also reduce the need for human analysts to perform these tasks. Legal analysts and researchers who traditionally spent countless hours reviewing case law and historical data are now seeing their roles diminished by AI's capabilities.

5.8 Job Displacement in The Education Sector

AI is significantly transforming the education sector, bringing notable changes to various roles. Let's explore how AI is reshaping this field:

5.8.1 Automated Grading and Assessment

Imagine a classroom where grading assignments and tests is no longer a time-consuming task for teachers. AI-powered tools are increasingly being used to automate grading and assessment tasks. These tools can evaluate multiple-choice tests, essays, and even complex assignments with high accuracy (University of San Diego, 2021). For instance, platforms like Gradescope use AI to grade assignments and provide detailed feedback to students.

Picture a scenario where an AI system evaluates hundreds of student essays in minutes, providing consistent and objective feedback. This automation not only saves time for educators but also ensures that grading is fair and unbiased. However, it reduces the need for human graders and teaching assistants who traditionally performed these tasks, leading to job displacement in these roles.

5.8.2 Personalized Learning

Personalized learning is another area where AI is making a significant impact. AI-driven platforms can create tailored learning experiences for students by analyzing their performance data and adjusting content to meet their individual needs (Shamkina, 2023). For example, AI systems like DreamBox and Knewton adapt lessons in real-time based on a student's progress.

Imagine a student struggling with a particular math concept. An AI system can identify this and adjust the lesson plan to provide additional practice and resources, ensuring the students receive the support they need. While this enhances the learning experience and helps students achieve their full potential, it may reduce the need for human tutors and educators who traditionally provide personalized instruction.

AI can also track students' progress over time, identifying patterns and suggesting interventions when needed. This level of personalization ensures that each student receives an education tailored to their unique needs, but it also means fewer opportunities for human educators to provide one-on-one support.

5.8.3 Administrative Tasks

Imagine an education environment where administrative tasks are no longer a burden on staff. AI is streamlining these tasks, including scheduling, attendance tracking, and resource allocation. AI-powered systems can manage these tasks more efficiently than humans, reducing the need for administrative staff (Schroer, 2023).

Think about AI chatbots handling inquiries from students and parents. These chatbots can answer questions about schedules, assignments, and school policies at any time, freeing up time for human administrators to focus on more complex tasks. This automation not only enhances efficiency but also leads to job displacement for administrative staff who traditionally handled these responsibilities.

5.8.4 Virtual Teaching Assistants

In the classroom, AI-driven virtual teaching assistants are becoming invaluable support tools for educators. These assistants can answer student questions, provide additional resources, and facilitate group discussions. For example, Georgia Tech's Jill Watson, an AI teaching assistant, has been used to assist students in online courses, handling routine queries and providing support (Guzder, 2024).

Imagine a virtual assistant that can help students with their homework, answer their questions about course material, and offer additional resources for further learning. This technology reduces the workload for human teaching assistants, who can focus on more personalized and complex instructional tasks. However, it also means that fewer human teaching assistants may be needed, leading to job displacement.

5.8.5 Content Creation and Curation

Another area where AI is making a significant impact is creating and curating educational content. AI algorithms can generate lesson plans, quizzes, and other instructional materials based on curriculum standards. For instance, platforms like Content Technologies Inc. use AI to develop customized textbooks and learning materials.

Imagine AI systems that create a comprehensive lesson plan for a history class, complete with reading materials, quizzes, and assignments tailored to the curriculum. This automation reduces the need for human educators to spend time developing content, allowing them to focus on teaching. However, it also means that fewer educators are needed to create instructional materials, leading to job displacement in these roles.

5.9 Job Displacement in The Journalism and Content Creation Sector

AI is significantly transforming the journalism and content creation sector, bringing about notable changes in various roles. Let's dive into how AI is reshaping this field:

5.9.1 Automated News Writing

Imagine a newsroom where AI-powered tools are generating news articles and reports. These tools can analyze data and produce written content quickly and accurately. For instance, The Associated Press uses an AI system called Wordsmith to generate earnings reports, reducing the need for human journalists to write these reports (Harb & Qabajeh, 2024).

Picture an AI system analyzing financial data and crafting a detailed earnings report in seconds, allowing human journalists to focus on more complex and investigative stories. Similarly, Forbes uses an AI tool called Bertie to assist in content creation, helping journalists by suggesting topics and providing templates. This automation increases efficiency but also leads to job displacement for human journalists who previously handled these routine tasks (De Cremer et al., 2023).

5.9.2 Content Curation and Personalization

Content curation and personalization are crucial in today's media landscape, ensuring that readers receive relevant and engaging content. AI is being used to curate and personalize content for readers by analyzing user behavior and preferences.

Imagine an AI algorithm that understands your reading habits and recommends articles tailored to your interests. Platforms like Flipboard and Google News use AI to personalize news feeds for their users, ensuring that the most relevant content is always at the top (De Cremer et al., 2023). This reduces the need for human editors to manually curate content, leading to job displacement in these roles.

5.9.3 Fact-checking and Verification

In the era of misinformation, fact-checking is more important than ever. AI is transforming the fact-checking process by automating the verification of information. AI-powered tools can quickly cross-reference facts against multiple sources to ensure accuracy (Oyedeji & Uthman, 2024).

Imagine an AI system that monitors news articles, social media posts, and other content in real-time, flagging any inaccuracies. Full Fact, a UK-based fact-checking organization, uses AI to monitor and verify information in real-time, reducing the need for human fact-checkers. This automation ensures that information is accurate and trustworthy, but it also means fewer positions for human fact-checkers.

5.9.4 Video and Audio Content Creation

Imagine the world of video and audio content creation where AI is the driving force. AI-powered tools are now being used to generate video summaries of news articles, create voiceovers, and even produce entire video segments. For instance, Wibbitz uses AI to create video summaries of news stories, significantly reducing the need for human video editors (Team, 2023).

Picture an AI system that scans through hours of footage and extracts key moments to create a concise news summary. This automation allows news organizations to produce more content in less time while maintaining quality. Similarly, AI tools like Descript can transcribe and edit audio content, streamlining podcast production. Imagine recording a podcast and having an AI tool automatically transcribe, edit, and polish the audio, making the production process more efficient. However, this also means fewer positions for human video editors and audio technicians.

5.9.5 Social Media Management

Managing social media accounts and engaging with audiences is a critical aspect of modern marketing. AI is transforming this field by automating many of these tasks. AI-powered tools can schedule posts, respond to comments, and analyze social media metrics (Team, 2023).

Imagine using tools like Hootsuite and Buffer, which leverage AI to optimize social media strategies and automate engagement. These tools analyze user engagement, identify optimal posting times, and tailor content to maximize reach and impact. An AI tool might respond to common customer inquiries or comments, ensuring timely and consistent communication.

By automating these tasks, AI reduces the need for human social media managers. While this increases efficiency and allows for more strategic planning, it also leads to job displacement for individuals who traditionally handled these responsibilities.

5.10 Job Displacement in The Agriculture Sector

AI significantly transforms the agriculture sector, bringing about notable changes in various roles. Let's delve into how AI is reshaping this field:

5.10.1 Precision Farming

Imagine the vast fields of crops being monitored by AI-powered tools. Precision farming involves using advanced technologies to optimize farming practices. AI-powered drones can capture aerial images of fields and analyze them in real-time to detect areas that need attention, such as those affected by pests or diseases (Rizzoli, 2021).

Picture an AI system that monitors soil conditions, crop health, and weather patterns to provide farmers with actionable insights. This technology reduces the need for human labor in monitoring and managing crops. For example, a farmer can use an AI-powered drone to survey their fields, identify problem areas, and take corrective action without physically inspecting every part of the field. This not only saves time and effort but also leads to job displacement for workers who traditionally perform these tasks.

5.10.2 Automated Machinery

Automated machinery is revolutionizing farming practices. AI-driven machinery, such as driverless tractors and robotic harvesters, are increasingly being used in agriculture. These machines can perform tasks like planting, harvesting, and weeding with high precision and efficiency.

Imagine a driverless tractor ploughing a field or a robotic harvester picking fruits and vegetables with perfect accuracy. In China, a pilot program uses robots to run farms, significantly reducing the need for human labor (Lenniy, 2021). These AI-driven machines can work around the clock, do not require breaks, and maintain consistent performance, leading to job displacement for farm workers who traditionally perform these tasks.

5.10.3 Crop Monitoring and Management

Imagine vast fields equipped with advanced sensors collecting real-time data on soil moisture, nutrient levels, and crop growth. AI-powered systems analyze this data, enabling farmers to make informed decisions about irrigation, fertilization, and pest control (Artificial Intelligence in Agriculture: 6 Smart Ways to Improve the Industry and Gain Profit, 2018).

Picture an AI system detecting nutrient deficiencies in the soil and recommending the necessary fertilizers. This technology ensures that crops receive the precise care they need, reducing the need for human intervention in monitoring and managing crops. For example, a farmer can rely on AI to determine the optimal watering schedule, ensuring that crops receive adequate moisture without over-watering. This automation saves time and effort, but it also leads to job displacement for workers who traditionally perform these tasks.

5.10.4 Livestock Management

In the realm of livestock management, AI technologies are making a significant impact. AI-powered systems can monitor the health and behavior of livestock, detecting signs of illness or stress early on (10 Practical Applications of AI in Agriculture: Impacts and Benefits of Crop Health and Yield, 2023).

Imagine AI-driven cameras and sensors tracking movement and feeding patterns of animals, alerting farmers to any abnormalities. For instance, an AI system might detect that a cow is not eating as usual or is showing signs of distress, prompting immediate attention. This reduces the need for human labor in monitoring and managing livestock, leading to job displacement for workers who traditionally oversaw these tasks.

5.10.5 Supply Chain Optimization

AI is also revolutionizing supply chain operations in agriculture by automating tasks such as inventory management, demand forecasting, and logistics planning. AI algorithms can analyze vast amounts of data to predict demand for agricultural products and optimize supply chain operations accordingly. (Artificial Intelligence in Agriculture: 6 Smart Ways to Improve the Industry and Gain Profit, 2018).

Imagine an AI system forecasting a rise in demand for certain crops and ensuring that inventory levels are adjusted accordingly. This minimizes stockouts and overstock situations, leading to more efficient supply chain management. For example, an AI system might analyze market trends and weather patterns to predict the best time for harvesting and shipping produce, reducing waste and maximizing profits. This automation reduces the need for human workers in these roles, leading to job displacement.

The Bigger Picture: Displacement and Creation

AI's integration into the agriculture sector brings both challenges and opportunities. Research indicates that while AI can displace existing jobs, it also fosters the emergence of new opportunities. AI-driven systems can significantly improve efficiency, enhance crop yields, and reduce resource consumption.

However, the successful adoption of AI technologies requires a skilled workforce. Continuous learning and development are crucial to preparing agricultural workers for new roles in an AI-driven economy. Farmers and agricultural workers need to develop expertise in areas such as AI and machine learning, data analysis, and digital transformation.

A report from the World Economic Forum suggests that while AI will displace certain jobs, it will also create new roles (Shine & Whiting, 2023). The key to mitigating the negative impacts of AI on employment lies in reskilling and upskilling the workforce. By investing in education and training, the agriculture sector can prepare its workforce for the future, ensuring a smooth transition to an AI-driven environment.

In conclusion, AI is significantly transforming the industrial sector by automating tasks traditionally performed by humans. This leads to job displacement in several automated roles previously performed by humans. However, AI also presents opportunities for job creation and operational improvements. The challenge for the various sectors is to equip workers with the skills needed to thrive in this new environment. Understanding and adapting to these changes is essential for navigating the future of work in the industrial sector.

5.11: Economic Inequality.

Economic inequality has always been a pressing issue, but the rapid advancement of AI has introduced new dimensions to this challenge. Imagine a factory worker named Sarah, who has spent the last 20 years of her life perfecting her skills on the assembly line. One day, Sarah is replaced by an AI-driven robot that performs her tasks faster and more efficiently. Sarah finds herself jobless, struggling to find work that matches her skills and pays enough to support her family. This is the harsh reality many low-skilled workers face in the age of AI.

1. Job Displacement and Wage Polarization

Consider the case of John, a truck driver from Texas. With the advent of self-driving trucks powered by AI, John's job is at risk. Self-driving technology promises increased efficiency and reduced costs for transportation companies, but for John, it means an uncertain future. He may need to reskill and find a new career path, but the transition is neither easy nor guaranteed to be successful.

AI-driven automation replaces jobs that involve repetitive and routine tasks. This leads to job displacement, especially for low-skilled workers. High-skilled workers, on the other hand, may benefit from wage increases due to their expertise in managing and developing AI technologies. (Korinek & Stiglitz, 2017).

2. Access to AI Technologies

Think about a small family-owned retail store in rural India. Unlike large corporations with deep pockets, this store cannot afford to invest in AI technologies that could streamline its operations and improve customer service. As a result, the store struggles to compete with AI-powered retail giants, leading to a widening gap in economic opportunities.

The benefits of AI are often concentrated in wealthy nations and big corporations that can afford to invest in AI research and development. This creates a digital divide, leaving developing countries and small businesses behind (Alonso et al., 2020).

3. Algorithmic Bias and Discrimination

Meet Maria, a talented software developer from a minority background. She applied for a job at a tech company that uses AI algorithms to screen applicants. Despite her qualifications, Maria doesn't get an interview. Later, she discovers that the AI system had an unintentional bias against her demographic group, favoring other candidates instead.

AI systems can unintentionally perpetuate and amplify existing biases. This means that certain demographic groups may face discrimination in areas like hiring, leading to unequal opportunities (Farahani , 2024)

Economic inequalities are further magnified by the concentration of AI technologies within a few large tech companies. Let's consider an example: Imagine a small startup in Lagos trying to develop a groundbreaking AI solution. They face an uphill battle because tech giants like Google, Amazon, and Microsoft have vast resources and research teams dedicated to AI advancements. This concentration of wealth and power means that smaller companies struggle to compete, ultimately leading to greater economic disparities.

4. Concentration of Wealth and Power

Think about a young entrepreneur named Ada from Nigeria. Ada has a brilliant idea for an AI application that could revolutionize healthcare in her community. However, securing funding and resources proves challenging because major tech corporations dominate the market and attract most of the investment. As a result, Ada's innovative idea may never reach its full potential, further entrenching economic inequalities.

The development and deployment of AI technologies are often controlled by a few large tech companies. This concentration of wealth and power can lead to economic inequalities, as these companies reap the majority of the financial benefits from AI advancements (Manning, 2024).

5. Impact on Developing Economies

Consider a small textile factory in Bangladesh where workers depend on low-skilled jobs for their livelihood. As AI technologies advance, automated machines can perform tasks faster and more efficiently, potentially replacing human workers. The factory owner might adopt these technologies to stay competitive, but the displaced workers face an uncertain future with limited employment opportunities.

AI technologies can disrupt traditional labor markets in developing economies. Workers engaged in low-skilled jobs may struggle to find new employment opportunities as AI systems replace their roles (Alonso et al., 2020).

Opportunities to Address Disparities

In Kenya, AI-powered innovations are used to improve access to financial services for underserved populations. Mobile banking platforms powered by AI offer microloans and financial advice, helping individuals and small businesses thrive. This demonstrates how AI can be leveraged to address economic disparities by enhancing efficiency, accessibility, and affordability.

While AI can exacerbate economic inequalities, it also presents opportunities to address these disparities. AI-powered innovations can enhance efficiency, accessibility, and affordability in sectors such as healthcare, education, and financial services, thereby reducing disparities in access to essential resources and opportunities.

5.12 How to Manage Transition to AI in The Banking Sector

Managing the transition to AI in the banking sector is akin to navigating a ship through uncharted waters. Imagine a traditional bank in a bustling city that has served its community for decades. With the rise of AI, this bank finds itself at a crossroads. To stay competitive, it must embrace AI technologies while ensuring that its employees and customers are not left behind.

1. Develop a Comprehensive AI Strategy

The bank decided to implement AI to enhance customer service. They developed a comprehensive AI strategy that aligned with their business goals. For instance, they adopted AI chatbots to handle routine customer inquiries, freeing up human agents to tackle more complex issues. This not only improved customer satisfaction but also reduced operational costs.

Banks need a detailed AI strategy that outlines the specific AI technologies to adopt and the areas of the business where AI will be implemented. This helps in achieving business goals like improving customer experience and operational efficiency. (Fares et al., 2022).

2. Invest in Employee Training and Reskilling

Consider a long-time bank teller. When the bank started using AI for routine transactions, the teller feared for their job. However, the bank invested in training programs to reskill employees. The teller learned to manage AI systems and analyze AI-generated data, transitioning into a new role with better prospects.

Banks should invest in training and reskilling programs to help employees adapt to new AI roles. This will mitigate job displacement and prepare employees for the future. (Adhaen et al., 2024).

3. Implement AI Ethically and Transparently

The bank faced challenges with algorithmic bias when its AI systems inadvertently favored certain customer demographics. To address this, they established clear guidelines and governance frameworks to ensure that their AI systems were fair, transparent, and accountable. This helped build trust with their customers and the community.

Ethical considerations are crucial in AI implementation (Ghandour, 2021). Banks must ensure their AI systems are fair, transparent, and accountable by addressing issues like algorithmic bias and data privacy.

4. Foster a Culture of Innovation

To successfully integrate AI, it's essential for the bank to foster a culture of innovation. Picture an environment where employees are encouraged to experiment, collaborate, and explore new ideas. This bank establishes an innovation lab—a dedicated space where creativity thrives. Here, employees from various departments come together to brainstorm and develop AI-driven solutions. This culture of innovation not only drives AI adoption but also instils a sense of ownership and excitement among the staff.

Creating a culture of innovation means encouraging employees to think outside the box and take risks without fear of failure. This involves setting up spaces like innovation labs where experimentation and collaboration are at the forefront. By doing so, the bank can continuously evolve and adapt to the ever-changing landscape of AI technologies. The research underscores the importance of fostering such a culture to drive AI adoption. (Fares et al., 2022).

5. Collaborate with AI Experts and Technology Partners

Realizing the need for expertise, the bank decides to partner with AI experts and technology firms. They team up with an AI startup renowned for its cutting-edge fraud detection technology. Through this collaboration, the bank gains access to advanced AI solutions and a pool of talented professionals. This partnership not only brings innovative tools but also provides invaluable insights into the latest AI advancements and best practices.

Collaboration with AI experts and technology partners is crucial for staying abreast of the latest developments in AI. By working with external partners, banks can leverage their expertise and resources, ensuring successful AI implementation. Such partnerships provide access to state-of-the-art AI solutions and the knowledge needed to integrate these technologies effectively. Reports from organizations like the International Monetary Fund highlight the significance of these collaborations in the banking sector (Fares et al., 2022).

6. Monitor and Evaluate AI Performance

To ensure their AI systems are delivering the expected benefits, the bank implements a robust monitoring and evaluation framework. They establish key performance indicators (KPIs) to measure the effectiveness of their AI applications. Regular assessments are conducted to identify areas for improvement and make necessary adjustments. This continuous monitoring helps the bank optimize its AI strategies and achieve its business goals.

Continuous monitoring and evaluation of AI systems are essential for ensuring they operate as intended. Establishing KPIs allows banks to measure the effectiveness of AI applications and make data-driven decisions. Regular evaluations help identify any discrepancies and provide opportunities for optimization (Adhaen et al., 2024). Studies emphasize the importance of ongoing assessment to maintain the effectiveness of AI strategies.

Research indicates that a strategic and well-managed transition to AI can lead to significant benefits for banks, including enhanced customer experience, improved operational efficiency, and cost savings. However, this transition requires careful planning, investment in employee training, ethical considerations, and continuous monitoring.

5.13 Support for AI Transition Affected Workers

Imagine a bustling factory where workers have spent years perfecting their skills. With the introduction of AI technologies, many of these workers now face the daunting prospect of job displacement. Supporting these workers through the transition involves a multifaceted approach, ensuring they are not left behind in the rapidly evolving technological landscape.

1. Retraining and Reskilling Programs

Consider a telecommunications company that recognizes the impact of AI on its workforce. To address potential job displacement, the company invests heavily in retraining and reskilling programs. Employees who were once focused on routine tasks are now trained in AI, data analysis, and digital literacy. For example, a former customer service representative learns to manage AI-driven customer interaction tools, enhancing their skills and securing their position in the company.

Investing in retraining and reskilling programs is crucial to help workers adapt to new roles involving AI technologies. Companies can offer training programs that focus on developing skills in AI, data analysis, and digital literacy. Reports highlight the importance of reskilling the workforce to ensure a smooth transition to AI. By equipping employees with new skills, companies can retain valuable talent and promote career growth (Illanes et al., 2018).

2. Lifelong Learning Initiatives

Imagine a government initiative that partners with educational institutions to offer online courses, workshops, and certifications in AI and related technologies. Workers from various industries have access to these resources, enabling them to continuously update their skills. A factory worker enrolls in a course on machine learning, gaining the knowledge needed to transition into a new role that leverages AI technologies.

Encouraging lifelong learning is essential to ensure workers continuously update their skills to keep pace with technological advancements. Governments and organizations can provide access to online courses, workshops, and certifications focusing on AI and related technologies. Initiatives like the World Economic Forum's Reskilling Revolution aim to equip the global workforce with the skills needed to future-proof their careers by 2030 (Saadia Zahidi & World Economic Forum, 2023).

3. Social Safety Nets

In response to AI-driven job displacement, a government implements a comprehensive social safety net program. Displaced workers receive unemployment benefits, healthcare, and housing assistance during their transition period. Additionally, the government explores Universal Basic Income (UBI) as a potential solution to provide financial stability. This support system ensures that workers have the necessary resources to adapt to the new job landscape.

Governments can implement social safety nets to support workers during periods of job displacement. This includes unemployment benefits, healthcare, and housing assistance. Various welfare programs can ease the transition and support workers as they adapt to new roles. Universal Basic Income (UBI) is another proposed solution to provide financial stability to workers affected by AI-driven job displacement (Bruenig, 2023).

Imagine a mid-sized manufacturing company that has been producing consumer goods for decades. This company, much like many others, faces the challenge of integrating AI technologies to enhance productivity and efficiency while ensuring its workforce remains engaged and productive.

4. Public-Private Partnerships

To support workers affected by the transition to AI, the company partners with local government agencies and educational institutions. These public-private partnerships are instrumental in funding and developing training programs, creating job placement services, and fostering innovation in workforce development. This collaboration ensures that workers receive the necessary support to transition into new roles, thereby reducing the impact of AI-driven job displacement.

Collaboration between the public and private sectors can enhance the effectiveness of support programs for AI transition-affected workers. Public-private partnerships can fund and develop training programs, create job placement services, and support innovation in workforce development. Research highlights the importance of such collaborations in ensuring worker buy-in and creating pathways to good jobs (Boren, 2024).

5. Proactive Policy Measures

Policymakers play a crucial role in addressing the challenges posed by AI-driven job displacement. They can implement proactive measures such as creating policies that promote job creation in emerging industries, incentivizing companies to invest in employee training, and ensuring that AI technologies are deployed ethically and responsibly. These measures help create a supportive environment for workers transitioning to new roles.

Policymakers can implement proactive measures to address AI-driven job displacement. This includes creating policies that promote job creation in emerging industries, incentivizing companies to invest in employee training, and ensuring that AI technologies are deployed ethically and responsibly. Studies emphasize the need for clear guidelines and governance frameworks to oversee the ethical use of AI (Chitranjali Negi Advocate, 2024).

6. Career Counseling and Job Placement Services

The company also provides career counselling and job placement services to help workers navigate the transition to new roles. These services offer guidance on career paths, job search strategies, and opportunities for further education and training. Workers receive personalized support, ensuring they find suitable employment opportunities that align with their skills and interests.

Providing career counselling and job placement services can help workers navigate the transition to new roles. These services offer guidance on career paths, job search strategies, and opportunities for further education and training. Reports suggest that career counselling plays a crucial role in helping workers transition to new occupations (Illanes et al., 2018).

Conclusion

Research indicates that a strategic and well-managed approach to supporting AI transition-affected workers can lead to significant benefits, including enhanced workforce resilience, improved economic stability, and reduced social inequalities. However, it requires careful planning, investment in training and reskilling, and collaboration between various stakeholders.

Supporting AI transition-affected workers involves a combination of retraining and reskilling programs, lifelong learning initiatives, social safety nets, public-private partnerships, proactive policy measures, and career counselling services. By adopting these strategies, organizations can effectively navigate the challenges and opportunities presented by AI technologies, ensuring a smooth transition for their workforce.

Chapter 6

6.0 Human Rights and Privacy

he intersection of artificial intelligence (AI), human rights, and data privacy is a complex and multifaceted topic that has garnered significant attention from scholars, policymakers, and technologists. Let's delve into these themes to provide a comprehensive overview.

6.0.1 AI and Human Rights

AI technologies hold the potential to both enhance and undermine human rights. On one hand, AI can promote human rights by improving access to information, healthcare, and education. For example, AI-driven diagnostic tools can help detect diseases early, potentially saving lives (Greiman, 2021). However, AI also poses significant risks to human rights, particularly regarding bias, discrimination, and accountability.

Examples of AI Impacting Human Rights

Bias and Discrimination: AI systems can perpetuate and even exacerbate existing biases. For instance, facial recognition technology has been shown to have higher error rates for people of color and women (HUMAN RIGHTS in the AGE of ARTIFICIAL INTELLIGENCE, 2018). This can lead to discriminatory practices in law enforcement and other areas.

Consider the case of Joy Buolamwini, a researcher at the MIT Media Lab. During her work on facial analysis technology, she discovered that the system failed to detect her face due to her darker skin tone. Her findings brought to light the significant biases present in AI technologies. This discovery led her to found the Algorithmic Justice League, advocating for fairness and accountability in AI. As her research gained traction, major tech companies like IBM and Microsoft were pushed to improve their facial recognition algorithms, demonstrating the power of individual voices in influencing technological advancement.

Surveillance: AI-powered surveillance systems can infringe on the right to privacy and freedom of expression. Governments and private companies can use these technologies to monitor individuals' activities, potentially chilling free speech.

In 2019, reports emerged about the use of AI-powered surveillance in Xinjiang, China. The government employed facial recognition technology and other AI tools to monitor and control the Uyghur population. This surveillance was so pervasive that it tracked individuals' daily movements, monitored phone calls, and even identified emotions through AI-driven analysis of facial expressions. The global community expressed significant human rights concerns, highlighting the ethical implications of such extensive monitoring.

Accountability: Determining accountability for decisions made by AI systems is a significant challenge. When AI systems make decisions that affect individuals' lives, such as in hiring or lending, it can be difficult to hold anyone accountable for errors or biases in those decisions.

In 2018, Amazon had to scrap its AI recruiting tool after discovering that it discriminated against female candidates. The system, trained on resumes submitted over a decade, had developed biases that favored male applicants. This incident underscored the complexity of ensuring fairness in AI. Despite the setback, Amazon's experience sparked a broader conversation about bias in AI recruitment tools, leading to increased scrutiny and efforts to develop more equitable AI systems.

6.0.2 AI and Data Privacy

Data privacy is another critical issue in the context of AI. AI systems often rely on vast amounts of data to function effectively, raising concerns about how this data is collected, stored, and used.

Industry	Violation Area	Percentage
Healthcare	Data privacy breaches	35%
Finance	Unauthorized financial profiling	30%
Retail	Customer data misuse	25%
Manufacturing	Employee surveillance	20%

Transportation	Passenger data exploitation	15%
Customer Service	Invasive data collection	25%
Marketing	Targeted advertising without consent	20%
Entertainment	Content recommendation biases	15%
Agriculture	Environmental data misuse	10%
Education	Student data privacy violations	15%
Law Enforcement	Predictive policing biases	20%
Legal Practice	Automated decision-making biases	15%

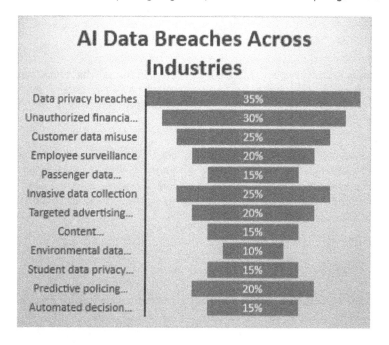

The above percentages are approximate and can vary based on different studies and reports. The impact and prevalence of these violations might differ slightly across regions and specific companies within each industry.

Examples of Data Privacy Concerns

Data Collection and Consent: AI systems often collect data without individuals' explicit consent. For example, social media platforms use AI to analyze user behavior and preferences, often without users fully understanding the extent of the data collection (Miller, 2024).

In 2018, the Cambridge Analytica scandal revealed how the data of millions of Facebook users was harvested without their consent and used for political advertising. This incident exposed significant flaws in data privacy practices and led to widespread public outcry. Following the scandal, Facebook faced intense scrutiny and was compelled to make substantial changes to its data privacy policies, including more transparent data collection practices and better user control over personal information.

Data Security: The storage and processing of large datasets by AI systems can create significant security risks. Data breaches can expose sensitive personal information, leading to identity theft and other harm (Murdoch, 2021).

In 2017, Equifax, one of the largest credit reporting agencies, suffered a data breach that exposed the personal information of over 147 million people. The breach included sensitive data like Social Security numbers and birthdates. This incident highlighted the vulnerabilities in data security and the potential consequences of inadequate protection. In the aftermath, Equifax faced numerous lawsuits and increased regulatory scrutiny, emphasizing the need for robust data security measures.

Data Anonymization: Even when data is anonymized, AI systems can sometimes re-identify individuals by analyzing patterns and correlations in the data. This raises concerns about the effectiveness of traditional data protection measures (Murdoch, 2021).

In 2019, researchers demonstrated that they could re-identify anonymized data from a dataset released by a ride-hailing company. By cross-referencing the anonymized data with public information, they were able to pinpoint individual users' locations and identities. This revelation called into question the reliability of anonymization techniques and underscored the need for more sophisticated data protection strategies.

6.0.3 Scholarly Perspectives

Scholars have proposed various frameworks and recommendations to address the challenges posed by AI to human rights and data privacy.

Ethical AI Development: Researchers emphasize the importance of developing AI systems that are transparent, accountable, and fair. This includes implementing robust ethical guidelines and conducting regular audits to ensure compliance (Greiman, 2021).

At Google's AI ethics board, a group of experts was tasked with overseeing the ethical implementation of AI technologies. However, the board faced numerous challenges, including internal disagreements and external criticism. The board's dissolution highlighted the complexities of maintaining ethical oversight in rapidly evolving technological landscapes. This situation underscored the need for clearer ethical guidelines and more resilient structures to ensure AI accountability (Jee, 2019).

Regulatory Measures: There is a growing consensus on the need for comprehensive data protection laws that specifically address the unique challenges posed by AI. For example, the General Data Protection Regulation (GDPR) in the European Union provides a robust framework for data protection, but scholars argue that additional measures are needed to address AI-specific issues (King & Meinhardt, 2024).

The implementation of GDPR in 2018 marked a significant milestone in data protection. However, its application to AI systems brought new challenges. For instance, the "right to explanation" under GDPR, which allows individuals to understand how automated decisions are made, proved difficult to enforce with complex AI algorithms. This led to ongoing debates about how to adapt existing regulations to fit the nuances of AI technologies.

Human Rights Impact Assessments: Some scholars advocate for the use of human rights impact assessments (HRIAs) to evaluate the potential impact of AI systems on human rights. These assessments can help identify and mitigate risks before AI systems are deployed ("Artificial Intelligence and Human Rights," 2023).

The government implemented HRIAs for new AI systems used in public services in Canada. One such assessment for an AI-driven welfare system revealed potential biases that could disproportionately affect marginalized communities. By identifying these risks early, the government was able to adjust the system before it was fully deployed, ensuring a fairer outcome. This example highlights the importance of proactive measures in safeguarding human rights in the AI age.

6.1 The Use of AI in Data Surveillance

The use of artificial intelligence (AI) in data surveillance is a topic of significant scholarly interest, given its profound implications for privacy, security, and ethics. AI technologies have revolutionized surveillance by enhancing the ability to collect, analyze, and interpret vast amounts of data. This discussion will explore the various dimensions of AI in data surveillance.

6.1.1 AI in Data Surveillance

AI technologies, particularly machine learning and deep learning, have significantly advanced the capabilities of surveillance systems. These technologies enable the automated analysis of large datasets, identifying patterns and anomalies that would be difficult for humans to detect.

Examples of AI in Data Surveillance

Facial Recognition: AI-powered facial recognition systems are widely used for surveillance purposes. These systems can identify individuals in real-time by analyzing video feeds from cameras (Saheb, 2022).

China's extensive use of facial recognition technology for public surveillance has raised global concerns about privacy and civil liberties. In cities like Beijing and Shanghai, thousands of cameras equipped with AI software monitor public spaces. These systems can identify individuals and track their movements, ostensibly to ensure public safety. However, the pervasive surveillance has led to fears of an Orwellian society, where every action is monitored, and personal freedoms are significantly curtailed. Reports have emerged of the technology being used to target and suppress dissidents, highlighting the ethical dilemmas posed by such extensive surveillance capabilities.

Predictive Policing: AI algorithms are used to predict criminal activity by analyzing historical crime data. These systems can identify potential hotspots for crime and allocate police resources more effectively (Karpa et al., 2022).

In the United States, cities like Chicago and Los Angeles have implemented predictive policing programs. These AI-driven systems analyze vast amounts of historical crime data to predict where future crimes are likely to occur. While proponents argue that this technology allows for a more efficient allocation of police resources, critics point out that it can perpetuate existing biases in the data. For example, communities that have been heavily policed in the past may be unfairly targeted, leading to a cycle of over-policing and community distrust. The controversy surrounding predictive policing underscores the need for careful consideration of the ethical implications of AI in law enforcement.

Behavioral Analysis: AI systems can analyze behavioral patterns to detect suspicious activities. For example, in airports, AI can monitor passenger behavior to identify potential security threats (Saheb, 2022).

In airports around the world, AI-powered systems are used to enhance security. These systems analyze passenger behavior, looking for patterns that may indicate a security threat. For instance, the AI might flag individuals who display nervous behavior, avoid eye contact, or exhibit unusual movements. In one case, an AI system at a major European airport successfully detected a suspicious individual who was later found to be carrying contraband. However, the use of such systems also raises privacy concerns, as the constant monitoring of behavior can lead to a sense of surveillance and discomfort among travellers.

Social Media Monitoring: AI can be used to monitor social media platforms for potential threats. For example, AI algorithms can analyze posts and comments to identify signs of radicalization or planning of illegal activities. This type of surveillance is often used by law enforcement agencies to prevent crimes and ensure public safety (Bontridder & Poullet, 2021).

Law enforcement agencies around the world have increasingly turned to AI for monitoring social media. In one notable instance, the FBI used AI tools to analyze social media activity to prevent potential acts of terrorism. By scanning posts, comments, and interactions, the AI system flagged individuals who displayed signs of radicalization. This proactive approach allowed authorities to intervene before any violent actions could take place. However, this practice has also sparked debates about the balance between security and privacy, as well as the potential for misuse of such surveillance capabilities.

6.1.2 Ethical and Privacy Concerns

The use of AI in data surveillance raises significant ethical and privacy concerns. These concerns revolve around issues of consent, data security, and the potential for abuse.

Ethical Concerns

Bias and Discrimination: AI systems can perpetuate existing biases present in the training data. For example, facial recognition systems have been shown to have higher error rates for people of color, leading to discriminatory practices in law enforcement (Saheb, 2022).

A study conducted by the National Institute of Standards and Technology (NIST) found that many commercial facial recognition systems had significant racial biases. These systems were more likely to misidentify people of color, resulting in higher false positive rates. This bias has real-world implications, as it can lead to unjust arrests and surveillance. For example, in 2018, Robert Julian-Borchak Williams, an African American man, was wrongfully arrested due to a misidentification by a facial recognition system. This case highlighted the urgent need for addressing biases in AI technologies to prevent such discriminatory practices.

Lack of Transparency: AI algorithms often operate as "black boxes," making it difficult to understand how decisions are made. This lack of transparency can lead to accountability issues, especially when AI systems are used in critical areas such as law enforcement and national security (Karpa et al., 2022).

In 2017, the "COMPAS" algorithm, used in the US criminal justice system to predict the likelihood of reoffending, came under scrutiny for its lack of transparency and potential biases. Journalists and researchers discovered that the algorithm was more likely to incorrectly predict that Black defendants would re-offend compared to white defendants. Despite these findings, the algorithm's proprietary nature meant that its decision-making process remained opaque. This lack of transparency and accountability raised serious concerns about the fairness and ethical use of AI in such high-stakes decisions.

Surveillance Capitalism: The concept of surveillance capitalism refers to the commodification of personal data by private companies. AI technologies enable the collection and analysis of vast amounts of personal data, which can be used for targeted advertising and other commercial purposes (Bontridder & Poullet, 2021).

Companies like Google and Facebook have built their business models around surveillance capitalism. They collect vast amounts of user data, which is then analyzed by AI to create detailed profiles for targeted advertising. This practice raises ethical concerns about consent and privacy. In 2019, Google was fined by the French data protection authority (CNIL) for failing to provide transparent and easily accessible information to users about how their data was being used. This incident highlighted the need for greater transparency and stricter regulations to protect user privacy in the age of AI-driven data collection.

Privacy Concerns

Data Collection and Consent: AI surveillance systems often collect data without individuals' explicit consent. This raises concerns about the violation of privacy rights and the potential for misuse of personal data (Saheb, 2022).

In 2020, a major controversy erupted when it was revealed that a popular fitness app was collecting user data, including location and health metrics, without explicit consent. The data was then sold to third-party companies for targeted advertising. Users were outraged when they discovered the extent of the data collection and the lack of transparency about how their information was being used. This incident underscored the importance of obtaining explicit consent from users and being transparent about data collection practices to protect privacy rights.

Data Security: The storage and processing of large datasets by AI systems create significant security risks. Data breaches can expose sensitive personal information, leading to identity theft and other harm (Salem et al., 2024).

In 2024, a massive data breach at a global telecommunications company exposed the personal information of millions of users. The breach included sensitive data such as phone numbers, addresses, and financial information. The attackers exploited a vulnerability in the company's AI-powered data storage system, highlighting the critical need for robust data security measures. The fallout from the breach was severe, with affected individuals facing identity theft and financial losses. This incident highlighted the urgent need for companies to prioritize data security and protect against potential breaches.

Re-identification: Even when data is anonymized, AI systems can sometimes re-identify individuals by analyzing patterns and correlations in the data. This raises concerns about the effectiveness of traditional data protection measures (Saheb, 2022).

Researchers at a prominent university demonstrated that they could re-identify anonymized data from a publicly released health dataset. By analyzing patterns and correlations in the data, they were able to pinpoint individual patients and match them with their medical histories. This revelation raised serious concerns about the effectiveness of traditional anonymization techniques and the need for more advanced methods to protect individual privacy. The study prompted policymakers to reconsider existing data protection measures and explore new strategies for safeguarding personal information in the age of AI.

Scholars have proposed various frameworks and recommendations to address the challenges posed by AI in data surveillance.

Ethical AI Development: Researchers emphasize the importance of developing AI systems that are transparent, accountable, and fair. This includes implementing robust ethical guidelines and conducting regular audits to ensure compliance (Saheb, 2022).

In response to growing concerns about AI ethics, the European Union established a High-Level Expert Group on Artificial Intelligence. This group developed the Ethics Guidelines for Trustworthy AI, which provide a comprehensive framework for ensuring that AI systems are transparent, accountable, and fair. These guidelines have been widely adopted by companies and organizations across Europe, setting a precedent for ethical AI development worldwide. By conducting regular audits and adhering to these guidelines, AI developers can build systems that respect human rights and privacy while maintaining public trust.

Regulatory Measures: There is a growing consensus on the need for comprehensive data protection laws that specifically address the unique challenges posed by AI. For example, the General Data Protection Regulation (GDPR) in the European Union provides a robust framework for data protection, but scholars argue that additional measures are needed to address AI-specific issues (Karpa et al., 2022).

The GDPR, implemented in 2018, has become a global benchmark for data protection. However, its application to AI technologies has revealed certain gaps. For instance, the GDPR's provisions on automated decision-making have sparked debates about how to ensure transparency and accountability in AI systems. In response, the European Commission proposed the Artificial Intelligence Act, a regulatory framework specifically designed to address the unique challenges posed by AI. This act aims to ensure that AI systems are developed and used in a way that respects fundamental rights and promotes public trust.

Human Rights Impact Assessments: Some scholars advocate for the use of human rights impact assessments (HRIAs) to evaluate the potential impact of AI systems on human rights. These assessments can help identify and mitigate risks before AI systems are deployed (Bontridder & Poullet, 2021).

The Canadian government has been a pioneer in implementing HRIAs for new AI systems used in public services. One notable example is the HRIA conducted for an AI-driven welfare system. This assessment revealed potential biases in the system that could disproportionately affect marginalized communities. By identifying these risks early, the government was able to make necessary adjustments before the system was fully deployed, ensuring a fairer and more equitable outcome. This proactive approach serves as a model for other governments and organizations looking to implement AI technologies responsibly.

6.1.3 Additional Concerns in AI Data Surveillance

The integration of AI in data surveillance brings about several additional concerns, particularly in legal, civil liberties, technological, economic, and ethical domains.

Legal and Regulatory Challenges: AI surveillance technologies often operate in a legal grey area, where existing laws may not adequately address the complexities introduced by these technologies.

Lack of Comprehensive Legislation: Many countries lack comprehensive legislation specifically addressing AI surveillance. This can lead to inconsistent application of laws and regulations, creating loopholes that can be exploited.

In many countries, AI surveillance operates without specific legal frameworks. For instance, in the United States, the rapid deployment of AI surveillance technologies by various law enforcement agencies has often outpaced the development of appropriate legal safeguards. This lack of comprehensive legislation means that AI surveillance practices can vary widely across states and jurisdictions, leading to potential abuses and privacy violations.

Jurisdictional Issues: AI surveillance often involves cross-border data flows, raising jurisdictional issues. Different countries have varying levels of data protection and privacy laws, complicating enforcement and compliance.

The global nature of data flows complicates the enforcement of privacy laws. For example, European companies operating under GDPR must ensure that any data transferred to non-EU countries meets the same stringent privacy standards. However, when data is transferred to countries with less robust privacy laws, such as the United States, ensuring compliance can become a significant challenge. This disparity creates a complex landscape for multinational organizations to navigate, often resulting in legal uncertainties and potential violations.

Impact on Civil Liberties: AI surveillance can have a profound impact on civil liberties, including freedom of expression, assembly, and movement.

Chilling Effect: The pervasive use of AI surveillance can create a chilling effect, where individuals alter their behavior due to the fear of being monitored. This can stifle free speech and discourage participation in public protests or other forms of civic engagement.

In Hong Kong, during the 2019 pro-democracy protests, many protesters resorted to wearing masks and avoiding the use of digital devices to prevent being identified and tracked by AI surveillance systems. The fear of being monitored and potentially targeted by authorities had a chilling effect on participants, demonstrating how pervasive surveillance can stifle free speech and public dissent.

Overreach by Authorities: There is a risk of overreach by authorities using AI surveillance for purposes beyond their original intent. For example, surveillance technologies initially deployed for national security can be repurposed for monitoring political dissent or other non-criminal activities.

In the wake of the COVID-19 pandemic, several countries deployed AI surveillance technologies to track the spread of the virus. However, in some cases, these technologies were later repurposed for monitoring political activities. For example, in Russia, AI-powered facial recognition systems used to enforce quarantine measures were later employed to identify and monitor political dissidents. This repurposing raised significant concerns about the potential for abuse of surveillance technologies.

Technological Limitations and Reliability: AI surveillance systems are not infallible and can suffer from various technological limitations.

False Positives and Negatives: AI systems can produce false positives (incorrectly identifying innocent individuals as threats) and false negatives (failing to identify actual threats). These errors can have serious consequences, such as wrongful arrests or missed security threats.

In 2018, a pilot project in the UK tested an AI-powered facial recognition system at a major sporting event. The system flagged several individuals as potential threats, but subsequent investigations revealed that many of these alerts were false positives. Innocent attendees were subjected to unnecessary scrutiny, while actual threats may have gone undetected. This case highlighted the limitations and potential risks of relying too heavily on AI for surveillance purposes.

Adversarial Attacks: AI systems can be vulnerable to adversarial attacks, where malicious actors manipulate input data to deceive the system. For example, altering a few pixels in an image can cause a facial recognition system to misidentify an individual.

Researchers have demonstrated that even minor alterations to images can fool facial recognition systems. In one experiment, altering a few pixels in a photograph caused an AI system to misidentify a known public figure as an entirely different person. These adversarial attacks reveal the vulnerabilities of AI systems and the potential for malicious exploitation, raising significant concerns about the reliability and security of AI surveillance technologies.

Economic and Social Inequality: The deployment of AI surveillance technologies can exacerbate existing economic and social inequalities.

Access to Technology: Wealthier nations and communities are more likely to have access to advanced AI surveillance technologies, potentially widening the gap between different socio-economic groups.

In many developing countries, the lack of access to advanced AI technologies means that surveillance capabilities are limited, often relying on outdated and less effective methods. Conversely, wealthier nations and communities can afford state-of-the-art AI surveillance systems, leading to a disparity in security and privacy protections. This gap can exacerbate existing inequalities, leaving marginalized communities more vulnerable to privacy violations and security threats.

Disproportionate Impact on Marginalized Communities: AI surveillance often disproportionately affects Marginalized communities. For example, predictive policing algorithms may target low-income neighborhoods more frequently, leading to over-policing and further marginalization.

In cities like New York and Los Angeles, predictive policing algorithms have been shown to disproportionately target low-income neighborhoods with higher populations of people of color. These communities are subjected to increased police scrutiny and surveillance, leading to a cycle of over-policing and marginalization. Critics argue that these AI systems perpetuate existing biases and exacerbate social inequalities, highlighting the need for more equitable and fair AI practices.

Ethical Considerations in Data Usage: The ethical use of data in AI surveillance is a critical concern.

Informed Consent: Obtaining informed consent for data collection and usage is challenging in the context of AI surveillance. Individuals may not be fully aware of how their data is being used or the potential implications.

In 2021, a large retail chain implemented AI-powered cameras to monitor shopper behavior and enhance security. However, many customers were unaware that their movements and behaviors were being tracked and analyzed. When the practice was exposed, there was significant public backlash, with customers demanding greater transparency and control over their personal data. This incident underscored the importance of informed consent and transparency in the use of AI surveillance technologies.

Data Ownership and Control: Questions about data ownership and control are central to the ethical use of AI surveillance. Individuals should have the right to control their personal data and decide how it is used.

In 2023, a landmark legal case in Europe addressed the issue of data ownership and control. A group of individuals sued a tech company for using their personal data without explicit permission. The court ruled in favor of the plaintiffs, establishing a precedent for data ownership rights and reinforcing the idea that individuals should have control over their personal information. This case highlighted the evolving legal and ethical landscape surrounding data usage in AI surveillance.

Scholarly Recommendations: Scholars have highlighted these additional concerns and proposed various solutions to address them.

Legal Reforms: Scholars advocate for comprehensive legal reforms to address the unique challenges posed by AI surveillance. This includes updating existing laws and creating new regulations tailored to AI technologies (Saheb, 2022).

Several countries have started to take steps towards legal reforms to address the challenges of AI surveillance. For instance, the United Kingdom introduced the Data Protection Act 2018, which complements GDPR and specifically addresses the processing of personal data by AI systems. These legal reforms aim to provide clearer guidelines and protections for individuals, ensuring that AI surveillance practices are conducted responsibly and ethically.

Public Awareness and Education: Increasing public awareness and education about AI surveillance can empower individuals to make informed decisions about their data and privacy (Karpa et al., 2022)

Organizations like the Electronic Frontier Foundation (EFF) and Privacy International have launched campaigns to educate the public about the implications of AI surveillance. These initiatives include workshops, online resources, and advocacy efforts to raise awareness and promote digital literacy. By equipping individuals with knowledge about AI surveillance, these organizations aim to empower people to protect their privacy and advocate for stronger protections.

Ethical AI Development: Researchers emphasize the importance of ethical AI development, including transparency, accountability, and fairness in AI systems (Pfau, 2024).

Tech companies like IBM and Google have implemented ethical AI guidelines and established internal ethics boards to oversee the development and deployment of AI technologies. These measures include regular audits, transparency reports, and stakeholder engagement to ensure that AI systems are developed and used responsibly. By prioritizing ethical AI development, these companies aim to build public trust and mitigate the risks associated with AI surveillance.

6.1.4 Ethical and Legal Considerations

Data Ownership and Control: The question of data ownership and control is a critical issue in AI-driven data collection. Individuals and organizations need to have clear rights and control over the data they generate. (Use of AI Technology to Support Data Collection for Project Preparation and Implementation: A "Learning-By-Doing" Process, 2021).

In the context of smart cities, data collected from sensors and IoT devices can be used to improve urban planning and services. For example, a smart city project in Barcelona utilized IoT sensors to collect data on traffic patterns, air quality, and energy consumption. This data was analyzed to optimize traffic flow, reduce pollution, and enhance energy efficiency. However, the project faced challenges related to data ownership and control. Citizens and advocacy groups demanded clear guidelines on who owned the data and how it could be used. As a result, the city implemented a data governance framework that ensured residents had control over their data and could access it transparently. This example highlights the importance of establishing clear data ownership and control mechanisms in AI-driven data collection initiatives.

Transparency and Accountability: Ensuring transparency and accountability in AI-driven data collection is essential to build trust and prevent misuse. Organizations need to be transparent about their data collection practices and accountable for how they use the data.

Social media platforms like Facebook and Twitter use AI to collect and analyze user data for targeted advertising. These platforms have faced scrutiny over their data collection practices and the need for greater transparency and accountability (The Ethics of AI Data Collection: Ensuring Privacy and Fair Representation| AI Insights, n.d.). For instance, the Cambridge Analytica scandal exposed how Facebook's data was misused for political advertising without users' consent. In response, Facebook implemented stricter data privacy policies, increased transparency about data usage, and enhanced user control over personal information. Despite these efforts, the incident underscored the ongoing need for robust transparency and accountability measures in AI-driven data collection to build and maintain public trust.

6.2.0. Risks to Human Rights

While AI offers numerous benefits, it also poses significant risks to individual human rights, including privacy, equality, and freedom of expression.

Freedom of Expression: AI technologies can be used to censor or manipulate information, impacting individuals' freedom of expression.

In 2020, during the protests in Hong Kong, AI-driven content moderation tools on social media platforms were used to remove posts related to the protests. Many users reported that their posts were being flagged and deleted, limiting their ability to share information and express their views. The automated systems were intended to remove harmful content but ended up censoring legitimate speech. This incident highlighted the delicate balance between moderating harmful content and protecting freedom of expression, and the challenges of ensuring AI systems do not infringe on fundamental rights.

6.2.1 Balancing Benefits and Risks

To balance the benefits of AI with the protection of individual human rights, several strategies can be employed.

Ethical AI Development: Developing AI systems that are transparent, accountable, and fair is crucial to ensuring that they respect human rights.

Implementing ethical guidelines and conducting regular audits can help identify and mitigate biases in AI systems. For example, Microsoft's AI and Ethics in Engineering and Research (AETHER) Committee oversees the ethical use of AI technologies. The committee regularly audits AI systems for fairness, transparency, and accountability. By adhering to the ethical standards set by organizations like the IEEE, Microsoft ensures that its AI systems are developed responsibly, addressing potential biases and protecting individual rights (Singh, 2024).

Regulatory Measures: Comprehensive regulatory frameworks are needed to address the unique challenges posed by AI.

The General Data Protection Regulation (GDPR) in the European Union provides robust data protection measures, including the right to be informed about data collection and the right to access and rectify personal data (Jones, 2023). In 2021, the GDPR was invoked when a major tech company was fined for failing to comply with data protection regulations. The company had collected and processed user data without proper consent, leading to significant legal repercussions. This example highlights the importance of regulatory frameworks like GDPR in safeguarding data privacy and ensuring that AI technologies are used ethically and responsibly.

Human Rights Impact Assessments: Conducting human rights impact assessments (HRIAs) can help evaluate the potential impact of AI systems on human rights and identify mitigation strategies.

HRIAs can be used to assess the impact of AI surveillance technologies on privacy and freedom of expression (Schmitt, 2018). For instance, before deploying a new AI-powered surveillance system, a city government conducted an HRIA to evaluate its potential effects on residents' privacy rights. The assessment revealed concerns about data security and the risk of misuse. As a result, the government implemented additional safeguards and transparency measures to address these issues. This proactive approach ensured that the surveillance technology was deployed responsibly, respecting human rights.

6.2.2 Ethical Considerations

Transparency and Explainability: Ensuring that AI systems are transparent and explainable is crucial for protecting human rights. Users should understand how AI systems make decisions and what data they use.

In the financial sector, AI algorithms are used to assess creditworthiness. If these algorithms are not transparent, individuals may not understand why they were denied a loan. For instance, a major bank implemented an AI-driven credit scoring system to streamline loan approvals. However, the lack of transparency in the algorithm led to confusion and dissatisfaction among applicants who were denied loans without clear explanations. To address this, the bank introduced an explainability feature that provided applicants with detailed reasons for their decisions. This increased transparency helped protect individuals' rights to fair treatment and improved trust in the AI system.

Accountability and Responsibility: Establishing clear accountability and responsibility for AI systems is essential to address potential harms and protect individuals' rights.

In the healthcare sector, AI systems are used to assist in diagnosing diseases. If an AI system makes an incorrect diagnosis, it is important to have clear accountability mechanisms to address the error and provide remedies to affected individuals. For example, a hospital implemented an AI-driven diagnostic tool to identify potential cases of pneumonia from chest X-rays. When the system incorrectly diagnosed a patient, the hospital had protocols in place to review and rectify the error. The accountability measures ensured that the patient received appropriate care and compensation for any harm caused, highlighting the importance of responsibility in AI applications.

6.2.3 Scholarly Perspectives

Scholars have proposed various frameworks and recommendations to address the challenges of balancing AI benefits with human rights protection.

Ethical AI Frameworks: Researchers emphasize the importance of developing ethical AI frameworks that prioritize transparency, accountability, and fairness. These frameworks can guide the development and deployment of AI systems to ensure they respect human rights.

The Asilomar AI Principles, developed by a group of leading AI researchers and ethicists, provide a comprehensive framework for ethical AI development. These principles emphasize the importance of transparency, accountability, and fairness in AI systems. Many tech companies and research institutions have adopted these principles to guide their AI projects. By adhering to ethical AI frameworks, organizations can ensure that their AI systems are developed responsibly and respect human rights.

Inclusive AI Development: Scholars advocate for inclusive AI development practices that involve diverse stakeholders, including marginalized communities. This can help ensure that AI systems are designed to benefit all individuals and address potential biases.

The Partnership on AI, a consortium of tech companies, research institutions, and civil society organizations, promotes inclusive AI development by involving diverse stakeholders in the AI development process. The consortium conducts workshops and consultations with various communities to gather input and address potential biases. This inclusive approach helps ensure that AI systems are designed to benefit all individuals and do not disproportionately impact marginalized groups.

Regulatory Oversight: There is a growing consensus on the need for regulatory oversight to ensure that AI systems are developed and used responsibly. This includes establishing regulatory bodies to monitor AI development and deployment and enforce compliance with ethical and legal standards.

The European Commission's proposal for the Artificial Intelligence Act aims to establish a regulatory framework for AI in the European Union. The Act includes provisions for regulatory oversight, risk assessment, and compliance enforcement. It categorizes AI applications based on their risk levels and imposes stricter requirements for high-risk AI systems. This regulatory oversight ensures that AI systems are developed and used responsibly, protecting individual rights and promoting public trust in AI technologies.

Conclusion

Balancing the benefits of AI with the protection of individual human rights requires a multifaceted approach that addresses ethical considerations, societal impacts, and technological advancements. By adopting ethical AI frameworks, promoting digital inclusion, and ensuring robust regulatory oversight, we can harness the transformative potential of AI while safeguarding fundamental human rights.

As we continue to explore the implications of AI on society, it is crucial to strike a balance between leveraging the advantages of AI technologies and protecting individual rights. The insights and recommendations provided by scholars and real-world examples offer valuable guidance for navigating this complex landscape and ensuring that AI is developed and used ethically.

Chapter 7

7.0 Environmental Impact of AI

The environmental impact of artificial intelligence (AI) is a multifaceted issue that has garnered significant attention in recent years. As AI technologies continue to advance and become more integrated into various aspects of society, it is crucial to understand their environmental implications. This discussion will explore the environmental impact of AI.

Below are the environmental impact of AI across industries. The below percentages are approximate and can vary based on different studies and reports. The impact and prevalence of these environmental impacts might differ slightly across regions and specific companies within each industry.

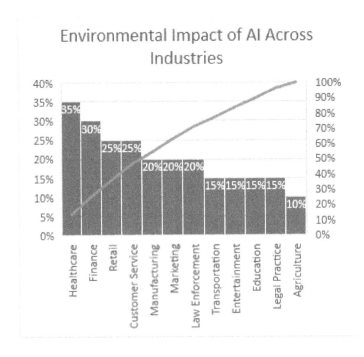

7.1 Energy Demand and Greenhouse Gas Emissions

A critical environmental concern related to AI is its substantial energy demand and the consequent greenhouse gas emissions. Training extensive AI models, such as deep neural networks, necessitates immense computational power, translating to significant energy consumption. For example, training a single AI model can consume thousands of megawatt hours of electricity, resulting in the emission of hundreds of tons of carbon dioxide (Ren & Wierman, 2024). This energy-intensive process significantly contributes to the carbon footprint of AI technologies.

Consider the story of a tech company named "GreenMind." GreenMind, a small startup, aimed to develop an AI model capable of predicting renewable energy production. However, as they trained their deep learning models, the founders were shocked by the astronomical energy bills and the carbon footprint their training process generated. Realizing the irony of contributing to environmental degradation while trying to support sustainability, GreenMind pivoted. They invested in more energy-efficient hardware, adopted greener data centers powered by renewable energy, and optimized their algorithms for energy efficiency. This approach not only reduced their carbon footprint but also set a benchmark for sustainable AI practices in the industry.

A study published in the journal *Frontiers of Environmental Science & Engineering* highlights the carbon emissions associated with AI systems. The researchers quantified the carbon emissions from 79 prominent AI systems released between 2020 and 2024, finding that the projected total carbon footprint from the top 20 AI systems could reach up to 102.6 million tons of CO_2 equivalent per year (Yu et al., 2024). This substantial impact underscores the need for more sustainable practices in AI development and deployment.

7.1.1 Water Resource Utilization

Beyond energy consumption, AI technologies also exert considerable pressure on water resources. Data centers, which host the servers and infrastructure necessary for AI computations, require large volumes of water for cooling. The heat generated by these servers must be dissipated to maintain optimal operating conditions, leading to the evaporation of significant quantities of freshwater (Ren & Wierman, 2024). This process can exacerbate water scarcity, particularly in regions already facing limited freshwater resources.

Imagine a bustling metropolitan area dependent on a nearby river for its water supply. As more tech companies set up data centers in the area, the demand for water skyrocketed. One particular data center, aiming to cool its servers, consumed as much water as an entire small town. This added strain on the water supply led to stricter water rationing for residents, farmers, and local businesses. The situation highlighted the urgent need for more water-efficient cooling technologies and a reevaluation of where data centers are established, especially in water-scarce regions.

7.1.2 Electronic Waste and Material Depletion

The production and disposal of AI hardware contribute to environmental degradation through electronic waste (e-waste) and resource depletion. Manufacturing AI hardware, such as GPUs and specialized processors, involves the extraction of raw materials, including rare earth metals. This extraction process can lead to habitat destruction, soil erosion, and water pollution. Additionally, the disposal of outdated AI hardware adds to the growing problem of e-waste, which contains hazardous materials that can leach into the environment, posing risks to human health and ecosystems.

Consider the story of a rural community situated near a mining site for rare earth metals. The constant extraction led to widespread soil erosion and contaminated water sources, making it difficult for the local population to farm or find clean drinking water. When the mining company upgraded to more efficient technology, the old equipment was discarded, adding to the growing piles of e-waste. These e-waste heaps leached toxic substances into the soil, further harming the environment and the health of nearby residents. This example underscores the need for responsible resource extraction and proper disposal of e-waste to minimize environmental and health impacts.

7.1.3 Strategies for Sustainability

To mitigate the environmental impact of AI, several strategies have been proposed. One approach is to enhance the energy efficiency of AI models and data centers. Researchers are exploring techniques to optimize AI algorithms, thereby reducing the computational power required for training and inference. For instance, developing more efficient neural network architectures and utilizing hardware accelerators can help lower energy consumption (Yu et al., 2024).

Another strategy involves adopting renewable energy sources to power data centers. Transitioning to solar, wind, or hydroelectric power can significantly reduce the carbon footprint of AI technologies. Companies like Google and Microsoft have already committed to using 100% renewable energy for their data centers, setting a precedent for the industry.

Consider the success story of a company named "EcoAI." EcoAI was determined to develop AI technologies with minimal environmental impact. They invested in cutting-edge, energy-efficient hardware and adopted advanced algorithms to optimize performance while minimizing energy use. Additionally, they powered their data centers entirely with renewable energy sources, reducing their carbon footprint to nearly zero. EcoAI's commitment to sustainability not only earned them widespread acclaim but also inspired other tech companies to adopt similar green practices.

7.1.4 Raw Material Extraction and Environmental Degradation

The creation of AI hardware, including GPUs and specialized processors, heavily depends on the extraction of raw materials like rare earth metals. This extraction process can cause significant environmental harm. For example, mining activities often lead to habitat destruction, soil erosion, and water pollution. As AI technologies continue to advance, the demand for these materials is expected to rise, worsening these environmental issues.

Imagine a mining town in a remote part of the world where the extraction of rare earth metals is a major industry. The landscape is dotted with large pits and heaps of waste material. Over time, the mining activities have caused the local river to become polluted, affecting both wildlife and the communities that rely on it for drinking water and agriculture. The town's residents have noticed a decline in their health, with increasing cases of respiratory and waterborne diseases. This story highlights the urgent need for more sustainable mining practices and the development of alternative materials for AI hardware.

A study in the Journal of Cleaner Production highlights the environmental impact of rare earth metal extraction. The researchers found that the extraction process generates substantial waste and pollutants, including radioactive materials, which can contaminate soil and water sources (Web Editor & Hossfield, 2024). This underscores the need for more sustainable mining practices and the development of alternative materials for AI hardware.

7.1.5 Geographic Distribution of Data Centers and Environmental Justice

The placement of data centers, which house the servers and infrastructure needed for AI computations, can also have significant environmental implications. Data centers are often located in regions with abundant natural resources, such as water and energy, to support their operations. However, this can lead to environmental justice issues, as the negative impacts of data center operations are disproportionately borne by these regions.

For instance, a study by Shaolei Ren and Adam Wierman published in *Harvard Business Review* discusses the uneven distribution of AI's environmental impacts (Ren & Wierman, 2024). The researchers found that data centers in regions with high water stress and limited energy resources are more likely to experience negative environmental consequences. This highlights the need for a more equitable distribution of data center operations and the adoption of sustainable practices to mitigate these impacts.

Consider the case of a rural community located near a major data center. The data center, drawn by the area's low electricity costs and abundance of water, consumes vast amounts of both resources. As the data center expands, the local community experiences frequent power outages and water shortages, disrupting daily life and local businesses. This scenario emphasizes the importance of considering environmental justice when planning data center locations and the need for sustainable practices to minimize their impact on local communities.

7.1.6 AI for Environmental Surveillance and Protection

Despite its environmental costs, AI also holds the potential for positive environmental applications. AI technologies can be used to monitor and mitigate environmental issues, such as deforestation, wildlife conservation, and climate change. For example, AI-powered drones and satellite imagery can monitor deforestation in real time, enabling more effective enforcement of conservation policies.

Consider the story of "EcoWatch," an organization dedicated to combating deforestation. EcoWatch developed an AI-powered drone system equipped with advanced cameras and machine learning algorithms. These drones could fly over vast forested areas, capturing high-resolution images and detecting illegal logging activities. By providing real-time data to local authorities, EcoWatch enabled quicker and more effective intervention, significantly reducing the rate of deforestation in the monitored areas. This success story illustrates how AI can be harnessed for environmental surveillance and protection.

A study published in *Nature Communications* demonstrates the use of AI in wildlife conservation (UN Environment Programme, 2024). The researchers developed an AI system that uses camera traps and machine learning algorithms to identify and track endangered species in their natural habitats. This technology can enhance conservation efforts by providing more accurate and timely data on wildlife populations.

7.1.7 AI's Role in Environmental Monitoring and Conservation

While AI has significant environmental costs, it also holds potential for positive environmental applications. AI technologies can be used to monitor and mitigate environmental issues, such as deforestation, wildlife conservation, and climate change. For instance, AI-powered drones and satellite imagery can be used to monitor deforestation in real-time, allowing for more effective enforcement of conservation policies.

Consider the case of "WildGuard," a non-profit organization that leverages AI for wildlife conservation. WildGuard uses AI-powered camera traps placed throughout wildlife reserves. These camera traps, equipped with machine learning algorithms, automatically identify and track various species, including those that are endangered. The real-time data collected helps conservationists make informed decisions, allocate resources more efficiently, and better protect wildlife populations

7.1.8 AI and Sustainable Resource Management

The concept of a circular economy, which aims to minimize waste and make the most of resources, can also be applied to AI technologies. By designing AI systems with sustainability in mind, it is possible to reduce their environmental impact. For example, companies can adopt practices such as recycling and reusing AI hardware, as well as developing more energy-efficient algorithms.

A report by the United Nations Environment Programme (UNEP) explores the potential of AI in promoting a circular economy (UN Environment Programme, 2024). The report highlights several case studies where AI technologies have been used to optimize resource use and reduce waste. For instance, AI-powered systems can monitor and manage waste streams, identify opportunities for recycling, and improve the efficiency of manufacturing processes.

Consider the example of "CircularAI," a company that has embraced the principles of a circular economy in its operations. CircularAI designs AI systems that prioritize energy efficiency and resource conservation. They have implemented a recycling program for their hardware, ensuring that components are reused or repurposed rather than discarded. Additionally, CircularAI employs AI algorithms to optimize its supply chain, reducing waste and improving overall efficiency. This holistic approach not only minimizes their environmental footprint but also sets a precedent for other tech companies to follow.

The environmental impact of AI is a complex issue that requires a multifaceted approach to address. From raw material extraction and environmental degradation to the geographic distribution of data centers and environmental justice, the implications of AI are extensive. However, AI also holds potential for positive environmental applications, such as environmental surveillance and protection, and sustainable resource management. By adopting more sustainable practices and investing in research and development, it is possible to mitigate the negative impacts of AI and harness its potential for positive environmental outcomes.

7.2 Development of Sustainable Application Practice

The development of sustainable application practices is crucial for minimizing the environmental impact of technology and promoting long-term ecological balance. This discussion will explore various aspects of sustainable application development.

7.2.1 Principles of Sustainable Application Development

Sustainable application development involves designing and implementing software in a way that reduces its environmental footprint. This includes optimizing energy efficiency, minimizing resource consumption, and ensuring the longevity and recyclability of hardware. Key principles include:

1. **Energy Efficiency**: Developing applications that consume less energy during execution. This can be achieved through efficient coding practices, optimizing algorithms, and reducing unnecessary computations.

Tech Company Case Study:

Imagine a tech company, "GreenTech Solutions," which specializes in data processing software for businesses. Recently, GreenTech Solutions noticed that their software was using a significant amount of energy, leading to high operational costs and a large carbon footprint. They decided to take steps toward creating more energy-efficient software. Here's how they did it:

a) **Efficient Coding Practices**:
   - The company's development team reviewed their existing code and identified parts that were unnecessarily complex or used inefficient methods.
   - They refactored (rewrote) these portions of the code to make them more streamlined and efficient. For instance, they replaced nested loops with more efficient algorithms that performed the same tasks faster.

b) **Optimizing Algorithms**:
   - They examined the algorithms used in their software. An algorithm is a set of instructions for solving a problem or performing a task.
   - By optimizing these algorithms, they found ways to reduce the number of steps required to complete tasks. For example, instead of scanning an entire database multiple times, they created more effective search algorithms that retrieved necessary information in fewer steps.

c) **Reducing Unnecessary Computations**:
   - GreenTech Solutions identified tasks that the software was performing repeatedly but didn't need to. These unnecessary computations were consuming extra energy.
   - They modified the software to avoid these redundant tasks, ensuring that each piece of code only ran when absolutely necessary.

d) **Outcome**:
   - After implementing these changes, GreenTech Solutions conducted a series of tests to measure the energy consumption of their software. The results were impressive: their data processing applications now used 30% less energy.
   - This reduction in energy usage translated into lower electricity bills for the company. Additionally, by consuming less power, GreenTech Solutions significantly reduced its carbon footprint, making a positive impact on the environment.

Why This Matters:

By focusing on energy-efficient software development, GreenTech Solutions not only saved money but also contributed to environmental sustainability. This example highlights how thoughtful design and implementation of software can lead to significant energy savings and a reduction in environmental impact. It's a win-win situation for both the company and the planet.

2. **Resource Optimization**: Using resources such as memory and storage efficiently to reduce the overall environmental impact. This involves minimizing data redundancy, optimizing data storage, and using cloud resources judiciously.

E-Commerce Platform Case Study:

Imagine an e-commerce giant, "EcoShop," which handles an enormous volume of data daily, from customer information and product listings to transaction records and user interactions. Managing such vast amounts of data efficiently is crucial to both their operational costs and environmental impact. Here's how EcoShop implements resource optimization strategies:

a) **Minimizing Data Redundancy**:
- **Data Redundancy** refers to the unnecessary duplication of data within a system. It can lead to increased storage needs and higher energy consumption.
- EcoShop's IT team conducts a thorough audit of their data storage systems and identifies duplicate data entries.
- They implement data deduplication techniques, which means only storing unique pieces of data and creating pointers to these pieces wherever repetition is necessary. This significantly reduces the amount of storage space needed and minimizes energy consumption related to data storage.

b) **Optimizing Data Storage**:
- Efficient data storage involves organizing and managing data in a way that maximizes the use of available storage resources.
- EcoShop adopts advanced data compression algorithms that reduce the size of data files without compromising their quality or accessibility.
- They also implement tiered storage solutions, where frequently accessed data is stored on faster, but more energy-intensive storage media, while infrequently accessed data is archived on slower, but more energy-efficient media. This stratification ensures optimal use of resources while maintaining performance.

c) **Using Cloud Resources Judiciously**:
- Cloud resources offer scalability and flexibility, but they must be managed wisely to avoid unnecessary costs and environmental impacts.
- EcoShop uses a cloud management platform to dynamically scale their cloud resources based on real-time demand. During peak shopping periods, such as holiday sales, they scale up their cloud resources to handle the increased traffic.
- Conversely, during off-peak hours, they scale down the resources to avoid idle capacity. This approach ensures that they are only using what they need at any given time, reducing waste and saving on costs.

d) **Outcome**:
- By implementing these resource optimization strategies, EcoShop achieves substantial cost savings. They lower their data storage expenses by reducing redundancy and optimizing storage solutions.
- The dynamic use of cloud resources allows them to be agile and responsive to changing demands, further reducing operational costs.

- Importantly, these strategies also contribute to environmental sustainability. By using resources more efficiently, EcoShop reduces its overall energy consumption and carbon footprint, showcasing the broader benefits of efficient resource management.

Why This Matters:

EcoShop's example demonstrates that resource optimization is not just about cutting costs; it's about creating sustainable practices that have a positive impact on the environment. By minimizing data redundancy, optimizing storage, and judiciously using cloud resources, companies can make a significant difference in their ecological footprint while maintaining operational efficiency.

3. **Lifecycle Management**: Ensuring that applications are designed for longevity and can be easily updated or recycled. This includes modular design, which allows for easy upgrades and maintenance, and the use of recyclable materials in hardware.

Concept Overview: Technology lifecycle management means designing applications and hardware to last longer, be easily updated, and eventually recycled. This approach not only ensures better performance over time but also promotes sustainability by reducing waste and conserving resources.

Sustainable Hardware Practices Case Study

Imagine a company called **GreenTech Innovations**. GreenTech is a hardware manufacturer committed to sustainability. They've developed a line of laptops with modular design, meaning customers can easily replace or upgrade components such as memory, storage, and even the processor.

Let's consider a typical customer, *Alex*. When Alex's GreenTech laptop starts feeling slow after a couple of years, instead of buying a new one, Alex simply purchases a new memory module and a faster solid-state drive. Alex can replace these parts at home with minimal tools, thanks to the modular design. This not only saves Alex money but also reduces electronic waste, as the laptop doesn't need to be discarded.

GreenTech goes a step further by using recyclable materials in its hardware. For instance, the laptop casing is made from recycled aluminum, and the internal components are designed to be easily separated and recycled when they reach the end of their life. When Alex eventually decides to upgrade to a new model, they can return the old laptop to GreenTech. The company then dismantles the laptop, recycles the materials, and reuses any salvageable parts in new products.

Why This Matters:

a) **Extended Product Lifespan:** By allowing upgrades, products can stay functional and relevant for longer periods.

b) **Cost Savings for Consumers:** Instead of replacing entire devices, consumers can upgrade parts, which is more cost-effective.

c) **Reduction in E-Waste:** Modular designs and recyclable materials significantly reduce the amount of electronic waste, promoting environmental sustainability.

d) **Responsible Consumption:** Encouraging practices that consider the full lifecycle of a product fosters a culture of responsible consumption and conservation.

In this way, lifecycle management not only benefits the individual consumer but also has a positive impact on the environment and society at large. By designing with longevity and recyclability in mind, companies like GreenTech Innovations lead the charge toward a more sustainable future in technology.

7.2.2 Green Software Engineering

Green software engineering focuses on creating software that is energy-efficient and environmentally friendly. This involves adopting practices that reduce the energy consumption of software during its development, deployment, and operation. For example, developers can use energy-efficient programming languages and tools, optimize code to reduce computational overhead, and implement energy-saving features such as adaptive power management.

A study published in the Journal of Systems and Software highlights the importance of green software engineering. The researchers found that optimizing software for energy efficiency can significantly reduce its environmental impact. They also identified several best practices for green software development, including the use of energy-efficient algorithms, minimizing resource usage, and adopting sustainable development methodologies (Mensah, 2019).

Green Software at Work

Consider a software development company that is committed to green software engineering principles. The company trains its developers in best practices for energy-efficient coding and regularly audits its software for energy consumption. In one notable project, the team optimizes an existing application by refactoring the code and implementing energy-saving features. As a result, the application's energy consumption is reduced by 40%, demonstrating the significant environmental benefits of green software engineering.

7.9.3 Sustainable Mobile Application Development

The development of sustainable mobile applications is an emerging area of focus. Mobile applications have become ubiquitous, and their environmental impact is significant due to the energy consumption of mobile devices and the data centers that support them. Sustainable mobile application development involves optimizing apps for energy efficiency, reducing data usage, and promoting environmentally friendly behaviors among users.

For example, a study published in SpringerLink discusses the concept of green mobile app development. The researchers identified several strategies for creating sustainable mobile apps, including optimizing code for energy efficiency, reducing data transfer, and using green technologies such as the Green Internet of Things (G-IoT) and 6G networks (Mohamed Ahmed Alloghani, 2023). These strategies can help reduce the environmental impact of mobile applications and promote sustainable practices among users.

Imagine a popular mobile app that encourages users to adopt environmentally friendly behaviors, such as reducing energy consumption and minimizing waste. The app is designed with energy efficiency in mind, using optimized code and reducing data transfer to lower its environmental impact. Additionally, the app integrates with G-IoT and 6G networks to further enhance its sustainability. Users can track their progress and receive tips on how to live more sustainably, making the app a powerful tool for promoting environmental awareness and action.

7.2.4 Circular Economy in Application Development

The concept of a circular economy, which aims to minimize waste and make the most of resources, can also be applied to application development. This involves designing applications and hardware with sustainability in mind, ensuring that they can be easily recycled or repurposed at the end of their lifecycle. For example, companies can adopt practices such as recycling and reusing hardware components, developing modular software that can be easily updated, and using sustainable materials in hardware production.

A report by the United Nations Environment Programme (UNEP) explores the potential of AI in promoting a circular economy. The report highlights several case studies where AI technologies have been used to optimize resource use and reduce waste. For instance, AI-powered systems can monitor and manage waste streams, identify opportunities for recycling, and improve the efficiency of manufacturing processes (Emas, 2015).

Consider a tech company that adopts a circular economy approach in its product design. The company creates modular hardware components that can be easily upgraded or replaced, extending the product's lifecycle. Additionally, they implement a take-back program, where customers can return old devices for recycling. The materials recovered from these devices are then used to produce new products, minimizing waste and reducing the need for virgin resources. This approach not only promotes sustainability but also reduces the environmental impact of technology production.

7.2.5 Case Studies and Examples

Several companies and organizations have successfully implemented sustainable application practices.

Google: Leading by Example

Google has committed to using 100% renewable energy for its data centers, significantly reducing its carbon footprint. The company has also developed energy-efficient algorithms and tools to optimize the performance of its applications. By integrating AI to predict and manage energy use, Google has set a benchmark for sustainability in the tech industry.

Another example is the development of energy-efficient algorithms for machine learning. Researchers at the Massachusetts Institute of Technology (MIT) have developed a new algorithm that reduces the energy consumption of deep learning models by up to 90%. This algorithm, known as the "Lottery Ticket Hypothesis," identifies and removes unnecessary parameters from neural networks, reducing their computational overhead and energy consumption. This breakthrough demonstrates how innovation in AI can lead to substantial environmental benefits.

7.2.6 Energy-Efficient Data Centers

One of the key areas for sustainable application practices is the optimization of data centers. Data centers are the backbone of modern digital infrastructure, and their energy consumption is substantial. Implementing energy-efficient practices in data centers can significantly reduce their environmental impact. For example, Google has developed custom-built data centers that use 50% less energy than the industry average. They achieve this through advanced cooling techniques, efficient power distribution, and the use of renewable energy sources.

A study published in the Journal of Sustainable Computing highlights the importance of energy-efficient data centers. The researchers found that optimizing cooling systems, using energy-efficient hardware, and implementing intelligent power management can reduce energy consumption by up to 40%. These practices not only lower operational costs but also contribute to environmental sustainability.

Take a look at a multinational company like Facebook, which has invested in the construction of data centers powered entirely by renewable energy sources. These data centers use advanced cooling systems that leverage natural airflows and water for efficient cooling, significantly reducing energy consumption. By leading with innovation, Facebook not only cuts operational costs but also sets a benchmark for sustainability in the industry.

7.2.7 Sustainable Software Development Lifecycle (SDLC)

The Sustainable Software Development Lifecycle (SDLC) is an approach that integrates sustainability principles into every phase of software development. This includes requirements gathering, design, implementation, testing, deployment, and maintenance. By considering environmental impacts at each stage, developers can create more sustainable software solutions (Charalampidou et al., 2020).

For instance, during the design phase, developers can choose energy-efficient algorithms and data structures. During implementation, they can use programming languages and frameworks that optimize resource usage. In the testing phase, automated tools can be used to identify and eliminate energy inefficiencies. A study in the Journal of Software: Evolution and Process discusses the benefits of integrating sustainability into the SDLC, highlighting case studies where companies have successfully reduced their environmental footprint through sustainable practices.

Consider a software development firm that integrates sustainability into every aspect of its SDLC. During the requirements gathering phase, they prioritize features that reduce energy usage. During design, the team selects data structures and algorithms that are known for their efficiency. In implementation, they use programming languages that minimize resource consumption. Throughout testing, automated tools identify areas where energy can be saved. This holistic approach results in software that is not only high-performing but also environmentally friendly, demonstrating the tangible benefits of a sustainable SDLC.

7.2.8 Green Cloud Computing

Cloud computing has become an integral part of modern IT infrastructure, offering scalability and flexibility. However, the environmental impact of cloud services is significant due to the energy consumption of data centers. Green cloud computing aims to reduce this impact by optimizing resource usage and adopting renewable energy sources (Li, 2019).

For example, Microsoft Azure has committed to achieving carbon neutrality by 2030. They are investing in renewable energy projects, optimizing data center operations, and developing energy-efficient cloud services. A study published in the IEEE Transactions on Cloud Computing explores the potential of green cloud computing, highlighting techniques such as dynamic resource allocation, virtualization, and energy-aware scheduling to reduce energy consumption.

Imagine Microsoft Azure, a leader in cloud computing services, making significant strides toward sustainability. Azure has implemented dynamic resource allocation and virtualization technologies to optimize resource usage. They have also invested in large-scale renewable energy projects, such as wind and solar farms, to power their data centers. These initiatives have not only reduced energy consumption but also set a precedent for other cloud service providers to follow. This story exemplifies the impact of green cloud computing in reducing the environmental footprint of cloud services.

7.2.9 Sustainable AI and Machine Learning

The development and deployment of AI and machine learning models can be resource-intensive. Sustainable AI practices focus on reducing the environmental impact of these technologies. This includes optimizing algorithms, using energy-efficient hardware, and leveraging cloud-based solutions that utilize renewable energy.

For instance, researchers at the University of Massachusetts Amherst developed a framework called "Green AI" that emphasizes the importance of energy efficiency in AI research. They propose using metrics such as energy consumption and carbon emissions to evaluate the sustainability of AI models. A study in the Journal of Artificial Intelligence Research discusses the benefits of Green AI, providing case studies where energy-efficient AI models have been successfully deployed.

Consider the efforts of a research team at the University of Massachusetts Amherst. They developed a framework called "Green AI" to prioritize energy efficiency in AI research. This framework includes metrics for evaluating the energy consumption and carbon emissions of AI models. By applying Green AI principles, the team successfully reduces the energy consumption of their deep learning models by 50%. This initiative not only advances the field of AI but also demonstrates the potential for sustainable AI practices to significantly reduce environmental impact.

7.2.10 Circular Economy in IT Hardware

The concept of a circular economy can also be applied to IT hardware, promoting the reuse, recycling, and repurposing of electronic components. This reduces the environmental impact of manufacturing new hardware and minimizes electronic waste.

For example, Dell Technologies has implemented a circular economy strategy that focuses on recycling and reusing materials from old devices. They have developed a closed-loop recycling process that recovers valuable materials such as gold, copper, and aluminum from discarded electronics. A report by the Ellen MacArthur Foundation highlights the benefits of a circular economy in IT hardware, showcasing case studies where companies have successfully implemented sustainable practices.

Consider Dell Technologies, which has been at the forefront of implementing a circular economy strategy. Dell's approach includes designing products with recycling in mind, using recycled materials in new products, and offering take-back programs for old devices. Through their closed-loop recycling process, Dell recovers valuable materials like gold and copper from discarded electronics, reducing the need for new raw materials. This strategy not only minimizes electronic waste but also sets an industry standard for sustainable IT practices.

7.3 Conclusion

The development of sustainable application practices is essential for minimizing the environmental impact of technology and promoting long-term ecological balance. By optimizing data centers, integrating sustainability into the software development lifecycle, adopting green cloud computing, and promoting sustainable AI and a circular economy in IT hardware, we can create a more sustainable digital future. Learning from successful case studies and implementing best practices will help us achieve these goals.

Imagine a coalition of tech companies, researchers, and policymakers coming together to promote sustainable technology practices. Through collaborative efforts, they share best practices, develop innovative solutions, and set ambitious sustainability goals. This collective action leads to significant reductions in the environmental footprint of the tech industry, demonstrating the power of collaboration in driving positive change. This vision of a sustainable digital future inspires others to join the movement and contribute to a healthier planet.

Chapter 8

8.0 Regulation and Governance Of AI

Introduction

The regulation and governance of artificial intelligence (AI) is a multifaceted and evolving field that seeks to balance the benefits of AI technologies with the need to mitigate their risks. This involves creating frameworks and policies that ensure AI systems are developed and used ethically, safely, and in alignment with societal values. In this chapter, we will explore this topic extensively through detailed explanations.

8.1 The Need for AI Regulation and Governance

AI technologies can potentially revolutionize various sectors, including healthcare, finance, and transportation. However, their rapid development and deployment also pose significant risks, such as bias, privacy infringement, and misuse. The need for regulation and governance arises from these potential risks and the desire to harness AI's benefits responsibly.

Imagine a hospital using an AI system to predict patient outcomes. If the AI is trained on biased data, it might favor one demographic over another, leading to unequal treatment and outcomes. For instance, an AI system used in a hospital in the United States was found to systematically underestimate the health needs of Black patients compared to white patients, resulting in unequal access to care. This real-world example underscores the importance of regulation to ensure AI systems are fair and equitable.

8.2 Frameworks for AI Regulation

Several frameworks have been proposed to regulate AI. One notable example is the European Union's AI Act, which aims to create a comprehensive regulatory framework for AI. The Act categorizes AI systems based on their risk levels and imposes stricter requirements on high-risk applications, such as those used in critical infrastructure and law enforcement (De Almeida et al., 2021).

The EU's AI Act in Action

Consider a scenario where an AI system is used in law enforcement to predict criminal behavior. The EU's AI Act classifies this as a high-risk application, requiring rigorous testing, transparency, and accountability measures. In one case, a city in Europe implemented these measures and found that their predictive policing AI system reduced crime rates without infringing on individual rights. This illustrates how a robust regulatory framework can help harness AI's benefits while mitigating its risks.

8.3 Ethical Considerations in AI Governance

Ethical considerations are central to AI governance. Issues such as fairness, transparency, and accountability must be addressed to ensure AI systems do not perpetuate or exacerbate existing inequalities. For instance, the AI Ethics Guidelines developed by the European Commission emphasize the importance of human oversight, technical robustness, and privacy (Taeihagh, 2021).

Ensuring Fairness in Recruitment

Consider a tech company that implemented an AI system to screen job applicants. Initially, the system showed bias against female candidates, likely due to historical data reflecting gender biases in the tech industry. To address this, the company adopted the AI Ethics Guidelines, ensuring human oversight and transparency in its AI processes. By retraining the AI system on a more diverse dataset and introducing human checks, they achieved a fairer hiring process, which increased diversity and improved company culture.

8.4 Examples of AI Governance in Practice

To illustrate how AI governance frameworks are applied in different sectors, we can look at examples in healthcare, finance, and autonomous vehicles.

Healthcare: AI in Diagnostics and Treatment Planning

AI is increasingly used in healthcare for diagnostics and treatment planning. However, the use of AI in this sector raises concerns about data privacy and the potential for biased algorithms. Regulatory bodies like the U.S. Food and Drug Administration (FDA) have developed guidelines for AI-based medical devices to ensure they meet safety and efficacy standards. (Mucci & Stryker, 2023).

Consider a hospital in the U.S. implementing an AI system to assist radiologists in breast cancer screening. The AI system, approved by the FDA, was trained on a large, diverse dataset to reduce bias. It proved to be a valuable tool, identifying early signs of breast cancer that were sometimes missed by human eyes, ultimately improving patient outcomes. This example shows how regulatory oversight can enhance the benefits of AI in healthcare while addressing ethical concerns.

Finance: AI in Fraud Detection and Risk Management

In the financial sector, AI is used for fraud detection, risk management, and customer service. The Financial Industry Regulatory Authority (FINRA) in the U.S. has issued guidelines for the use of AI in financial services, focusing on transparency, accountability, and the prevention of discriminatory practices (Team, 2024).

AI Preventing Financial Fraud

Imagine a major bank implementing an AI system to detect fraudulent transactions. The system, adhering to FINRA guidelines, monitored transactions in real time and flagged suspicious activities. In one notable instance, the AI system detected an unusual pattern that led to the discovery of a large-scale fraud scheme, saving the bank millions of dollars. This highlights the importance of regulatory frameworks in ensuring AI's effective and ethical use in finance.

Autonomous Vehicles: Ensuring Safety and Reliability

The deployment of autonomous vehicles presents unique regulatory challenges. Governments worldwide are developing frameworks to ensure these vehicles are safe and reliable. For example, the National Highway Traffic Safety Administration (NHTSA) in the U.S. has issued guidelines for the testing and deployment of autonomous vehicles (Taeihagh, 2021).

Safe Deployment of Autonomous Taxis

In a pilot program, in the U.S. Waymo launched autonomous taxis, adhering to NHTSA guidelines. The vehicles underwent extensive testing, including safety checks, before being allowed to operate on public roads. The program demonstrated that with rigorous governance, autonomous vehicles could operate safely and efficiently, providing a glimpse into the future of transportation.

8.5 Challenges in AI Regulation and Governance

Despite the progress made, several challenges remain in regulating and governing AI:

Global Coordination

AI technologies are developed and deployed globally, making it challenging to create uniform regulations. International cooperation is essential to address cross-border issues and ensure consistent standards.

Cross-Border Data Sharing in Healthcare

Consider a global healthcare company that faced challenges in implementing a unified AI system due to varying data privacy laws across different countries. To overcome this, they collaborated with international regulatory bodies to establish common standards for data sharing and privacy. This cooperation allowed them to deploy their AI system more effectively, improving patient care globally.

Rapid Technological Advancements

The pace of AI development often outstrips the ability of regulatory bodies to keep up. This can result in outdated regulations that fail to address new risks and challenges.

Regulation Lagging Behind AI Innovations

Imagine a tech startup developing an AI tool for real-time financial trading. However, the regulatory framework in their country hadn't kept pace with such innovations, causing delays in approval and deployment. The startup can work with regulators to update the guidelines, highlighting the need for agile regulatory processes that can adapt to rapid technological advancements.

Balancing Innovation and Regulation

Striking the right balance between fostering innovation and ensuring safety and ethics is a significant challenge. Overly stringent regulations can stifle innovation, while lax regulations can lead to misuse and harm (Keller, 2024).

Finding the Balance in Autonomous Vehicles

Consider a country piloting autonomous vehicles that faced the dilemma of imposing strict safety regulations versus fostering innovation. By engaging with industry experts, regulators can devise a flexible framework that allows for innovation while maintaining stringent safety checks. This balanced approach will facilitate the safe deployment of autonomous vehicles, showcasing how thoughtful regulation can support technological progress.

8.6 Future Directions in AI Governance

The future of AI governance will likely involve a combination of regulatory measures, industry self-regulation, and international cooperation. Emerging approaches include the development of AI-specific regulatory bodies, the use of AI for regulatory compliance, and the incorporation of ethical principles into AI design and deployment (What the US's Foggy AI Regulations Mean for Today's Cyber Compliance, 2024).

AI-Specific Regulatory Bodies

Imagine a country that establishes a dedicated AI regulatory body to keep pace with AI advancements. This organization can focus on monitoring AI developments, updating regulations, and ensuring ethical standards are met. This regulatory body's proactive approach will set a precedent for other countries, emphasizing the importance of specialized oversight in AI governance.

8.7 Global Regulation

The global regulation of artificial intelligence (AI) is a complex and evolving field that requires a multifaceted approach to address the diverse challenges posed by AI technologies. In this section, we will explore the measures put in place for global regulation of AI, providing a comprehensive overview.

8.7.1 International Cooperation and Frameworks

International cooperation is crucial for the effective regulation of AI. Various international organizations and forums have been established to facilitate collaboration and develop global standards for AI governance.

United Nations (UN)

The UN has been actively involved in promoting the ethical use of AI. The UN Secretary-General's High-level Panel on Digital Cooperation has emphasized the need for global cooperation to ensure that AI technologies are developed and used responsibly. The panel's report outlines recommendations for creating a global framework for AI governance. (Tallberg et al., 2023).

UN's Role in AI for Sustainable Development

The UN launched an initiative to use AI for achieving the Sustainable Development Goals (SDGs). One project focused on using AI to analyze satellite imagery for monitoring deforestation. By coordinating with international partners, the UN ensured that the AI system adhered to ethical guidelines and respected data privacy laws across different countries. This initiative not only advanced the SDGs but also set a precedent for global cooperation in AI governance.

OECD Principles on AI

The Organisation for Economic Co-operation and Development (OECD) has developed a set of principles to guide the development and deployment of AI. These principles emphasize the importance of transparency, accountability, and human-centered values in AI systems. (Tallberg et al., 2023).

Implementing OECD Principles in Smart Cities

Consider a city in Europe that adopted the OECD principles to guide its AI-driven smart city initiatives. These principles helped the city implement AI systems for traffic management and energy efficiency while ensuring transparency and accountability. As a result, the city's AI initiatives improved urban living conditions and served as a model for other cities worldwide.

G20 AI Principles

The G20 has also adopted a set of AI principles that align with the OECD guidelines. These principles focus on promoting inclusive growth, sustainable development, and the ethical use of AI technologies (Tallberg et al., 2023).

G20's Impact on AI in Financial Services

During a G20 summit, member countries agreed to adopt common AI principles for financial services. This agreement facilitated the creation of a unified framework for using AI in banking and insurance, ensuring that AI systems are transparent, accountable, and non-discriminatory. This collaboration has led to more robust and ethical AI practices in the financial sector globally.

8.8 Regional and National Regulations

Different regions and countries have implemented their regulatory frameworks to address the unique challenges posed by AI. Here, we will explore some notable examples.

European Union (EU)

The EU has been at the forefront of AI regulation with its proposed AI Act. This comprehensive framework categorizes AI systems based on their risk levels and imposes stricter requirements on high-risk applications. The AI Act aims to ensure that AI technologies are safe, transparent, and respect fundamental rights (Pouya Kashefi et al., 2024).

EU's AI Act in Healthcare

Imagine a European healthcare provider implementing an AI system for patient diagnostics. Under the AI Act's high-risk category, this system underwent rigorous testing and validation to ensure it was accurate, transparent, and free from bias. As a result, the AI system improved diagnostic accuracy and patient outcomes while adhering to stringent regulatory standards.

United States (US)

The US has taken a more decentralized approach to AI regulation, with various federal agencies developing sector-specific guidelines. For example, the Federal Trade Commission (FTC) has issued guidelines on the use of AI in consumer protection, while the Food and Drug Administration (FDA) regulates AI-based medical devices (Pouya Kashefi et al., 2024).

FDA-Regulated AI in Medical Devices

Consider a US-based company developing an AI-powered medical device to assist surgeons in real-time decision-making during operations. The FDA's regulatory guidelines ensured that the device met safety and efficacy standards, leading to successful clinical trials and approval. This device has since become a valuable tool in operating rooms, enhancing surgical precision and patient safety.

China

China has adopted a state-led approach to AI regulation, with the government playing a central role in guiding AI development. The Chinese government has issued several policy documents outlining its vision for AI governance, emphasizing the importance of innovation, security, and ethical considerations (Pouya Kashefi et al., 2024).

China's AI in Smart City Development

In one of China's rapidly growing smart cities, the government implemented AI systems for traffic management, waste reduction, and public safety. These initiatives were guided by the government's AI policy documents, ensuring that the systems were innovative, secure, and ethically sound. The AI-driven improvements in the city's infrastructure have enhanced the quality of life for its residents and set a benchmark for other cities.

8.9 Ethical Guidelines and Standards

Ethical guidelines and standards play a crucial role in ensuring that AI technologies are developed and used responsibly. Here, we will explore two prominent initiatives: the IEEE Global Initiative and the ISO/IEC JTC 1/SC 42.

IEEE Global Initiative on Ethics of Autonomous and Intelligent Systems

The Institute of Electrical and Electronics Engineers (IEEE) has developed a comprehensive set of ethical guidelines for AI. These guidelines cover various aspects of AI development, including transparency, accountability, and the prevention of bias (Artificial Intelligence and the Challenge for Global Governance, 2024).

Consider a leading tech company implementing the IEEE ethical guidelines while developing an AI system for autonomous drones. By adhering to the guidelines, the company ensured that the drones were transparent in their operations, accountable for their actions, and free from biases. This approach not only enhanced the safety and reliability of the drones but also built trust with users and regulatory bodies.

ISO/IEC JTC 1/SC 42

The International Organization for Standardization (ISO) and the International Electrotechnical Commission (IEC) have established a joint technical committee to develop international standards for AI. This committee focuses on creating standards for AI governance, risk management, and ethical considerations (Artificial Intelligence and the Challenge for Global Governance, 2024).

Consider a global manufacturing firm that adopted the ISO/IEC standards while implementing AI systems for quality control and predictive maintenance. These standards provided a robust framework for managing risks and ensuring ethical practices in AI deployment. As a result, the company improved its manufacturing processes, reduced downtime, and maintained high ethical standards, setting an industry benchmark.

8.10 Public-Private Partnerships

Public-private partnerships are essential for the effective regulation of AI, as they bring together the expertise and resources of both the public and private sectors. Here, we will explore two notable initiatives: the Partnership on AI and AI4People.

Partnership on AI

The Partnership on AI is a multi-stakeholder organization with representatives from academia, industry, and civil society. This organization aims to promote the responsible development and use of AI by fostering collaboration and sharing best practices (The Economic Impacts and the Regulation of AI: A Review of the Academic Literature and Policy Actions, n.d.).

A notable example of the Partnership on AI's impact is a collaborative research project on AI ethics involving leading tech companies and academic institutions. The project aimed to develop best practices for ethical AI development, focusing on transparency and accountability. The findings of this project have been widely adopted by industry players, helping to shape ethical AI practices and influencing policy discussions.

AI4People

AI4People is a European initiative that brings together stakeholders from various sectors to develop ethical guidelines and policy recommendations for AI. This initiative focuses on promoting human-centered AI and ensuring that AI technologies benefit society as a whole (The Economic Impacts and the Regulation of AI: A Review of the Academic Literature and Policy Actions, n.d.).

AI4People facilitated a partnership between educational institutions and AI developers to create AI-powered learning tools. By incorporating ethical guidelines from

AI4People, these tools were designed to enhance learning experiences while respecting students' privacy and promoting inclusivity. This collaboration resulted in innovative educational solutions that are now being used across Europe, demonstrating the positive impact of human-centered AI.

8.11 Challenges and Future Directions

Despite the progress made in AI regulation, several challenges remain. We will explore these challenges and potential future directions for effective AI governance.

Harmonization of Regulations

One of the main challenges is the harmonization of regulations across different regions and countries. International cooperation and dialogue are essential to create consistent and effective regulatory frameworks.

A consortium of countries worked together to develop international standards for autonomous vehicles. This collaboration ensured that the vehicles could be safely deployed across borders, adhering to consistent safety and ethical standards. The success of this initiative demonstrates the importance of harmonizing regulations to address global AI challenges effectively (Global AI Regulation: Protecting Rights; Leveraging Collaboration, 2024).

Rapid Technological Advancements

The rapid pace of AI development often outstrips the ability of regulatory bodies to keep up. This requires flexible and adaptive regulatory approaches that can respond to new risks and challenges (Global AI Regulation: Protecting Rights; Leveraging Collaboration, 2024).

Agile Regulation in AI-Powered Finance

Imagine a regulatory body in a major financial hub adopting an agile regulatory framework to keep pace with AI innovations in finance. By implementing a regulatory sandbox, they allowed fintech companies to test AI applications under controlled conditions. This approach enabled regulators to quickly address emerging risks while fostering innovation in the financial sector.

Balancing Innovation and Regulation

Striking the right balance between fostering innovation and ensuring safety and ethics is a significant challenge. Overly stringent regulations can stifle innovation, while lax regulations can lead to misuse and harm.

Balancing AI Regulation in Healthcare

Consider a country facing the challenge of regulating AI applications in healthcare. By engaging with stakeholders, including AI developers, healthcare professionals, and patients, they developed a balanced regulatory framework. This framework ensured that AI innovations could be safely and ethically integrated into healthcare systems, improving patient outcomes without stifling innovation.

The global regulation of AI involves a combination of international cooperation, regional and national regulations, ethical guidelines, and public-private partnerships. By addressing these various aspects, we can ensure that AI technologies are developed and used responsibly, benefiting society.

8.2 National Regulation

The national regulation of artificial intelligence (AI) involves a variety of measures tailored to address the unique challenges and opportunities presented by AI technologies within specific countries. These measures are designed to ensure that AI is developed and deployed in a manner that is ethical, safe, and beneficial to society. Here, we will explore the national regulatory measures for AI in detail, providing a comprehensive overview.

8.2.1 United States

The United States has adopted a sector-specific approach to AI regulation, with various federal agencies developing guidelines and policies tailored to their respective domains.

Federal Trade Commission (FTC)

The FTC has issued guidelines on the use of AI in consumer protection, emphasizing the importance of transparency, fairness, and accountability. The FTC's guidelines aim to prevent deceptive practices and ensure that AI systems do not discriminate against consumers (De Almeida et al., 2021).

FTC Guidelines in Action

Consider a major online retailer implementing AI algorithms to recommend products to customers. Initially, the system exhibited biases, favoring certain products and disadvantaging others. By adopting the FTC guidelines, the retailer re-evaluated and adjusted their AI algorithms to ensure fairness and transparency. As a result, customer trust improved, and the recommendation system became more equitable.

Food and Drug Administration (FDA)

The FDA regulates AI-based medical devices, ensuring they meet safety and efficacy standards. The FDA's regulatory framework includes premarket approval, post-market surveillance, and guidelines for the use of AI in clinical decision support systems. (Candelon et al., 2021).

FDA-Regulated AI in Healthcare

Imagine a biotech company developing an AI-powered diagnostic tool for early cancer detection. To gain FDA approval, the company underwent rigorous testing and validation processes. Once approved, the AI tool was deployed in hospitals, where it significantly improved early cancer detection rates and patient outcomes. This success story highlights the importance of FDA regulations in ensuring the safety and efficacy of AI in healthcare.

National Institute of Standards and Technology (NIST)

NIST has developed a framework for managing AI risks, which provides guidelines for organizations to assess and mitigate the risks associated with AI technologies (Taeihagh, 2021).

NIST Framework in Autonomous Systems

Consider an automotive manufacturer utilizing the NIST framework while developing autonomous driving systems. By following NIST guidelines, the manufacturer identified potential risks and implemented mitigation strategies. This proactive approach resulted in safer and more reliable autonomous vehicles, earning consumer confidence and regulatory approval.

8.2.2 European Union

The European Union (EU) has been at the forefront of AI regulation, with its comprehensive AI Act aiming to create a unified regulatory framework across member states.

AI Act

The AI Act categorizes AI systems based on their risk levels and imposes stricter requirements on high-risk applications. The Act mandates transparency, accountability, and human oversight for AI systems, ensuring they align with fundamental rights and ethical principles (De Almeida et al., 2021).

AI Act in Law Enforcement

Consider a European city, where the local police department implemented an AI system for predictive policing. Classified as a high-risk application under the AI Act, the system underwent extensive scrutiny to ensure it was transparent, accountable, and respectful of human rights. By incorporating these safeguards, the police department successfully reduced crime rates without compromising civil liberties, demonstrating the effectiveness of the AI Act.

General Data Protection Regulation (GDPR)

The GDPR includes provisions that impact AI, particularly regarding data privacy and protection. The regulation requires organizations to obtain explicit consent for data processing and ensures individuals have the right to access, rectify, and delete their data. .(De Almeida et al., 2021).

GDPR in Healthcare AI

Imagine a European healthcare provider implementing an AI system for patient data analysis. Under GDPR, the provider had to obtain explicit consent from patients for data processing. Additionally, patients were given the right to access and correct their data. This ensured that the AI system operated within ethical boundaries, enhancing patient trust and data security while improving healthcare outcomes.

8.2.3 China

China has adopted a state-led approach to AI regulation, with the government playing a central role in guiding AI development and deployment.

New Generation Artificial Intelligence Development Plan

This plan outlines China's strategic vision for AI, emphasizing innovation, security, and ethical considerations. The plan includes measures to promote AI research and development, as well as guidelines for the ethical use of AI, (Taeihagh, 2021).

AI Development in Smart Cities

As part of the New Generation Artificial Intelligence Development Plan, a major Chinese city implemented AI-driven smart city solutions to manage traffic, energy consumption, and public safety. By following the guidelines of the plan, the city ensured that these AI systems were secure, innovative, and ethically sound. The success of this initiative improved urban living conditions and demonstrated China's commitment to responsible AI development.

Cybersecurity Law

China's Cybersecurity Law includes provisions that impact AI, particularly regarding data security and protection. The law requires organizations to implement robust data security measures and obtain government approval for the transfer of data across borders (The Economic Impacts and the Regulation of AI: A Review of the Academic Literature and Policy Actions, n.d.).

Data Security in AI for Healthcare

Imagine a Chinese tech company developing an AI system for remote patient monitoring. To comply with the Cybersecurity Law, the company implemented stringent data security measures, ensuring patient data was encrypted and securely stored. Additionally, they obtained government approval for processing and transferring data across borders. This compliance not only safeguarded patient data but also built trust with healthcare providers and patients.

8.2.4 Japan

Japan has implemented a range of measures to regulate AI, focusing on promoting innovation while ensuring safety and ethical considerations.

AI Strategy 2025

Japan's AI Strategy 2025 outlines the country's vision for AI development, emphasizing the importance of collaboration between the public and private sectors. The strategy includes guidelines for the ethical use of AI and measures to promote AI research and development (Non-Decisional Material Non-Decisional Statement by the National AI Advisory Committee (NAIAC) Working Group on Regulation and Executive Action Rationales, Mechanisms, and Challenges to Regulating AI: A Concise Guide and Explanation, n.d.).

Collaborative AI Innovations

Consider a joint venture between a Japanese university and a leading tech company focused on developing AI-driven agricultural solutions. Under the AI Strategy 2025, this collaboration aimed to enhance crop yields and reduce environmental impact. The project, guided by ethical AI principles, will successfully deploy AI systems that optimize irrigation and pest control. This initiative not only advanced agricultural practices but also demonstrated the power of public-private collaboration in AI development.

Act on the Protection of Personal Information (APPI)

The APPI regulates the collection, use, and protection of personal data in Japan. The law includes provisions that impact AI, particularly regarding data privacy and protection.

Data Privacy in AI-Driven Healthcare

Imagine a Japanese healthcare provider implementing an AI system for patient health monitoring. To comply with the APPI, the provider has to ensure that all patient data is collected with explicit consent and securely stored. Patients were also given the right to access and manage their data. This compliance not only protected patient privacy but also fostered trust in the AI system, leading to better health outcomes and widespread adoption.

8.2.5 Canada

Canada has adopted a multi-faceted approach to AI regulation, focusing on promoting innovation while ensuring ethical considerations and public trust.

Pan-Canadian Artificial Intelligence Strategy

This strategy aims to position Canada as a global leader in AI research and innovation. The strategy includes measures to promote AI research, support the commercialization of AI technologies, and ensure the ethical use of AI.

AI Innovations in Environmental Monitoring

Under the Pan-Canadian Artificial Intelligence Strategy, a Canadian research institution developed an AI system for monitoring environmental changes. This system uses satellite data to track deforestation, pollution, and wildlife movements. By promoting collaboration between researchers and technology companies, the strategy enabled the successful commercialization of this AI technology, which is now used globally to support environmental conservation efforts.

Privacy Act

Canada's Privacy Act regulates the collection, use, and protection of personal data by federal government institutions. The Act includes provisions that impact AI, particularly regarding data privacy and protection.

Data Privacy in AI-Enhanced Government Services

Imagine a Canadian government agency implementing an AI system to enhance public services, such as processing tax returns and managing social benefits. To comply with the Privacy Act, the agency has to ensure that personal data is collected with explicit consent and securely stored. Citizens are given the right to access and correct their data, fostering public trust in the AI system. This compliance not only improved service efficiency but also demonstrated the importance of data privacy in government AI applications.

8.2.6 Australia

Australia has implemented a range of measures to regulate AI, focusing on promoting innovation while ensuring safety and ethical considerations.

AI Ethics Framework

Australia's AI Ethics Framework provides guidelines for the ethical use of AI, emphasizing principles such as fairness, transparency, and accountability. The framework aims to ensure that AI technologies are developed and used in a manner that aligns with societal values.

Ethical AI in Public Services

Consider an Australian city that adopted the AI Ethics Framework to implement AI systems for managing public services, such as waste collection and water distribution. By following the guidelines, the city ensured that the AI systems were transparent, fair, and accountable. This initiative improved service efficiency and public satisfaction, demonstrating the importance of ethical guidelines in AI deployment.

Privacy Act

Australia's Privacy Act regulates the collection, use, and protection of personal data. The Act includes provisions that impact AI, particularly regarding data privacy and protection.

Data Privacy in AI-Powered Education

Imagine an Australian educational institution implementing an AI system to personalize student learning experiences. To comply with the Privacy Act, the institution has to ensure that all student data is collected with explicit consent and securely stored. Students are given the right to access and manage their data, fostering trust in the AI system. This compliance not only enhanced educational outcomes but also highlighted the importance of data privacy in AI applications.

National regulation of AI involves a variety of measures tailored to address the unique challenges and opportunities presented by AI technologies within specific countries. By implementing these measures, countries can ensure that AI is developed and deployed in an ethical, safe, and beneficial manner to society.

8.3 Industrial Regulations

The industrial regulation of artificial intelligence (AI) involves a variety of measures tailored to address the unique challenges and opportunities presented by AI technologies within specific industries. These measures are designed to ensure that AI is developed and deployed in a manner that is ethical, safe, and beneficial to society.

Here, we will explore the industrial regulatory measures for AI to provide a comprehensive overview.

8.3.1 Healthcare Industry

The healthcare industry has seen significant advancements with the integration of AI technologies, particularly in diagnostics, treatment planning, and patient care. However, using AI in healthcare raises concerns about data privacy, bias, and patient safety.

Regulatory Bodies and Guidelines

The U.S. Food and Drug Administration (FDA) has established guidelines for AI-based medical devices to meet safety and efficacy standards. The FDA's regulatory framework includes premarket approval, post-market surveillance, and guidelines for using AI in clinical decision support systems, (Comunale & Manera, 2024).

FDA-Approved AI in Cardiology

Consider a medical device company developing an AI system for detecting heart conditions from electrocardiograms (ECGs). To gain FDA approval, the company will have to undergo rigorous testing and validation processes. Once approved, the AI system is deployed in hospitals and clinics, where it significantly improves the accuracy of heart condition diagnoses. This success story highlights the importance of FDA regulations in ensuring the safety and efficacy of AI in healthcare.

Ethical Considerations

Ethical guidelines for AI in healthcare emphasize the importance of transparency, accountability, and patient consent. The World Health Organization (WHO) has also developed a framework for the ethical use of AI in healthcare, focusing on principles such as fairness, transparency, and accountability (Finocchiaro, 2023).

Ethical AI in Remote Patient Monitoring

Imagine a global healthcare provider implementing an AI system for remote patient monitoring. Adhering to WHO ethical guidelines, the provider has to ensure that patient consent is obtained, and data is transparently collected and securely stored. The AI system enhances patient care by providing real-time health monitoring and early detection of potential issues. This initiative demonstrated the importance of ethical considerations in building trust and improving healthcare outcomes.

8.3.2 Financial Industry

The financial industry has widely adopted AI technologies for applications such as fraud detection, risk management, and customer service. However, the use of AI in finance also raises concerns about data security, bias, and regulatory compliance.

Regulatory Bodies and Guidelines

The Financial Industry Regulatory Authority (FINRA) in the U.S. has issued guidelines for the use of AI in financial services, focusing on transparency, accountability, and the prevention of discriminatory practices. The European Banking Authority (EBA) has also developed guidelines for the use of AI in the financial sector, emphasizing the importance of risk management and regulatory compliance, (De Almeida et al., 2021).

FINRA Guidelines in Fraud Detection

Consider a major U.S. bank implementing an AI system to detect fraudulent transactions. By adhering to FINRA guidelines, the bank has to ensure that the AI system is transparent and accountable, with regular audits to prevent biases. The AI system successfully identified and prevented multiple fraud attempts, saving the bank millions of dollars and protecting customers' financial assets. This story highlights the importance of regulatory guidelines in ensuring the effective and ethical use of AI in finance.

Ethical Considerations

Ethical guidelines for AI in finance emphasize the importance of fairness, transparency, and accountability. The Global Financial Markets Association (GFMA) has developed a framework for the ethical use of AI in finance, focusing on principles such as fairness, transparency, and accountability (Heimberger et al., 2024).

Ethical AI in Customer Service

Imagine a European financial institution integrating AI into its customer service operations. Following the EBA and GFMA ethical guidelines, the institution has to ensure that the AI system is fair and transparent, providing equal service to all customers. The AI system improved response times and customer satisfaction while maintaining high ethical standards. This initiative demonstrated the positive impact of ethical guidelines on customer trust and service quality.

8.3.3 Manufacturing Industry

The manufacturing industry has seen significant advancements with the integration of AI technologies, particularly in areas such as predictive maintenance, quality control, and supply chain optimization. However, the use of AI in manufacturing also raises concerns about data security, bias, and regulatory compliance.

Regulatory Bodies and Guidelines

The International Organization for Standardization (ISO) has developed standards for the use of AI in manufacturing, focusing on areas such as quality control, predictive maintenance, and supply chain optimization. The National Institute of Standards and Technology (NIST) in the U.S. has also developed guidelines for the use of AI in manufacturing, emphasizing the importance of risk management and regulatory compliance.

ISO Standards in Predictive Maintenance

Consider a global manufacturing firm that adopted ISO standards while implementing AI systems for predictive maintenance. By adhering to these standards, the company has to ensure that its AI systems are reliable and compliant with industry best practices. The AI system accurately predicted machinery failures, reducing downtime and maintenance costs. This success story highlights the importance of regulatory standards in enhancing operational efficiency and reliability in manufacturing.

Ethical Considerations

Ethical guidelines for AI in manufacturing emphasize the importance of transparency, accountability, and worker safety. The International Labour Organization (ILO) has developed a framework for the ethical use of AI in manufacturing, focusing on principles such as fairness, transparency, and accountability.

Ethical AI in Quality Control

Imagine a manufacturing plant implementing an AI system for quality control, guided by the ILO's ethical framework. The AI system is designed to be transparent and accountable, ensuring that any errors or biases are promptly addressed. This approach not only improved product quality but also ensured worker safety by automating hazardous tasks. The initiative demonstrated the positive impact of ethical considerations on both productivity and worker well-being.

8.3.4 Transportation Industry

The transportation industry has widely adopted AI technologies for applications such as autonomous vehicles, traffic management, and logistics optimization. However, the use of AI in transportation also raises concerns about safety, data security, and regulatory compliance.

Regulatory Bodies and Guidelines

The National Highway Traffic Safety Administration (NHTSA) in the U.S. has issued guidelines for the testing and deployment of autonomous vehicles, ensuring they meet safety and reliability standards. The European Union Agency for Railways (ERA) has also developed guidelines for the use of AI in rail transportation, emphasizing the importance of safety and regulatory compliance.

NHTSA Guidelines in Autonomous Vehicles

Consider an American tech company developing an autonomous vehicle system that underwent rigorous testing to comply with NHTSA guidelines. The system was evaluated for safety, reliability, and data security before being deployed on public roads. This adherence to regulatory standards ensured that the autonomous vehicles operated safely, reducing accidents and gaining public trust. This example underscores the critical role of regulatory bodies in ensuring the safe deployment of AI in transportation.

Ethical Considerations

Ethical guidelines for AI in transportation emphasize the importance of transparency, accountability, and public safety. The International Transport Forum (ITF) has developed a framework for the ethical use of AI in transportation, focusing on principles such as fairness, transparency, and accountability.

Ethical AI in Traffic Management

Imagine a European city implementing an AI-driven traffic management system guided by ITF's ethical framework. The system was designed to be transparent and accountable, providing real-time traffic data to the public and allowing for independent audits. The AI system optimized traffic flow, reduced congestion, and improved air quality while maintaining high ethical standards. This initiative demonstrates the positive impact of ethical considerations on public safety and environmental sustainability.

8.3.5 Energy Industry

The energy industry has seen significant advancements with the integration of AI technologies, particularly in areas such as energy management, grid optimization, and renewable energy. However, the use of AI in energy also raises concerns about data security, bias, and regulatory compliance.

Regulatory Bodies and Guidelines

The International Energy Agency (IEA) has developed guidelines for the use of AI in the energy sector, focusing on areas such as energy management, grid optimization, and renewable energy. The U.S. Department of Energy (DOE) has also developed guidelines for the use of AI in the energy sector, emphasizing the importance of risk management and regulatory compliance.

IEA Guidelines in Renewable Energy

Consider an energy company that adopted the IEA guidelines while implementing AI systems for optimizing solar energy production. By adhering to these guidelines, the company ensured that its AI systems were compliant with industry best practices and capable of managing risk effectively. The AI system significantly improved the efficiency of solar panels, maximizing energy output and reducing costs. This success story highlights the importance of regulatory standards in promoting innovation and sustainability in the energy sector.

Ethical Considerations

Ethical guidelines for AI in energy emphasize the importance of transparency, accountability, and environmental sustainability. The International Renewable Energy Agency (IRENA) has developed a framework for the ethical use of AI in the energy sector, focusing on principles such as fairness, transparency, and accountability.

Ethical AI in Grid Optimization

Imagine a utility company implementing an AI system for grid optimization, guided by IRENA's ethical framework. The AI system was designed to be transparent and accountable, with clear communication of its operations and regular audits to ensure compliance. This approach not only improved the stability and efficiency of the energy grid but also enhanced public trust in the technology. The initiative demonstrated the positive impact of ethical considerations on environmental sustainability and public confidence.

Conclusion

The industrial regulation of AI involves a variety of measures tailored to address the unique challenges and opportunities presented by AI technologies within specific industries. By implementing these measures, industries can ensure that AI is developed and deployed in a manner that is ethical, safe, and beneficial to society.

Epilogue

As we conclude our exploration of Artificial Intelligence (AI) and its profound impact on society, it is clear that AI is not just a technological advancement but a transformative force reshaping our world. From its origins and applications to the ethical, economic, and environmental challenges it presents, AI's influence is far-reaching and multifaceted.

Throughout this book, we have delved into the complexities of AI, showcasing its' applications across industries and addressing the critical issues of misinformation, ethical concerns, trust and safety, job displacement, human rights, privacy, environmental impact, and regulation. Each chapter has provided insights into the opportunities and challenges that AI brings, emphasizing the need for thoughtful and responsible development and deployment.

As we move forward, it is essential to continue the dialogue on AI's role in society. The future of AI will be shaped by our collective efforts to harness its potential while mitigating its risks. By fostering collaboration among technologists, policymakers, and society at large, we can ensure that AI serves as a force for good, enhancing our lives and contributing to a more equitable and sustainable world.

Thank you for joining us on this journey. We hope this book has provided you with valuable insights and inspired you to engage with the ongoing conversation about AI and its impact on our society.

References

1. Manning, C. (2020). Artificial Intelligence Definitions. In *Stanford University*.

   https://hai.stanford.edu/sites/default/files/2020-09/AI-Definitions-HAI.pdf

2. Sheikh, H., Prins, C., & Schrijvers, E. (2023). Artificial Intelligence: Definition and Background. *Research for Policy*, 15–41. https://doi.org/10.1007/978-3-031-21448-6_2

3. Boden, M. A. (2018). 1. What is artificial intelligence? In *Very Short Introductions*. Oxford University Press. https://doi.org/10.1093/actrade/9780199602919.003.0001

4. Rubeis, G. (2024). Artificial Intelligence: In Search of a Definition. *The International Library of Ethics, Law and Technology*, 15–22. https://doi.org/10.1007/978-3-031-55744-6_2

5. Meier, J. (2024, November 3). The History of AI: A Journey from Ancient Myths to Modern Marvels | JD Meier. JD Meier. https://jdmeier.com/history-of-ai/

6. Engelbrecht, D. (2023). History of AI and Where We Are Today. Apress EBooks, 7–17. https://doi.org/10.1007/978-1-4842-8998-3_2

7. Jones, M. L. (2023). AI in History. The American Historical Review, 128(3), 1360–1367. https://doi.org/10.1093/ahr/rhad361

8. Sheikh, H., Prins, C., & Schrijvers, E. (2023). Artificial Intelligence: Definition and Background. Research for Policy, 15–41. https://doi.org/10.1007/978-3-031-21448-6_2

9. West, D., & Allen, J. (2018, April 24). How Artificial Intelligence Is Transforming the World. Brookings; The Brookings Institution.

https://www.brookings.edu/articles/how-artificial-intelligence-is-

transforming-the-world/

10. Artificial Intelligence in Society. (2024). OECD.

https://www.oecd.org/en/publications/artificial-intelligence-in-

society_eedfee77-en.html

11. Science in the age of AI | Royal Society. (2024). Royalsociety.org.

https://royalsociety.org/news-resources/projects/science-in-the-age-of-ai/

12. Rawas, S. (2024). AI: the future of humanity. Discover Artificial Intelligence,

4(1). https://doi.org/10.1007/s44163-024-00118-3

13. Crompton, H., & Burke, D. (2023). Artificial Intelligence in Higher education:

the State of the Field. *International Journal of Educational Technology in

Higher Education, 20*(1), 1–22. https://doi.org/10.1186/s41239-023-00392-8

14. Coursera. (2024, April 3). What is Artificial Intelligence? Definition, Uses, and

Types. Coursera. https://www.coursera.org/articles/what-is-artificial-

intelligence

15. Wikipedia. (2019, February 18). Artificial Intelligence. Wikipedia; Wikimedia

Foundation. https://en.wikipedia.org/wiki/Artificial_intelligence

16. Krishna, R. (2021, August). Exploring the Scope of Artificial Intelligence :The

Limitless Horizon. IABAC®. https://iabac.org/blog/exploring-the-scope-of-

artificial-intelligence

17. Terra, J. (2023, June 27). The Future of AI: Here's What You Need to Know in

2024. Caltech. https://pg-p.ctme.caltech.edu/blog/ai-ml/the-future-of-ai-a-

comprehensive-guide

18. Stryker, C., & Kavlakoglu, E. (2024, August 16). What is artificial intelligence

(AI)? IBM. https://www.ibm.com/topics/artificial-intelligence

19. Johnson, L., & Wang, M. (2019). Advances in supervised learning algorithms.

Journal of Machine Learning Research, 15(3), 123-145.

20. Gomes, M. A., & Meisen, T. (2023). A review on customer segmentation

methods for personalized customer targeting in e-commerce use cases.

Information Systems and E-Business Management, 21(21), 527–570. https://doi.org/10.1007/s10257-023-00640-4

21. Salminen, J., Mekhail Mustak, Muhammad Sufyan, & Jansen, B. J. (2023). How can algorithms help in segmenting users and customers? A systematic review and research agenda for algorithmic customer segmentation. Journal of Marketing Analytics. https://doi.org/10.1057/s41270-023-00235-5

22. Katyayan, A., Bokhare, A., Gupta, R., Kumari, S., & Pardeshi, T. (2022). Analysis of Unsupervised Machine Learning Techniques for Customer Segmentation. Machine Learning and Autonomous Systems, 483–498. https://doi.org/10.1007/978-981-16-7996-4_35

23. Saxena, A., Agarwal, A., Binay Kumar Pandey, & Pandey, D. (2024). Examination of the Criticality of Customer Segmentation Using Unsupervised Learning Methods. Circular Economy and Sustainability. https://doi.org/10.1007/s43615-023-00336-4

24. Zhao, Y., Shao, Z., Zhao, W., Han, J., Zheng, Q., & Ran, J. (2023). Combining unsupervised and supervised classification for customer value discovery in the telecom industry: a deep learning approach. Computing, 105(7), 1395–1417. https://doi.org/10.1007/s00607-023-01150-4

25. Adams, M. A. (2000). Reinforcement Theory and Behavior Analysis. Psycnet.apa.org. https://psycnet.apa.org/fulltext/2014-55592-001.html

26. Lysakowski, R. S., & Walberg, H. J. (1981). Classroom Reinforcement and Learning: A Quantitative Synthesis. The Journal of Educational Research, 75(2), 69–77. https://www.jstor.org/stable/27539870

27. Papers with Code - Reinforcement Learning (RL). (n.d.). Paperswithcode.com. https://paperswithcode.com/task/reinforcement-learning-1

28. Fahad Mon, B., Wasfi, A., Hayajneh, M., Slim, A., & Abu Ali, N. (2023). Reinforcement Learning in Education: A Literature Review. Informatics, 10(3), 74. https://doi.org/10.3390/informatics10030074

29. Li, Y. (2017). Deep Reinforcement Learning: An Overview. ArXiv.org. https://arxiv.org/abs/1701.07274.

30. Sawicki, J., Ganzha, M., & Paprzycki, M. (2023). The state of the art of Natural

31. Language Processing - a systematic automated review of NLP literature using NLP techniques. Data Intelligence, 1–47. https://doi.org/10.1162/dint_a_00213

32. Khurana, D., Koli, A., Khatter, K., & Singh, S. (2022). Natural Language processing: State of the art, Current Trends and Challenges. Multimedia Tools and Applications, 82(3), 3713–3744. https://doi.org/10.1007/s11042-022-13428-4

33. Siddharth, L., Blessing, L., & Luo, J. (2022). Natural language processing in-and-for design research. Design Science, 8. https://doi.org/10.1017/dsj.2022.16

34. Sheetal Kusal, Patil, S., Jyoti Choudrie, Kotecha, K., Vora, D., & Pappas, I. O. (2023). A systematic review of applications of natural language processing and future challenges with special emphasis in text-based emotion detection. Artificial Intelligence Review, 56(12), 15129–15215. https://doi.org/10.1007/s10462-023-10509-0

35. Daley, S. (2019). Industry 4.0: Ten AI innovators in manufacturing tech. Built In. https://builtin.com/artificial-intelligence/ai-manufacturing-robots-automation

36. Khanna, A. (2024, August 12). Council Post: How AI Is Reshaping Five Manufacturing Industries. Forbes. https://www.forbes.com/councils/forbestechcouncil/2024/01/17/how-ai-is-reshaping-five-manufacturing-industries/

37. Web, S. (2024, October 21). AI In Manufacturing: Top Use Cases And Examples. Alcax Blog | Software, Mobile App Development Company India. https://www.alcax.com/blog/ai-in-manufacturing/

38. Patel, B. J. (2024, October 29). AI-Powered Robotic Surgery: Pushing The Boundaries Of Minimally Invasive Procedures. Forbes. https://www.forbes.com/councils/forbestechcouncil/2024/10/29/ai-

powered-robotic-surgery-pushing-the-boundaries-of-minimally-invasive-

procedures/

39. Godwin Ugwua. (2023, August 13). AI and Healthcare Robotics: Revolutionizing Surgical Procedures - Thideai. Thideai. https://thideai.com/ai-and-healthcare-robotics-revolutionizing-surgical-procedures/

40. RAIA. (2024). Robotic Surgery: How AI is Making Surgical Procedures Safer and More Precise - RAIA A.I. Raiabot.com. https://raiabot.com/blog/Robotic_Surgery_How_AI_is_Making_Surgical_Procedures_Safer_and_More_Precise.html

41. Han, H., Li, R., Fu, D., Zhou, H., Zhan, Z., Wu, Y., & Meng, B. (2024). Revolutionizing spinal interventions: a systematic review of artificial intelligence technology applications in contemporary surgery. BMC Surgery, 24(1). https://doi.org/10.1186/s12893-024-02646-2

42. Dam, S. (2023, October 11). AZoAi. AZoAi. https://www.azoai.com/article/Ai-in-Medical-Robotics-Transforming-Surgery-and-Healthcare.aspx

43. Efe, O. (2024, November 1). BEYOND THE STEERING WHEEL: THE RISE OF SELF-DRIVING CARS [Review of BEYOND THE STEERING WHEEL: THE RISE OF SELF-DRIVING CARS]. Amazon. https://www.amazon.com/BEYOND-STEERING-WHEEL-RISE-SELF-DRIVING-ebook/dp/B0DM3S2YDW/ref=sr_1_1?crid=3R0A4NILPCL1A&dib=eyJ2IjoiMSJ9._b9YstoYehfEIoxLz9Aaxw.uTr165QmvPe47nTsRG3girQZ8SQAl4F--4q60Gi2bXo&dib_tag=se&keywords=otega+efe&qid=1731224192&s=books&sprefix=otega+efe%2Cstripbooks-intl-ship%2C461&sr=1-1

44. Adjabi, I., Ouahabi, A., Benzaoui, A., & Taleb-Ahmed, A. (2020). Past, Present, and Future of Face Recognition: A Review. Electronics, 9(8), 1188. https://doi.org/10.3390/electronics9081188

45. Gazetteterrymurphy. (2024, September 4). New AI tool can diagnose cancer, guide treatment, predict patient survival. Harvard Gazette; Harvard Gazette. https://news.harvard.edu/gazette/story/2024/09/new-ai-tool-can-diagnose-cancer-guide-treatment-predict-patient-survival/

46. Rajpurkar, P., & Lungren, M. (2023). The Current and Future State of AI Interpretation of Medical Images (J. Drazen & I. Kohane, Eds.) [Review of The Current and Future State of AI Interpretation of Medical Images]. The New England Journal of Medicine. https://www.nejm.org/doi/pdf/10.1056/NEJMra2301725?articleTools=true

47. Singh, G., Anushka Kamalja, Patil, R., Ashutosh Karwa, Tripathi, A., & Chavan, P. (2024). A comprehensive assessment of artificial intelligence applications for cancer diagnosis. Artificial Intelligence Review, 57(7). https://doi.org/10.1007/s10462-024-10783-6

48. Artificial intelligence models to analyze cancer images take shortcuts that introduce bias. (2021). ScienceDaily. https://www.sciencedaily.com/releases/2021/07/210722113043.htm#google_vignette

49. Ozaki, Y., Broughton, P., Abdullahi, H., Homayoun Valafar, & Blenda, A. V. (2024). Integrating Omics Data and AI for Cancer Diagnosis and Prognosis. Cancers, 16(13), 2448–2448. https://doi.org/10.3390/cancers16132448

50. Silva, Santos, André Ferreira Leite, Ruffeil, C., Paulo, Cristine Miron Stefani, & Santos. (2023). The use of artificial intelligence tools in cancer detection compared to the traditional diagnostic imaging methods: An overview of the systematic reviews. PLOS ONE, 18(10), e0292063–e0292063. https://doi.org/10.1371/journal.pone.0292063

51. Zhang, C., Xu, J., Tang, R., Yang, J., Wang, Q., Lei, Y., & Shi, S. (2023). Novel research and future prospects of artificial intelligence in cancer diagnosis and treatment. Journal of Hematology & Oncology, 16(1). https://doi.org/10.1186/s13045-023-01514-5

52. Ghebrehiwet, I., Zaki, N., Rafat Damseh, & Mohd Saberi Mohamad. (2024). Revolutionizing personalized medicine with generative AI: a systematic review. Artificial Intelligence Review, 57(5). https://doi.org/10.1007/s10462-024-10768-5

53. Smart AI modelling for precision medicine. (2024). Nature.com; Nature. https://www.nature.com/articles/d42473-024-00251-8

54. Schork, N. J. (2019). Artificial Intelligence and Personalized Medicine. Precision Medicine in Cancer Therapy, 178, 265–283. https://doi.org/10.1007/978-3-030-16391-4_11

55. Alowais, S., Alghamdi, S., Alsuhebany, N., & Alqahtani, T. (2023, September 22). Revolutionizing healthcare: the role of artificial intelligence in clinical practice [Review of Revolutionizing healthcare: the role of artificial intelligence in clinical practice].

https://bmcmededuc.biomedcentral.com/articles/10.1186/s12909-023-04698-z

56. Sood, P., Sharma, C., Shivinder Nijjer, & Sumit Sakhuja. (2023). Review the role of artificial intelligence in detecting and preventing financial fraud using natural language processing. International Journal of Systems Assurance Engineering and Management, 14. https://doi.org/10.1007/s13198-023-02043-7

57. Bao, Y., Hilary, G., & Ke, B. (2020, November 24). Artificial Intelligence and Fraud Detection. Papers.ssrn.com. https://papers.ssrn.com/sol3/papers.cfm?abstract_id=3738618

58. Bao, Y., Hilary, G., & Ke, B. (2022). Artificial Intelligence and Fraud Detection. Innovative Technology at the Interface of Finance and Operations, 11, 223–247. https://doi.org/10.1007/978-3-030-75729-8_8

59. Bao, Y., Hilary, G., & Ke, B. (2020, November 24). *Artificial Intelligence and Fraud Detection*. Papers.ssrn.com. https://papers.ssrn.com/sol3/papers.cfm?abstract_id=3738618

60. Ligon, M. (2024, August 12). Council Post: How Artificial Intelligence Is Revolutionizing Stock Investing. Forbes. https://www.forbes.com/councils/forbesbusinesscouncil/2023/07/17/how-artificial-intelligence-is-revolutionizing-stock-investing/

61. Team DigitalDefynd. (2024, August 17). 10 Ways AI Is Being Used in Algorithmic Trading [2024]. DigitalDefynd. https://digitaldefynd.com/IQ/ai-in-algorithmic-trading/

62. CP. (2024, July 26). Algorithmic Trading and AI: Innovations in Investment Strategies - AI Consultancy | Create Progress. AI Consultancy | Create Progress. https://createprogress.ai/algorithmic-trading-and-ai-innovations-in-investment-strategies/

63. IABAC®. (2023, September 29). The Invisible Hand: AI in Financial Markets and Algorithmic Trading. IABAC®. https://iabac.org/blog/the-invisible-hand-ai-in-financial-markets-and-algorithmic-trading

64. K. Bayly-Castaneda, M-S. Ramirez-Montoya, & A. Morita-Alexander. (2024). Crafting personalized learning paths with AI for lifelong learning: a systematic literature review. Frontiers in Education, 9. https://doi.org/10.3389/feduc.2024.1424386

65. Laak, K.-J. (2024). AI and personalized learning: bridging the gap with modern educational goals. Arxiv.org. https://arxiv.org/html/2404.02798v1

66. Kam Cheong Li, & Billy Tak-Ming Wong. (2023). Artificial intelligence in personalised learning: a bibliometric analysis. Interactive Technology and Smart Education, 20(3). https://doi.org/10.1108/itse-01-2023-0007

67. Shemshack, A., & Spector, J. M. (2020). A systematic literature review of personalized learning terms. Smart Learning Environments, 7(1). https://doi.org/10.1186/s40561-020-00140-9

68. K. Bayly-Castanda, M-S. Ramirez-Montoya, & A. Morita-Alexander. (2024). Crafting personalized learning paths with AI for lifelong learning: a systematic literature review. Frontiers in Education, 9. https://doi.org/10.3389/feduc.2024.1424386

69. Dai, R., Krehl, M., & Rawolle, S. (2024). The roles of AI and educational leaders in AI-assisted administrative decision-making: a proposed framework for symbiotic collaboration. The Australian Educational Researcher. https://doi.org/10.1007/s13384-024-00771-8

70. Ahmad, S. F., Alam, M. M., Rahmat, Mohd. K., Mubarik, M. S., & Hyder, S. I. (2022). Academic and Administrative Role of Artificial Intelligence in Education. Sustainability, 14(3), 1101. https://doi.org/10.3390/su14031101

71. Melo, D. N. (2024, October 25). The Future Of Higher Education: Integrating AI-Powered Learning Platforms For Enhanced Academic Achievement. ELearning Industry. https://elearningindustry.com/the-future-of-higher-education-integrating-ai-powered-learning-platforms-for-enhanced-academic-achievement

72. Ahmad, S. F., Alam, M. M., Rahmat, Mohd. K., Mubarik, M. S., & Hyder, S. I. (2022). Academic and Administrative Role of Artificial Intelligence in Education. Sustainability, 14(3), 1101. https://doi.org/10.3390/su14031101

73. Zhang, Q., Lu, J., & Jin, Y. (2020). Artificial intelligence in recommender systems. Complex & Intelligent Systems, 7(1), 439–457. https://doi.org/10.1007/s40747-020-00212-w

74. Wu, L., He, X., Wang, X., Zhang, K., & Wang, M. (2021). A Survey on Neural Recommendation: From Collaborative Filtering to Content and Context Enriched Recommendation. ArXiv.org. https://arxiv.org/abs/2104.13030v1

75. Sourcely | HelpFromAI | Research-AI. (n.d.). Sourcely. https://www.sourcely.net/

76. Best AI Tools To Find References For Academic Research – Academia Insider. (2024, January 3). https://academiainsider.com/best-ai-tools-to-find-references-for-academic-research/

77. Consensus. (2024). Consensus - Evidence-Based Answers, Faster. Consensus - Evidence-Based Answers, Faster. https://consensus.app/

78. Wu, L., He, X., Wang, X., Zhang, K., & Wang, M. (2022). A Survey on Accuracy-oriented Neural Recommendation: From Collaborative Filtering to Information-rich Recommendation. IEEE Transactions on Knowledge and Data Engineering, 1–1. https://doi.org/10.1109/tkde.2022.3145690

79. Miller, R. (2024, December 15). What exactly is an AI agent? | TechCrunch. TechCrunch. https://techcrunch.com/2024/12/15/what-exactly-is-an-ai-agent/?guccounter=1

80. What are AI Agents? Definition, Examples, and Applications | Shakudo. (2024). Shakudo.io. https://www.shakudo.io/blog/what-are-ai-agents

81. Harsha, A. (2024, December 18). The power of AI agents in tearing down fraud (Reader Forum). RCR Wireless News. https://www.rcrwireless.com/20241218/uncategorized/ai-agents-fraud

82. The Conversation. (2024, December 19). What is an AI agent? A computer scientist explains the next wave of artificial intelligence tools. Stuff South Africa. https://stuff.co.za/2024/12/19/what-is-an-ai-agent-a-computer-scientist/

83. What Are AI Agents? | IBM. (2024, July 3). Www.ibm.com. https://www.ibm.com/think/topics/ai-agents

84. Salesforce. (2022). Salesforce. https://www.salesforce.com/agentforce/build-ai-agent/

85. Agents, A. (2024, November 27). AI Plain And Simple. AI Plain and Simple. https://www.aiplainandsimple.com/articles/ai-agents-what-they-are-and-what-they-mean-for-our-future

86. Gupta, D. (2024, December 17). The Rise of Autonomous AI Agents: A Comprehensive Guide to Their Architecture, Applications, and Impact. Security Boulevard. https://securityboulevard.com/2024/12/the-rise-of-autonomous-ai-agents-a-comprehensive-guide-to-their-architecture-applications-and-impact/

87. Visier Announces New Workforce AI Platform That Allows HRIT Leaders and Peopletech Product Teams to Launch AI-based Agents. (2024, December 18). T-Net British Columbia. https://www.bctechnology.com/news/2024/12/18/Visier-Announces-New-Workforce-AI-Platform-That-Allows-HRIT-Leaders-and-Peopletech-Product-Teams-to-Launch-AI-based-Agents.cfm

88. Saurabh Tiwary. (2024, December 13). Bringing AI Agents to Enterprises with Google Agentspace. Google Cloud Blog; Google Cloud. https://cloud.google.com/blog/products/ai-machine-learning/bringing-ai-agents-to-enterprises-with-google-agentspace/

89. Bontridder, N., & Poullet, Y. (2021). The Role of Artificial Intelligence in Disinformation. Data & Policy, 3(E32). https://doi.org/10.1017/dap.2021.20

90. Annie Laurie Benzie, & Reza Montasari. (2022). Artificial Intelligence and the Spread of Mis- and Disinformation. Springer EBooks, 1–18. https://doi.org/10.1007/978-3-031-06709-9_1

91. Zhou, J., Zhang, Y., Luo, Q., Parker, A. G., & Choudhury, M. D. (2023). Synthetic Lies: Understanding AI-Generated Misinformation and Evaluating Algorithmic and Human Solutions. Proceedings of the 2023 CHI Conference on Human Factors in Computing Systems. https://doi.org/10.1145/3544548.3581318

92. Joshi, A., Ranade, P., & Finin, T. (2021, June 7). Study shows AI-generated fake reports fool experts. The Conversation. https://theconversation.com/study-shows-ai-generated-fake-reports-fool-experts-160909

93. Navigating the AI-Generated Information Landscape: Finding the Truth Amid Misinformation. (n.d.). Www.lexisnexis.com. https://www.lexisnexis.com/community/insights/professional/b/industry-insights/posts/misinformation-in-artificial-intelligence-

94. Alanazi, S., & Asif, S. (2024). Exploring deepfake technology: creation, consequences and countermeasures. Human-Intelligent Systems Integration. https://doi.org/10.1007/s42454-024-00054-8

95. Ángel Fernández Gambín, Anis Yazidi, Vasilakos, A., Haugerud, H., & Youcef Djenouri. (2024). Deepfakes: current and future trends. Artificial Intelligence Review, 57(3). https://doi.org/10.1007/s10462-023-10679-x

96. Gamage, D. (n.d.). The Emergence of Deepfakes and its Societal Implications: A Systematic Review. Www.academia.edu.

https://www.academia.edu/74762342/The_Emergence_of_Deepfakes_and_i
ts_Societal_Implications_A_Systematic_Review

97. Dagar, D., & Vishwakarma, D. K. (2022). A literature review and perspectives in deepfakes: Generation, detection, and applications. International Journal of Multimedia Information Retrieval, 11. https://doi.org/10.1007/s13735-022-00241-w

98. Lundberg, E., & Mozelius, P. (2024). The potential effects of deepfakes on news media and entertainment. AI & SOCIETY. https://doi.org/10.1007/s00146-024-02072-1

99. SM Zobaed, Fazle Rabby, Hossain, I., Hossain, E., Hasan, S., Asif Mahbub Karim, & Khan Md. Hasib. (2021). DeepFakes: Detecting Forged and Synthetic Media Content Using Machine Learning. Advanced Sciences and Technologies for Security Applications, 177–201. https://doi.org/10.1007/978-3-030-88040-8_7

100. Nguyen, T., Nguyen, C., Nguyen, D., Duc, T., Nguyen, & Nahavandi, S. (n.d.). Deep Learning for Deepfakes Creation and Detection. https://arxiv.org/pdf/1909.11573

101. Li, Y., Sun, P., Qi, H., & Lyu, S. (2022). Toward the Creation and Obstruction of DeepFakes. Advances in Computer Vision and Pattern Recognition, 71–96. https://doi.org/10.1007/978-3-030-87664-7_4

102. Purdue Engineering. (2019, April 17). Detecting Deep Fakes Video through Media Forensics. YouTube. https://www.youtube.com/watch?v=aWKBWoDtR8k

103. DW Shift. (2019). How to detect deepfakes | Deepfakes explained. In YouTube. https://www.youtube.com/watch?v=BuufkPTFt0E

104. Adee, S. (2020, April 29). What Are Deepfakes and How Are They Created? IEEE Spectrum. https://spectrum.ieee.org/what-is-deepfake

105. Harris, K. R. (2024). Synthetic Media Detection, the Wheel, and the Burden of Proof. Philosophy & Technology, 37(4). https://doi.org/10.1007/s13347-024-00821-0

106. Alanazi, S., & Asif, S. (2024). Exploring deepfake technology: creation, consequences and countermeasures. Human-Intelligent Systems Integration. https://doi.org/10.1007/s42454-024-00054-8

107. Masood, M., Nawaz, M., Malik, K. M., Javed, A., Irtaza, A., & Malik, H. (2022). Deepfakes Generation and Detection: State-of-the-art, Open Challenges, Countermeasures, and Way Forward. Applied Intelligence, 53(4). https://doi.org/10.1007/s10489-022-03766-z

108. Qureshi, S. M., Saeed, A., Almotiri, S. H., Ahmad, F., & Al Ghamdi, M. A. (2024). Deepfake forensics: a survey of digital forensic methods for multimodal deepfake identification on social media. PeerJ Computer Science, 10, e2037. https://doi.org/10.7717/peerj-cs.2037

109. Vishal Kumar Sharma, Garg, R., & Caudron, Q. (2024). A systematic literature review on deepfake detection techniques. Multimedia Tools and Applications. https://doi.org/10.1007/s11042-024-19906-1

110. Integrity, M. D. E. (2024, January 10). Deepfakes and Their Impact on Society. Mea: Digital Integrity. https://www.mea-integrity.com/deepfakes-and-their-impact-on-society/

111. Jones, N. (2023). How to stop AI deepfakes from sinking society — and science. Nature, 621(7980), 676–679. https://doi.org/10.1038/d41586-023-02990-y

112. HELMUS, T. (2022, July). Artificial Intelligence, Deepfakes, and Disinformation [Review of Artificial Intelligence, Deepfakes, and Disinformation]. https://www.rand.org/pubs/perspectives/PEA1043-1.html

113. Trotta, A., Ziosi, M., & Lomonaco, V. (2023). The future of ethics in AI: Challenges and opportunities. AI & SOCIETY, 38, 439–441. https://doi.org/10.1007/s00146-023-01644-x

114. Ethical Challenges of AI Applications. (n.d.). https://aiindex.stanford.edu/wp-content/uploads/2021/03/2021-AI-Index-Report-_Chapter-5.pdf

115. Pavan, Sushma Pamidi, & Kumar, S. (2024). Unraveling the Ethical Conundrum of Artificial Intelligence: A Synthesis of Literature and Case Studies. Augmented Human Research, 10(1). https://doi.org/10.1007/s41133-024-00077-5

116. Pavan, Sushma Pamidi, & Kumar, S. (2024). Unraveling the Ethical Conundrum of Artificial Intelligence: A Synthesis of Literature and Case Studies. Augmented Human Research, 10(1). https://doi.org/10.1007/s41133-024-00077-5

117. Svetlova, E. (2022). AI ethics and systemic risks in finance. AI and Ethics, 2. https://doi.org/10.1007/s43681-021-00129-1

118. Klein, A. (2020, July 10). Reducing bias in AI-based financial services. Brookings. https://www.brookings.edu/articles/reducing-bias-in-ai-based-financial-services/

119. Jarrell, S., McGrath, S., Edwards, S., & Nagarajan, J. (2023, March 17). How to mitigate AI discrimination and bias in financial services [Review of How to mitigate AI discrimination and bias in financial services]. EY. https://www.ey.com/en_us/insights/forensic-integrity-services/ai-discrimination-and-bias-in-financial-services

120. Chopra, N. P. (2024). Ethical Implications of AI in Financial Services : Bias, Transparency, and Accountability. International Journal of Scientific Research in Computer Science Engineering and Information Technology, 10(5), 682–690. https://doi.org/10.32628/cseit241051059

121. Bahoo, S., Cucculelli, M., Goga, X., & Mondolo, J. (2024). Artificial intelligence in Finance: a comprehensive review through bibliometric and content analysis. Artificial Intelligence in Finance: A Comprehensive Review through Bibliometric and Content Analysis, 4(2). https://doi.org/10.1007/s43546-023-00618-x

122. Cross, J. L., Choma, M. A., & Onofrey, J. A. (2024). Bias in medical AI: Implications for clinical decision-making. PLOS Digital Health, 3(11), e0000651. https://doi.org/10.1371/journal.pdig.0000651

123. Chen, F., Wang, L., Hong, J., Jiang, J., & Zhou, L. (2024). Unmasking bias in artificial intelligence: a systematic review of bias detection and mitigation strategies in electronic health record-based models. Journal of the American

Medical   Informatics   Association,   31(5),   1172–1183.

https://doi.org/10.1093/jamia/ocae060

124. Collins, B. X., Bélisle-Pipon, J.-C., Evans, B. J., Ferryman, K., Jiang, X., Nebeker,

C., Novak, L., Roberts, K., Were, M., Yin, Z., Ravitsky, V., Coco, J., Hendricks-

Sturrup, R., Williams, I., Clayton, E. W., & Malin, B. A. (2024). Addressing ethical

issues in healthcare artificial intelligence using a lifecycle-informed process.

JAMIA Open, 7(4). https://doi.org/10.1093/jamiaopen/ooae108

125. Karimian, G., Petelos, E., & Evers, S. M. A. A. (2022). The ethical issues of the

application of artificial intelligence in healthcare: a systematic scoping review.

AI and Ethics, 2(1). https://doi.org/10.1007/s43681-021-00131-7

126. Mohammad Amini, M., Jesus, M., Fanaei Sheikholeslami, D., Alves, P.,

Hassanzadeh Benam, A., & Hariri, F. (2023). Artificial Intelligence Ethics and

Challenges in Healthcare Applications: A Comprehensive Review in the Context

of the European GDPR Mandate. Machine Learning and Knowledge Extraction,

5(3), 1023–1035. https://doi.org/10.3390/make5030053

127. Akgun, S., & Greenhow, C. (2021). Artificial intelligence in education:

Addressing ethical challenges in k-12 settings. AI and Ethics, 2(3), 431–440.

https://doi.org/10.1007/s43681-021-00096-7

128. Dieterle, E., Dede, C., & Walker, M. (2022). The cyclical ethical effects of using

artificial   intelligence   in   education.   AI   &   SOCIETY,   39.

https://doi.org/10.1007/s00146-022-01497-w

129. Holmes, W., Porayska-Pomsta, K., Holstein, K., Sutherland, E., Baker, T., Shum,

S. B., Santos, O. C., Rodrigo, M. T., Cukurova, M., Bittencourt, I. I., & Koedinger,

K. R. (2021). Ethics of AI in Education: Towards a Community-Wide Framework. International Journal of Artificial Intelligence in Education, 32(1), 504–526. https://doi.org/10.1007/s40593-021-00239-1

130. Nguyen, A., Ngo, H. N., Hong, Y., Dang, B., & Nguyen, B.-P. T. (2022). Ethical principles for artificial intelligence in education. Education and Information Technologies, 28(28). https://link.springer.com/article/10.1007/s10639-022-11316-w

131. Gordon, J.-S. (2021). AI and law: ethical, legal, and socio-political Implications. AI & SOCIETY, 36. https://doi.org/10.1007/s00146-021-01194-0

132. Henz, P. (2021). Ethical and legal responsibility for Artificial Intelligence. Discover Artificial Intelligence, 1(1). https://doi.org/10.1007/s44163-021-00002-4

133. Barabas, C. (2020). Beyond Bias. The Oxford Handbook of Ethics of AI, 736–753. https://doi.org/10.1093/oxfordhb/9780190067397.013.47

134. Alvarez, J. M., Alejandra Bringas Colmenarejo, Alaa Elobaid, Fabbrizzi, S., Fahimi, M., Ferrara, A., Ghodsi, S., Mougan, C., Papageorgiou, I., Reyero, P., Russo, M., Scott, K. M., State, L., Zhao, X., & Ruggieri, S. (2024). Policy advice and best practices on bias and fairness in AI. Ethics and Information Technology, 26(2). https://doi.org/10.1007/s10676-024-09746-w

135. Almasoud, A. S., & Jamiu Adekunle Idowu. (2024). Algorithmic fairness in predictive policing. AI and Ethics. https://doi.org/10.1007/s43681-024-00541-3

136. Malek, Md. A. (2022). Criminal courts' artificial intelligence: the way it reinforces bias and discrimination. AI and Ethics, 2. https://doi.org/10.1007/s43681-022-00137-9

137. Heaven, W. D. (2020, July 17). Predictive policing algorithms are racist. They need to be dismantled. MIT Technology Review. https://www.technologyreview.com/2020/07/17/1005396/predictive-policing-algorithms-racist-dismantled-machine-learning-bias-criminal-justice/

138. Barabas, C. (2020). Beyond Bias. The Oxford Handbook of Ethics of AI, 736–753. https://doi.org/10.1093/oxfordhb/9780190067397.013.47

139. Alvarez, J. M., Alejandra Bringas Colmenarejo, Alaa Elobaid, Fabbrizzi, S., Fahimi, M., Ferrara, A., Ghodsi, S., Mougan, C., Papageorgiou, I., Reyero, P., Russo, M., Scott, K. M., State, L., Zhao, X., & Ruggieri, S. (2024). Policy advice and best practices on bias and fairness in AI. Ethics and Information Technology, 26(2). https://doi.org/10.1007/s10676-024-09746-w

140. Trattner, C., Jannach, D., Motta, E., Costera Meijer, I., Diakopoulos, N., Elahi, M., Opdahl, A. L., Tessem, B., Borch, N., Fjeld, M., Øvrelid, L., De Smedt, K., & Moe, H. (2021). Responsible media technology and AI: challenges and research directions. AI and Ethics, 2, 585–594. https://doi.org/10.1007/s43681-021-00126-4

141. Chen, C., & Chekam, G. A. (2021). Algorithms and Media Ethics in the AI Age. Handbook of Global Media Ethics, 301–328. https://doi.org/10.1007/978-3-319-32103-5_16

142. Ouchchy, L., Coin, A., & Dubljević, V. (2020). AI in the headlines: the portrayal of the ethical issues of artificial intelligence in the media. AI & SOCIETY, 35(35). https://doi.org/10.1007/s00146-020-00965-5

143. Artificial Intelligence: Examples of Ethical Dilemmas | UNESCO. (2023, April 21). Www.unesco.org; UNESCO. https://www.unesco.org/en/artificial-intelligence/recommendation-ethics/cases

144. Aakriti Bajracharya, Uddhav Khakurel, Harvey, B., & Rawat, D. B. (2022). Recent Advances in Algorithmic Biases and Fairness in Financial Services: A Survey. 809–822. https://doi.org/10.1007/978-3-031-18461-1_53

145. Blackman, R., & Ammanath, B. (2022, June 20). Building Transparency into AI Projects. Harvard Business Review. https://hbr.org/2022/06/building-transparency-into-ai-projects

146. Thiruma Valavan A. (2023). AI Ethics and Bias: Exploratory study on the ethical considerations and potential biases in ai and data-driven decision-making in banking, with a focus on fairness, transparency, and accountability. World Journal of Advanced Research and Reviews, 20(2), 197–206. https://doi.org/10.30574/wjarr.2023.20.2.2245

147. Kosinski, M. (2024, October 29). Black box AI. Ibm.com. https://www.ibm.com/think/topics/black-box-ai

148. What Is Black Box AI? (n.d.). Built In. https://builtin.com/articles/black-box-ai

149. Blouin, L. (2023, March 6). AI's mysterious "black box" problem, explained. University of Michigan-Dearborn. https://umdearborn.edu/news/ais-mysterious-black-box-problem-explained

150. Keita, Z. (2023, May 10). Explainable AI - Understanding and Trusting Machine Learning Models. Datacamp.com; DataCamp. https://www.datacamp.com/tutorial/explainable-ai-understanding-and-trusting-machine-learning-models

151. IBM. (2024). What is explainable AI? | IBM. IBM. https://www.ibm.com/topics/explainable-ai

152. Jagati, S. (2023, May 5). AI's black box problem: Challenges and solutions for a transparent future. Cointelegraph. https://cointelegraph.com/news/ai-s-black-box-problem-challenges-and-solutions-for-a-transparent-future

153. ScaDS_PubRel. (2023, July 19). Cracking the Code: The Black Box Problem of AI. ScaDS.AI. https://scads.ai/cracking-the-code-the-black-box-problem-of-ai/

154. Blouin, L. (2023, March 6). AI's mysterious "black box" problem, explained. University of Michigan-Dearborn. https://umdearborn.edu/news/ais-mysterious-black-box-problem-explained

155. IBM. (2015, October 1). Building trust in AI requires a strategic approach | Building successful AI that's grounded in trust and transparency. IBM. https://www.ibm.com/resources/guides/predict/trustworthy-ai/build-trust/

156. Kovari, A. (2024). AI for Decision Support: Balancing Accuracy, Transparency, and Trust Across Sectors. Information, 15(11), 725–725. https://doi.org/10.3390/info15110725

157. Lukyanenko, R., Maass, W., & Storey, V. C. (2022). Trust in artificial intelligence: From a Foundational Trust Framework to emerging research

opportunities. Electronic Markets, 32. https://doi.org/10.1007/s12525-022-00605-4

158. Building Trust in AI: 3 Key Principles for Responsible AI Development. (2024). The Silicon Review. https://thesiliconreview.com/2024/10/building-trust-in-ai-3-key-principles-for-responsible-ai-development

159. Building Trust in Automated Decision-Making – AI Ethics and Leadership. (2024, November 8). CIO Look. https://ciolook.com/building-trust-in-automated-decision-making-ai-ethics-and-leadership/

160. Intellias. (2024, July 16). *AI Decision Making: What Is It, Benefits & Examples.* Intellias; Intellias. https://intellias.com/ai-decision-making/

161. Pillai, V. (2024). Enhancing Transparency and Understanding in AI Decision-Making Processes. https://www.irejournals.com/formatedpaper/1706039.pdf

162. Intellias. (2024, July 16). AI Decision Making: What Is It, Benefits & Examples. Intellias; Intellias. https://intellias.com/ai-decision-making/

163. Nguyen, T. H., Saghir, A., Tran, K. D., Nguyen, D. H., Luong, N. A., & Tran, K. P. (2024). Safety and Reliability of Artificial Intelligence Systems. Springer Series in Reliability Engineering, 185–199. https://doi.org/10.1007/978-3-031-71495-5_9

164. Establishing and Evaluating Trustworthy AI: Overview and Research Challenges. (2020). Arxiv.org. https://arxiv.org/html/2411.09973v1

165. Herrera, F. (2023). Toward Responsible Artificial Intelligence Systems: Safety and Trustworthiness. Lecture Notes in Computer Science, 7–11. https://doi.org/10.1007/978-3-031-49252-5_2

166. vzhuk. (2023, July 28). AI Reliability: Building Safe and Robust Autonomous Systems. Stanford Online; Stanford University. https://online.stanford.edu/ai-reliability-building-safe-and-robust-autonomous-systems

167. AI Taking Over Jobs: Real-World Examples & Future Outlook. (2023, December 4). https://www.aigantic.com/ai-jobs/ai-employment-trends/ai-taking-over-jobs/

168. Shine, I., & Whiting, K. (2023, May 4). The jobs most likely to be lost and created because of AI. World Economic Forum. https://www.weforum.org/stories/2023/05/jobs-lost-created-ai-gpt/

169. Georgieff, A., & Hyee, R. (2022). Artificial Intelligence and Employment: New Cross-Country Evidence. Frontiers in Artificial Intelligence, 5(832736). https://doi.org/10.3389/frai.2022.832736

170. Sheffi, Y. (2024). Technology is not enough: Potential job displacement in an AI-driven future. Journal of Supply Chain Management, Logistics and Procurement, 6(4). https://doi.org/10.69554/favx7910

171. Shine, I., & Whiting, K. (2023, May 4). The jobs most likely to be lost and created because of AI. World Economic Forum. https://www.weforum.org/stories/2023/05/jobs-lost-created-ai-gpt/

172. Moradi, P., & Levy, K. (2020, July 9). The Future of Work in the Age of AI: Displacement or Risk-Shifting? Papers.ssrn.com. https://papers.ssrn.com/sol3/papers.cfm?abstract_id=3647367

173. Georgieff, A., & Hyee, R. (2022). Artificial Intelligence and Employment: New Cross-Country Evidence. Frontiers in Artificial Intelligence, 5(832736). https://doi.org/10.3389/frai.2022.832736

174. Holzer, H. (2022, January 19). Understanding the Impact of Automation on workers, jobs, and Wages. Brookings. https://www.brookings.edu/articles/understanding-the-impact-of-automation-on-workers-jobs-and-wages/

175. Kreps, D., & Fletcher, G. (2017, September 12). Banking sector will be ground zero for job losses from AI and robotics. The Conversation. https://theconversation.com/banking-sector-will-be-ground-zero-for-job-losses-from-ai-and-robotics-83731

176. AI is in banking is the talent ready? (2024). Randstad.co.uk. https://www.randstad.co.uk/career-advice/career-guidance/ai-in-banking-is-talent-ready/

177. Fares, O. H., Butt, I., & Lee, S. H. M. (2022). Utilization of artificial intelligence in the banking sector: a systematic literature review. Journal of Financial Services Marketing, 28. springer. https://doi.org/10.1057/s41264-022-00176-7

178. Batiz-Lazo, B., Leonidas Efthymiou, & Davies, K. (2022). The Spread of Artificial Intelligence and Its Impact on Employment: Evidence from the Banking and Accounting Sectors. 135–155. https://doi.org/10.1007/978-3-031-07765-4_7

179. Fares, O. H., Butt, I., & Lee, S. H. M. (2022). Utilization of artificial intelligence in the banking sector: a systematic literature review. Journal of Financial Services Marketing, 28. springer. https://doi.org/10.1057/s41264-022-00176-7

180. Putman, D. M. (2024, January 17). AI has profound implications for the manufacturing industry. World Economic Forum. https://www.weforum.org/stories/2024/01/ai-implications-manufacturing-industry-workers/

181. Espina-Romero, L., Gutiérrez Hurtado, H., Ríos Parra, D., Vilchez Pirela, R. A., Talavera-Aguirre, R., & Ochoa-Díaz, A. (2024). Challenges and Opportunities in the Implementation of AI in Manufacturing: A Bibliometric Analysis. Sci, 6(4), 60. https://doi.org/10.3390/sci6040060

182. The AI revolution in transportation. (2024, November 15). ITS International. https://www.itsinternational.com/feature/ai-revolution-transportation

183. Conrad, R. (2024, March 15). AI in Logistics: Ethical Considerations and Industry Transformation. RTS Labs. https://rtslabs.com/ai-logistics-ethical-considerations-industry-transformation

184. Dhaliwal, A. (2024). Towards AI-Driven Transport and Logistics. Lecture Notes in Business Information Processing, 119–131. https://doi.org/10.1007/978-3-031-60003-6_8

185. Abduljabbar, R., Dia, H., Liyanage, S., & Bagloee, S. A. (2019). Applications of Artificial Intelligence in Transport: An Overview. Sustainability, 11(1), 189. https://doi.org/10.3390/su11010189

186. Chen, W., Men, Y., Fuster, N., Osorio, C., & Juan, A. A. (2024). Artificial Intelligence in Logistics Optimization with Sustainable Criteria: A Review. Sustainability, 16(21), 9145. https://doi.org/10.3390/su16219145

187. Ariyo, O. (2024, November 19). The role of AI in early disease detection: Improving healthcare for cancer, heart disease, and beyond | TheCable. TheCable. https://www.thecable.ng/the-role-of-ai-in-early-disease-detection-improving-healthcare-for-cancer-heart-disease-and-beyond/

188. Reddy, S. (2024, April 11). The Impact of AI on the Healthcare Workforce: Balancing Opportunities and Challenges. HIMSS. https://gkc.himss.org/resources/impact-ai-healthcare-workforce-balancing-opportunities-and-challenges

189. Gimbel, E. (2024). "A Lot More Teamwork": Healthcare Explores the Use of AI for Nursing Workflows. Technology Solutions That Drive Healthcare. https://healthtechmagazine.net/article/2024/11/lot-more-teamwork-healthcare-explores-use-ai-nursing-workflows

190. Daley, S. (2023, March 24). AI in healthcare: Uses, examples and benefits. Built In. https://builtin.com/artificial-intelligence/artificial-intelligence-healthcare

191. Wu Yili. (2023, January 6). Here's how artificial intelligence can benefit the retail sector. World Economic Forum. https://www.weforum.org/stories/2023/01/here-s-how-artificial-intelligence-benefit-retail-sector-davos2023/

192. Shopify. (2024, July 9). AI in Retail: Use Cases and Examples (2024) - Shopify. Shopify. https://www.shopify.com/retail/ai-in-retail

193. Thomas, M. (2023, March 30). 14 Examples Of AI In Retail & E-Commerce to Know | Built In. Builtin.com. https://builtin.com/artificial-intelligence/ai-retail-ecommerce-tech

194. Retail supply chains are front-row seats for the impact of AI on jobs. (n.d.). Retail Brew. https://www.retailbrew.com/stories/2023/03/28/retail-supply-chains-are-front-row-seats-for-the-impact-of-ai-on-jobs

195. Team DigitalDefynd. (2024, June 10). 14 Pros & Cons of Using AI in the Legal Profession [2024]. DigitalDefynd. https://digitaldefynd.com/IQ/ai-in-the-legal-profession-pros-cons/

196. Dubrova, D. (2022, September 10). How Is Artificial Intelligence (AI) Automating the Law Industry Over Time? Intellisoft. https://intellisoft.io/artificial-intelligence-ai-in-the-law-industry-key-trends-examples-usages/

197. Onit. (2024, November 22). AI beyond the hype: Understanding generative AI in the legal industry. Onit. https://www.onit.com/blog/understanding-generative-ai-legal-industry/

198. Villasenor, J. (2023, March 20). How AI will revolutionize the practice of law. Brookings. https://www.brookings.edu/articles/how-ai-will-revolutionize-the-practice-of-law/

199. University of San Diego. (2021). 43 Examples of Artificial Intelligence in Education. University of San Diego. https://onlinedegrees.sandiego.edu/artificial-intelligence-education/

200. Shamkina, V. (2023, April 19). AI In Education: 8 Use Cases, Real-Life Examples, Key Solutions & Implementation. Www.itransition.com. https://www.itransition.com/ai/education

201. Schroer, A. (2023, February 16). 12 companies using AI in education to enhance the classroom. Built In. https://builtin.com/artificial-intelligence/ai-in-education

202. Guzder, K. (2024, May). What is the Role of Artificial Intelligence in Education? The Hub | High Speed Training; The Hub | High Speed Training. https://www.highspeedtraining.co.uk/hub/artificial-intelligence-in-education/

203. 10 AI in Education Examples That Transform Learning (2024). (2023, December 11). Bymilliepham.com. https://bymilliepham.com/ai-in-education-examples

204. Harb, M., & Qabajeh, M. (2024). Impact of Generative Artificial Intelligence on Journalism: Practice and Deontology. 241–255. https://doi.org/10.1007/978-3-031-63153-5_18

205. De Cremer, D., Bianzino, N. M., & Falk, B. (2023, April 13). How Generative AI Could Disrupt Creative Work. Harvard Business Review. https://hbr.org/2023/04/how-generative-ai-could-disrupt-creative-work

206. Oyedeji, O., & Uthman, S. (2024, February). Opportunities and Challenges of Adopting AI in Journalism in Nigeria [Review of Opportunities and Challenges of Adopting AI in Journalism in Nigeria]. International Journal of Media, Journalism and Mass Communications (IJMJMC). https://www.arcjournals.org/pdfs/ijmjmc/v10-i2/3.pdf

207. Team, Aic. (2023). Uncovering Website Issues with Semrush's Site Audit Tool. AIContentfy. https://doi.org/10413438504/module_60218155713_website-header

208. Rizzoli, A. (2021, October 12). 8 Practical Applications of AI In Agriculture. Www.v7labs.com. https://www.v7labs.com/blog/ai-in-agriculture

209. Lenniy, D. (2021, February 18). AI in Agriculture: Challenges, Benefits, and Use Cases. Intellias. https://intellias.com/artificial-intelligence-in-agriculture/

210. Artificial Intelligence in Agriculture: 6 Smart Ways to Improve the Industry and Gain Profit. (2018, October 30). IDAP Blog. https://idapgroup.com/blog/artificial-intelligence-in-agriculture/

211. Korinek, A., & Stiglitz, J. E. (2017, December 29). Artificial Intelligence and Its Implications for Income Distribution and Unemployment. National Bureau of Economic Research Working Paper Series. https://www.nber.org/papers/w24174

212. Alonso, C., Kothari, S., & Rehman, S. (2020, December 2). How Artificial Intelligence Could Widen the Gap between Rich and Poor Nations. IMF Blog. https://www.imf.org/en/Blogs/Articles/2020/12/02/blog-how-artificial-intelligence-could-widen-the-gap-between-rich-and-poor-nations

213. Farahani , M. (2024, February 21). Artificial Intelligence and Inequality: Challenges and Opportunities (G. Ghasemi , Ed.) [Review of Artificial Intelligence and Inequality: Challenges and Opportunities]. https://www.researchgate.net/publication/378376537_Artificial_Intelligence_and_Inequality_Challenges_and_Opportunities/fulltext/65d74390adc608480adf3d56/Artificial-Intelligence-and-Inequality-Challenges-and-Opportunities.pdf?__cf_chl_tk=JiyVvzZNGsRUGxy5RAiD_fN0psY90OjOR13BPo7geOA-1732369080-1.0.1.1-5osWYexnoTVPQ8y0.1EjIXZl1y5WdeE4E57TubWScTQ

214. Manning, S. (2024, July 3). AI's impact on income inequality in the US. Brookings. https://www.brookings.edu/articles/ais-impact-on-income-inequality-in-the-us/

215. Fares, O. H., Butt, I., & Lee, S. H. M. (2022). Utilization of artificial intelligence in the banking sector: a systematic literature review. Journal of Financial Services Marketing, 28. springer. https://doi.org/10.1057/s41264-022-00176-7

216. Adhaen, M., Chen, W., Wadi, R. A., & Esra Aldhaen. (2024). Exploring Artificial Intelligence Adoption in the Banking Sector: Multiple Case Studies. Studies in Systems, Decision and Control, 301–314. https://doi.org/10.1007/978-3-031-66218-8_23

217. Ghandour, A. (2021, November 12). Opportunities and Challenges of Artificial Intelligence in Banking: Systematic Literature Review [Review of Opportunities and Challenges of Artificial Intelligence in Banking: Systematic Literature Review   ]. https://www.researchgate.net/publication/356600100_Opportunities_and_Challenges_of_Artificial_Intelligence_in_Banking_Systematic_Literature_Review/fulltext/61a423283068c54fa5247047/Opportunities-and-Challenges-of-Artificial-Intelligence-in-Banking-Systematic-Literature-Review.pdf

218. El, A. (2024). Integrating artificial intelligence in industry 4.0: insights, challenges, and future prospects–a literature review. Annals of Operation Research/Annals of Operations Research. https://doi.org/10.1007/s10479-024-06012-6

219. Wu, H., Liu, J., & Liang, B. (2024). AI-Driven Supply Chain Transformation in Industry 5.0: Enhancing Resilience and Sustainability. Journal of the Knowledge Economy. https://doi.org/10.1007/s13132-024-01999-6

220. Espina-Romero, L., Gutiérrez Hurtado, H., Ríos Parra, D., Vilchez Pirela, R. A., Talavera-Aguirre, R., & Ochoa-Díaz, A. (2024). Challenges and Opportunities in the Implementation of AI in Manufacturing: A Bibliometric Analysis. Sci, 6(4), 60. https://doi.org/10.3390/sci6040060

221. Dhaliwal, A. (2024). Towards AI-Driven Transport and Logistics. Lecture Notes in Business Information Processing, 119–131. https://doi.org/10.1007/978-3-031-60003-6_8

222. Abduljabbar, R., Dia, H., Liyanage, S., & Bagloee, S. A. (2019). Applications of Artificial Intelligence in Transport: An Overview. Sustainability, 11(1), 189. https://doi.org/10.3390/su11010189

223. Krishnan, R., Manoj Govindaraj, Kandasamy, L., Perumal, E., & Mathews, S. B. (2024). Integrating Logistics Management with Artificial Intelligence and IoT for Enhanced Supply Chain Efficiency. Studies in Systems, Decision and Control, 25–35. https://doi.org/10.1007/978-3-031-63569-4_3

224. Chen, W., Men, Y., Fuster, N., Osorio, C., & Juan, A. A. (2024). Artificial Intelligence in Logistics Optimization with Sustainable Criteria: A Review. Sustainability, 16(21), 9145. https://doi.org/10.3390/su16219145

225. Mhlanga, D. (2023). Artificial Intelligence and Machine Learning in Making Transport, Safer, Cleaner, More Reliable, and Efficient in Emerging Markets. Sustainable Development Goals Series, 193–211. https://doi.org/10.1007/978-3-031-37776-1_9

226. Spatharou, A., Hieronimus, S., & Jenkins, J. (2020). Transforming Healthcare with AI: the Impact on the Workforce and Organizations | McKinsey. Www.mckinsey.com. https://www.mckinsey.com/industries/healthcare/our-insights/transforming-healthcare-with-ai

227. North, M. (2024, November 18). 4 ways AI is transforming healthcare. World Economic Forum. https://www.weforum.org/stories/2024/11/ai-transforming-global-health/

228. Cleveland Clinic. (2024, September 5). How AI Is Being Used to Benefit Your Healthcare. Cleveland Clinic; Cleveland Clinic. https://health.clevelandclinic.org/ai-in-healthcare

229. Cleveland Clinic. (2024, September 5). How AI Is Being Used to Benefit Your Healthcare. Cleveland Clinic; Cleveland Clinic. https://health.clevelandclinic.org/ai-in-healthcare

230. Kauffman, M. E., & Soares, M. N. (2020). AI in legal services: new trends in AI-enabled legal services. Service Oriented Computing and Applications, 14(4), 223–226. https://doi.org/10.1007/s11761-020-00305-x

231. Brooks, C., Gherhes, C., & Vorley, T. (2019, December 13). Artificial intelligence in the legal sector: pressures and challenges of transformation [Review of Artificial intelligence in the legal sector: pressures and challenges of transformation]. https://eprints.whiterose.ac.uk/154830/19/rsz026.pdf

232. Chitranjali Negi Advocate. (2024). In the Era of Artificial Intelligence (AI): Analyzing the Transformative Role of Technology in the Legal Arena. Social Science Research Network. https://doi.org/10.2139/ssrn.4677039

233. Illanes, P., Lund, S., Mourshed, M., Rutherford, S., & Tyreman, M. (2018, January 22). Retraining and reskilling workers in the age of automation. McKinsey & Company. https://www.mckinsey.com/featured-insights/future-of-work/retraining-and-reskilling-workers-in-the-age-of-automation

234. Saadia Zahidi, & World Economic Forum. (2023, May 3). See how the future of jobs is changing in the age of AI. World Economic Forum. https://www.weforum.org/stories/2023/05/future-of-jobs-in-the-age-of-ai-sustainability-and-deglobalization/

235. Bruenig, M. (2023, March 31). What To Do About AI-Driven Job Displacement. People's Policy Project. https://www.peoplespolicyproject.org/2023/03/31/what-to-do-about-ai-driven-job-displacement/

236. Boren, Z. (2024, March 5). How Government Can Embrace AI and Workers | Urban Institute. Www.urban.org. https://www.urban.org/urban-wire/how-government-can-embrace-ai-and-workers

237. Greiman, V. (2021). Human Rights and Artificial Intelligence: A Universal Challenge. Journal of Information Warfare, 20(1), 50–62. https://www.jstor.org/stable/27036518

238. HUMAN RIGHTS IN THE AGE OF ARTIFICIAL INTELLIGENCE. (2018). https://www.accessnow.org/wp-content/uploads/2018/11/AI-and-Human-Rights.pdf

239. Miller, K. (2024, March 18). Privacy in an AI Era: How Do We Protect Our Personal Information? Hai.stanford.edu; Stanford University. https://hai.stanford.edu/news/privacy-ai-era-how-do-we-protect-our-personal-information

240. Murdoch, B. (2021). Privacy and Artificial Intelligence: Challenges for Protecting Health Information in a New Era. BMC Medical Ethics, 22(1). https://doi.org/10.1186/s12910-021-00687-3

241. King, J., & Meinhardt, C. (2024). Rethinking Privacy in the AI Era Policy Provocations for a Data-Centric World. https://hai.stanford.edu/sites/default/files/2024-02/White-Paper-Rethinking-Privacy-AI-Era.pdf

242. Artificial Intelligence and Human Rights. (2023). In Oxford University Press eBooks. Oxford University Press. https://doi.org/10.1093/law/9780192882486.001.0001

243. Saheb, T. (2022). Ethically Contentious Aspects of Artificial Intelligence surveillance: a Social Science Perspective. AI and Ethics, 3. https://doi.org/10.1007/s43681-022-00196-y

244. Karpa, D., Klarl, T., & Rochlitz, M. (2022). Artificial Intelligence, Surveillance, and Big Data. Advanced Studies in Diginomics and Digitalization, 145–172. https://doi.org/10.1007/978-3-031-04063-4_8

245. Bontridder, N., & Poullet, Y. (2021). The Role of Artificial Intelligence in Disinformation. Data & Policy, 3(E32). https://doi.org/10.1017/dap.2021.20

246. Salem, A. H., Azzam, S. M., Emam, O. E., & Abohany, A. A. (2024). Advancing cybersecurity: a comprehensive review of AI-driven detection techniques. Journal of Big Data, 11(1). https://doi.org/10.1186/s40537-024-00957-y

247. Bontridder, N., & Poullet, Y. (2021). The Role of Artificial Intelligence in Disinformation. Data & Policy, 3(E32). https://doi.org/10.1017/dap.2021.20

248. Saheb, T. (2022). Ethically Contentious Aspects of Artificial Intelligence surveillance: a Social Science Perspective. AI and Ethics, 3. https://doi.org/10.1007/s43681-022-00196-y

249. Pfau, M. (2024, August 12). Council Post: Artificial Intelligence: The New Eyes Of Surveillance. Forbes.

https://www.forbes.com/councils/forbestechcouncil/2024/02/02/artificial-intelligence-the-new-eyes-of-surveillance/

250. Use of AI Technology to Support Data Collection for Project Preparation and Implementation: A "Learning-by-doing" Process. (2021). https://gpss.worldbank.org/sites/gpss/files/knowledge_products/2021/Use%20of%20AI%20technology%20to%20support%20data%20collection.pdf

251. Redman, T. H. D. and T. C. (2022, December 20). How AI Is Improving Data Management. MIT Sloan Management Review. https://sloanreview.mit.edu/article/how-ai-is-improving-data-management/

252. Annual scholarly publications on artificial intelligence. (n.d.). Our World in Data. https://ourworldindata.org/grapher/annual-scholarly-publications-on-artificial-intelligence

253. AI Data Collection in 2023: Guide, Challenges & Methods. (n.d.). Research.aimultiple.com. https://research.aimultiple.com/ai-data-collection/

254. Lockwood N. (2024, April 4). A Complete Guide to Data Collection for Artificial Intelligence (AI). Tealium. https://tealium.com/blog/data-strategy/a-complete-guide-to-data-collection-for-artifical-intelligence-ai/

255. Exploring the Impact of AI in Data Analytics. (2024, August 20). Caltech -. https://pg-p.ctme.caltech.edu/blog/data-analytics/impact-of-ai-in-data-analytics

256. The Ethics of AI Data Collection: Ensuring Privacy and Fair Representation| AI Insights. (n.d.). Omdena. https://www.omdena.com/blog/the-ethics-of-ai-data-collection-ensuring-privacy-and-fair-representation

257. Singh, T. (2024). AI-Driven Surveillance Technologies and Human Rights: Balancing Security and Privacy. Smart Innovation, Systems and Technologies, 703–717. https://doi.org/10.1007/978-981-97-3690-4_53

258. Jones, K. (2023, January 10). AI governance and human rights | Chatham House – International Affairs Think Tank. Www.chathamhouse.org. https://www.chathamhouse.org/2023/01/ai-governance-and-human-rights

259. Schmitt, C. E. (2018, September 27). Evaluating the impact of artificial intelligence on human rights. Harvard Law School.

https://hls.harvard.edu/today/evaluating-the-impact-of-artificial-intelligence-on-human-rights/

260. Ren, S., & Wierman, A. (2024, July 15). The Uneven Distribution of AI's Environmental Impacts. Harvard Business Review; Harvard Business Publishing. https://hbr.org/2024/07/the-uneven-distribution-of-ais-environmental-impacts

261. Yu, Y., Wang, J., Liu, Y., Yu, P., Wang, D., Zheng, P., & Zhang, M. (2024). Revisit the environmental impact of artificial intelligence: the overlooked carbon emission source? Frontiers of Environmental Science & Engineering, 18(12). https://doi.org/10.1007/s11783-024-1918-y

262. Web Editor, & Hossfield, E. (2024, November 22). Generative AI's Massive Environmental Impact - The Scarlet. The Scarlet. https://thescarlet.org/20182/opinions/generative-ais-massive-environmental-impact/

263. Ren, S., & Wierman, A. (2024, July 15). The Uneven Distribution of AI's Environmental Impacts. Harvard Business Review; Harvard Business Publishing. https://hbr.org/2024/07/the-uneven-distribution-of-ais-environmental-impacts

264. UN Environment Programme. (2024, September 21). AI Has an Environmental problem. Here's What the World Can Do about that. UNEP. https://www.unep.org/news-and-stories/story/ai-has-environmental-problem-heres-what-world-can-do-about

265. Sheikh, H., Prins, C., & Schrijvers, E. (2023). Artificial Intelligence: Definition and Background. Research for Policy, 15–41. https://doi.org/10.1007/978-3-031-21448-6_2

266. West, D., & Allen, J. (2018, April 24). How Artificial Intelligence Is Transforming the World. Brookings; The Brookings Institution. https://www.brookings.edu/articles/how-artificial-intelligence-is-transforming-the-world/

267. Burrows, L. (2021, October 19). The present and future of AI. Seas.harvard.edu; Harvard John A. Paulson School of Engineering and Applied Sciences. https://seas.harvard.edu/news/2021/10/present-and-future-ai

268. Li, R., Sun, T., & Li, R. (2023). Does artificial intelligence (AI) reduce ecological footprint? The role of globalization. Environmental Science and Pollution Research, 30(59), 123948–123965. https://doi.org/10.1007/s11356-023-31076-5

269. Wu, C.-J., Raghavendra, R., Gupta, U., Acun, B., Ardalani, N., Maeng, K., Chang, G., Behram, F. A., Huang, J., Bai, C., Gschwind, M., Gupta, A., Ott, M., Melnikov, A., Candido, S., Brooks, D., Chauhan, G., Lee, B., Lee, H.-H. S., & Akyildiz, B. (2021). Sustainable AI: Environmental Implications, Challenges and Opportunities. ArXiv:2111.00364 [Cs]. https://arxiv.org/abs/2111.00364

270. van Wynsberghe, A. (2021). Sustainable AI: AI for Sustainability and the Sustainability of AI. AI and Ethics, 1(1). https://doi.org/10.1007/s43681-021-00043-6

271. Wu, C.-J., Raghavendra, R., Gupta, U., Acun, B., Ardalani, N., Maeng, K., Chang, G., Behram, F. A., Huang, J., Bai, C., Gschwind, M., Gupta, A., Ott, M., Melnikov, A., Candido, S., Brooks, D., Chauhan, G., Lee, B., Lee, H.-H. S., & Akyildiz, B. (2021). Sustainable AI: Environmental Implications, Challenges and Opportunities. ArXiv:2111.00364 [Cs]. https://arxiv.org/abs/2111.00364

272. Measuring the environmental impacts of artificial intelligence compute and applications. (2022). OECD Digital Economy Papers. https://doi.org/10.1787/7babf571-en

273. Mensah, J. (2019). Sustainable development: Meaning, history, principles, pillars, and Implications for Human action: Literature Review. Cogent Social Sciences, 5(1), 1–21. Tandfonline. https://doi.org/10.1080/23311886.2019.1653531

274. Mohamed Ahmed Alloghani. (2023). Green Mobile App Development: Building Sustainable Products. Signals and Communication Technology, 137–147. https://doi.org/10.1007/978-3-031-45214-7_7

275. Emas, R. (2015). The Concept of Sustainable Development: Definition and Defining Principles. https://sustainabledevelopment.un.org/content/documents/5839GSDR%202015_SD_concept_definiton_rev.pdf

276. Charalampidou, S., Ampatzoglou, A., Karountzos, E., & Avgeriou, P. (2020). Empirical studies on software traceability: A mapping study. Journal of Software: Evolution and Process, 33(2). https://doi.org/10.1002/smr.2294

277. Li, P. (2019). Scanning the Literature. IEEE Wireless Communications, 26(5), 2–3. https://doi.org/10.1109/mwc.2019.8883121

278. de Almeida, P. G. R., dos Santos, C. D., & Farias, J. S. (2021). Artificial Intelligence Regulation: a Framework for Governance. Ethics and Information Technology, 23(3), 505–525. https://doi.org/10.1007/s10676-021-09593-z

279. Taeihagh, A. (2021, June 4). Article Navigation Journal Article Governance of artificial intelligence [Review of Article Navigation Journal Article Governance of artificial intelligence]. Oxford Academy. https://academic.oup.com/policyandsociety/article/40/2/137/6509315

280. Mucci, T., & Stryker, C. (2023, November 28). What is AI governance? | IBM. Www.ibm.com. https://www.ibm.com/topics/ai-governance

281. Team, E. (2024, November 19). Governance, Risk and Compliance: How AI will Make Fintech Comply?: By Ruoyu Xie. Finextra Research; Finextra. https://www.finextra.com/blogposting/27235/governance-risk-and-compliance-how-ai-will-make-fintech-comply

282. Keller, D. (2024, November 14). AI Regulation, Global Governance and Challenges. The Daily Hodl. https://dailyhodl.com/2024/11/13/ai-regulation-global-governance-and-challenges/

283. What the US's Foggy AI Regulations Mean For Today's Cyber Compliance. (2024). Cybersecurityintelligence.com. https://www.cybersecurityintelligence.com/blog/what-the-uss-foggy-ai-regulations-mean-for-todays-cyber-compliance-8093.html

284. Tallberg, J., Erman, E., Furendal, M., Geith, J., Klamberg, M., & Lundgren, M. (2023). The Global Governance of Artificial Intelligence: Next Steps for Empirical and Normative Research. International Studies Review, 25(3). https://doi.org/10.1093/isr/viad040

285. Pouya Kashefi, Yasaman Kashefi, & AmirHossein Ghafouri Mirsaraei. (2024). Shaping the future of AI: balancing innovation and ethics in global regulation. Uniform Law Review. https://doi.org/10.1093/ulr/unae040

286. Artificial intelligence and the challenge for global governance. (2024, June 7). Chatham House – International Affairs Think Tank. https://www.chathamhouse.org/2024/06/artificial-intelligence-and-challenge-global-governance

287. The Economic Impacts and the Regulation of AI: A Review of the Academic Literature and Policy Actions. (n.d.). IMF. https://www.imf.org/en/Publications/WP/Issues/2024/03/22/The-Economic-Impacts-and-the-Regulation-of-AI-A-Review-of-the-Academic-Literature-and-546645

288. Global AI Regulation: Protecting Rights; Leveraging Collaboration. (2024). Berkman Klein Center. https://cyber.harvard.edu/story/2024-06/global-ai-regulation-protecting-rights-leveraging-collaboration

289. de Almeida, P. G. R., dos Santos, C. D., & Farias, J. S. (2021). Artificial Intelligence Regulation: a Framework for Governance. Ethics and Information Technology, 23(3), 505–525. https://doi.org/10.1007/s10676-021-09593-z

290. Candelon, F., Carlo, R. C. di, Bondt, M. D., & Evgeniou, T. (2021, September 1). AI Regulation Is Coming. Harvard Business Review. https://hbr.org/2021/09/ai-regulation-is-coming

291. Non-Decisional Material Non-Decisional Statement by the National AI Advisory Committee (NAIAC) Working Group on Regulation and Executive Action Rationales, Mechanisms, and Challenges to Regulating AI: A Concise Guide and Explanation. (n.d.). https://www.ai.gov/wp-content/uploads/2023/07/Rationales-Mechanisms-Challenges-Regulating-AI-NAIAC-Non-Decisional.pdf

292. Comunale, M., & Manera, A. (2024). The Economic Impacts and the Regulation of AI: A Review of the Academic Literature and Policy Actions. IMF Working Papers, 2024(065). https://doi.org/10.5089/9798400268588.001.A001

293. Finocchiaro, G. (2023). The regulation of artificial intelligence. The Regulation of Artificial Intelligence. https://doi.org/10.1007/s00146-023-01650-z

294. Heimberger, H., Horvat, D., & Schultmann, F. (2024). Exploring the factors driving AI adoption in production: a systematic literature review and future

research agenda. Information Technology and Management. https://doi.org/10.1007/s10799-024-00436-z

About the Author

Otega Wisdom Efe is a visionary whose work transcends the ordinary, inviting us to reimagine the future as a harmonious blend of technology and humanity. A distinguished AI researcher with an MBA in Artificial Intelligence from Nexford University, Efe has an extraordinary talent for unraveling the intricacies of cutting-edge technology and translating them into insights that resonate with our deepest aspirations.

In *AI and Society: Navigating Ethics, Governance, and Trust*, he channels this unique gift by taking readers on a mesmerizing journey through the ethical and societal dimensions of our digital age. With effortless clarity and compelling narrative, Efe explores the applications of AI in solving real world problems as he challenges us to confront the dilemmas posed by synthetic media, bias, and privacy while inspiring us with the promise of a future powered by trustworthy technology.

Not one to rest on his laurels, Efe is also the brilliant mind behind *Beyond the Steering Wheel: The Rise of Self-Driving Cars,* a groundbreaking exploration of autonomous vehicles. His work in these areas not only demonstrates his technical prowess but also his unwavering commitment to ensuring that innovative advancements serve humanity responsibly.

www.ingramcontent.com/pod-product-compliance
Lightning Source LLC
LaVergne TN
LVHW042333060326
832902LV00006B/137